STRATEGIES
FOR TEACHING
Guide for
Music Methods Classes

STRATEGIES
FOR TEACHING

Guide for
Music Methods Classes

Compiled and edited by
Louis O. Hall with
Nancy R. Boone, John Grashel, and Rosemary C. Watkins

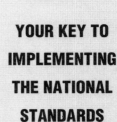

**YOUR KEY TO
IMPLEMENTING
THE NATIONAL
STANDARDS
FOR MUSIC
EDUCATION**

MENC MENC
MENC MENC

MUSIC EDUCATORS NATIONAL CONFERENCE

Series Editor: Carolynn A. Lindeman

Project Administrator: Margaret A. Senko

MENC wishes to thank
Carolynn A. Lindeman for developing and coordinating this series;
the Society for Music Teacher Education (SMTE),
especially chair *Mary Lou Van Rysselberghe* and past chair *Rosemary C. Watkins,*
for their leadership in developing this book;
Louis O. Hall and section leaders
Nancy R. Boone (choral), *John Grashel* (instrumental), and *Rosemary C. Watkins* (general music)
for selecting, writing, and editing the strategies for this book
with *Joe W. Grant, Joyce Eastlund Gromko,* and *Diane C. Persellin* (choral)
and *Barbara Lewis* and *Mary Lou Van Rysselberghe* (general music);
and the following teachers for submitting strategies:

William M. Anderson
Stephan P. Barnicle
Janet R. Barrett
Rodger J. Beatty
JoAnn A. Blyther-Powers
Anna Belle Bognar
Judy Bond
Madeline Bridges
J. Bryan Burton
Patricia Shehan Campbell
Lee Campbell-Towell
Jimmy A. Cheek II
William Clark
Patricia J. Cox
Gregory Cunningham
Carolee R. Curtright
Jo-Ann L. Decker-St. Pierre
Judith Delzell
Nelle Donahue
Lynn Drafall
Richard Dugger
Lane Dyke
Larry Eisman
Michael O. Ellingsen
Joanne Erwin
Don P. Ester

Jana R. Fallin
Todd Fallis
John Flohr
Marshall Forrester
Laurie Forsberg
Meg Franks
Craig S. Freeman
Mary Goetze
Kimberly M. Golden
Thomas W. Goolsby
Sharon Davis Gratto
Sara Hagen
Dianne Hardy
Brian Harris
Dennis Hayslett
Mark Heidel
Martha F. Hilley
Charles R. Hoffer
Mary Hoffman
Mary Hookey
Lloyd P. Hoover
Kathleen Jacobi-Karna
Catherine Jarjisian
Christine Jordanoff
Robert H. Klotman
Jerell Lambert

Carolyn Livingston
Joseph Manfredo
Rochelle Mann
Wendy L. Marsh
Claudia McCain
Claire McCoy
Carrie Miller
Randie Moore
Paul Mortenson
Glenn Nierman
Li Ying K. Noell
Katherine Norman
Emily Owen
Natalie Ozeas
Kathy Palmer
Vista J. Rainey
Darhyl S. Ramsey
James Rodde
Christine L. Rogers
Debbie Rohwer
Rosita M. Sands
Stanley L. Schleuter
Jennifer S. Scott
Tina Scott
David Sebald
Carol Sedgwick

Deborah Sheldon
Kim F. Shirey
Marcelyn Smale
Jennifer M. Starr
Barb Stevanson
Clint F. Taylor, Jr.
Mary Terrell
Keith P. Thompson
Gary Towne
Kathy Turay
Chuck Turner
Kathleen R. Vande Berg
Valerie Vander Mark
Kari Veblen
Kimberly C. Walls
Richard Watkins
Ran Whitley
Jackie Wiggins
Bonnie Blu Williams
Ramona M. Wis
Vance D. Wolverton
Marilyn Wood
Stephen F. Zdzinski

CONTENTS

PREFACE

The Music Educators National Conference (MENC) created the *Strategies for Teaching* series to help preservice and in-service music educators implement the K–12 National Standards for Music Education and the MENC Prekindergarten Standards. To address the many components of the school music curriculum, each book in the series focuses on a specific curricular area and a particular level. The result is eleven books spanning the K–12 areas of band, chorus, general music, strings/orchestra, guitar, keyboard, and specialized ensembles. A prekindergarten book and a guide for college music methods classes complete the series.

The purpose of the series is to seize the opportunity presented by the landmark education legislation of 1994. With the passage of the Goals 2000: Educate America Act, the arts were established for the first time in our country's history as a core, challenging subject in which all students need to demonstrate competence. Voluntary academic standards were called for in all nine of the identified core subjects—standards specifying what students need to know and be able to do when they exit grades 4, 8, and 12.

In music, content and achievement standards were drafted by an MENC task force. They were examined and commented on by music teachers across the country, and the task force reviewed their comments and refined the standards. While all students in grades K–8 are expected to meet the achievement standards specified for those levels, two levels of achievement—proficient and advanced—are designated for students in grades 9–12. Students who elect music courses for one to two years beyond grade 8 are expected to perform at the proficient level. Students who elect music courses for three to four years beyond grade 8 are expected to perform at the advanced level.

The music standards, together with the dance, theatre, and visual arts standards, were presented in final form—*National Standards for Arts Education*—to the U.S. Secretary of Education in March 1994. Recognizing the importance of early childhood education, MENC went beyond the K–12 standards and established content and achievement standards for the prekindergarten level as well, which are included in MENC's *The School Music Program: A New Vision*.

Now the challenge at hand is to implement the standards at the state and local levels. Implementation may require schools to expand the resources necessary to achieve the standards as specified in MENC's *Opportunity-to-Learn Standards for Music Instruction: Grades PreK–12*. Teachers will need to examine their curricula to determine if they lead to achievement of the standards. For many, the standards reflect exactly what has always been included in the school music curriculum—they represent best practice. For others, the standards may call for some curricular expansion.

To assist in the implementation process, this series offers teaching strategies illustrating how the music standards can be put into action in the music classroom. The strategies themselves do not suggest a curriculum. That, of course, is the responsibility of school districts and individual teachers. The strategies, however, are designed to help in curriculum development, lesson planning, and assessment of music learning.

The teaching strategies are based on the content and achievement standards specified in the *National Standards for Arts Education* (K–12) and *The School Music Program: A New Vision* (PreK–12). Although the strategies, like the standards, are designed primarily for four-year-olds, fourth graders, eighth graders, and high school seniors, many may be developmentally appropriate for students in other grades. Each strategy, a lesson appropriate for a portion of a class session or a complete class session, includes an objective (a clear statement of what the student will be able to do), a list of necessary materials, a description of what prior student learning and experiences are expected, a set of procedures, and the indicators of success. A follow-up section identifies ways learning may be expanded.

The *Guide for Music Methods Classes* contains strategies appropriate for preservice instructional settings in choral, instrumental, and general music methods classes. The teaching strategies in this guide relate to the other books in the series and reflect a variety of teaching/learning styles.

Bringing a series of thirteen books from vision to reality in a little over a year's time required tremendous commitment from many, many music educators—not to mention the tireless help of the MENC publications staff. Literally hundreds of music teachers across the country answered the call to participate in this project, the largest such participation in an MENC publishing endeavor. The contributions of these teachers and the books' editors are proudly presented in the various publications.

—*Carolynn A. Lindeman*
Series Editor

Carolynn A. Lindeman, professor of music at San Francisco State University and president of the Music Educators National Conference (1996–98), served on the MENC task force that developed the music education standards. She is the author of three college textbooks (The Musical Classroom, PianoLab, *and* MusicLab) *and numerous articles.*

INTRODUCTION TO THE *GUIDE*

In anticipation of the adoption of the Goals 2000: Educate America Act, representatives of the various academic and artistic disciplines set out to establish content and achievement standards by which both teaching and learning in the United States could be organized and monitored in a more effective way. The membership of the Music Educators National Conference was active in the development of the music standards and the consensus-building process that shaped their final form.

Shortly after the publication of the National Standards for Music Education, the MENC leadership issued a call for instructional strategies that music teachers nationwide could use in their classrooms. MENC members responded again by submitting strategies for this purpose in twelve specific areas. In conjunction with this effort, MENC's Society for Music Teacher Education (SMTE) was charged with the task of preparing this guide for music methods classes.

Strategies for Teaching: Guide for Music Methods Classes is intended for use in preparing preservice music teachers. It provides exemplary strategies and a wealth of resources that will enable teachers of methods courses to acquaint their students with the music standards so that they will be able to incorporate them into music instruction at all levels. The teaching strategies presented in the *Guide* address all areas of music teacher education—general music, choral music, and instrumental music—for the elementary, middle, and high school levels. Each content standard is addressed in all areas.

These strategies have come from a variety of sources that reflect the diverse interests and expertise of the music educators who submitted them. Materials needed to implement the standards in music methods classes are in keeping with those generally found in music classrooms across the country. The depth, variety, and quality of these strategies ensure continuity between materials developed for college methods classes and those used in implementation of the strategies in K–12 music instruction. Suggested readings, videos, recordings, and software are readily available through university and college libraries or are currently available from publishers.

Specifically designed for college music methods classes, this book offers some unique musical content and pedagogical applications:

- A number of the strategies involve cooperative learning. Studies have shown that the cooperative-learning setting is one of the most effective ways for college students to learn and apply knowledge.

- The three lists of resources summarize those included at the end of each strategy and represent the most authoritative writings in our profession. They include recent publications by respected music educators, as well as those that have come to be valued by music educators over time. Together with the list of MENC resources, they constitute a comprehensive checklist for any music teacher education library.

- In addition to extensive listings of materials from a variety of cultures, teacher educators will find numerous references to graded literature, texts, and recordings. Any music educator's professional library could be significantly enhanced by references suggested in the *Guide's* strategies.

- In line with the National Standards, a number of activities that traditionally have been outside the realm of the performing ensemble—such as composing and arranging—are incorporated into these strategies for methods classes.

- Strategies that address analyzing and evaluating music suggest to music educators and students that knowledge about music can be a significant factor in their own preferences. The nurturing of educated preference can help to eliminate the premature judgment often associated with musical choice.

- Because of the unprecedented collection of materials, ideas, activities, and exercises suggested here, methods teachers can expand considerably the scope and content of their classes.

- These strategies bring into focus the idea that excellence in performing is a result of balanced attention to all aspects of music, such as history, theory, and composition, as well as pedagogy. Many strategies suggest specific ways that help to show preservice music educators how to incorporate the many facets of music into its preparation and performance.

- Professional discussions among music methods instructors often focus extensively upon specific course content. Regardless of the type of methods course taught, the strategies presented here are appropriate and applicable, and they can considerably enhance methods course content. The *Guide* can serve to unify efforts in methods classes because it directly addresses the goals outlined in the music standards.

- Finally, this book is designed to be used with the eleven K–12 books in the *Strategies for Teaching* series. As each content and achievement standard is addressed by the methods instructor, methods students should reference the strategies in the *Strategies for Teaching* books that relate to the area and level under study.

Significant changes in the education of music teachers and their students are possible in the next few years if educators involved in teacher preparation assume a position of leadership in the implementation of the music standards. The *Guide for Methods Classes* is a timely and practical publication in this regard. The current generation of preservice teachers will be the first to receive formal training in implementing the music standards. The editors of the *Guide* hope that this book will not only prove to be a valuable addition to teaching resources but also provide a vital connection between the preparation of music educators and the practice of music education.

—Louis O. Hall and Rosemary C. Watkins

General Music

Section compiled and edited by:

Rosemary C. Watkins, Barbara Lewis, and Mary Lou Van Rysselberghe

INTRODUCTION

"The role that music will play in students' lives depends in large measure on the level of skills they achieve in creating, performing, and listening to music." That statement from *National Standards for Arts Education* (p. 42) encapsulates the goal of the National Standards for Music Education: to systematically set forth what students should know and be able to do in music classes, K–12.

A perspective of general music instruction as a continuum over elementary, middle, and high school levels is fundamental to the success of the implementation of the National Standards. Early music experiences alone will not be sufficient to perpetuate lifelong learning in music. At each level, the expectations for what a student should know and be able to do in music must be adapted to meet the unique needs and learning styles of each student.

Elementary general music seeks to reach every child. Its inclusive scope is unique to that level. Regular and continuing musical experiences afford all children opportunities to learn about music, to acquire basic skills for making music, and to realize the joy and satisfaction that come through involvement with music. Methods for designing these experiences reflect children's natural inclinations to sing, play instruments, move to music, and create music. Musical understanding, skills, and positive attitudes are developed through an interactive process during the elementary years.

For students at the middle level, general music is characterized as transitional, and this is reflected in the content of the standards for that age group. Basic skills must be reinforced during the time that students are exploring more sophisticated ways to perform, listen, and create, taking into account vocal changes, physical changes, and social needs. Students must build skills to participate individually and as members of ensembles. An exploratory approach to musical knowledge and skills allows students to prepare for lifelong music participation by performing, creating, and improvising using a variety of instruments, sightreading treble and bass clef, and playing melodies and harmonic accompaniments by ear. Middle-level students, through exploration, survey careers in music, learn to evaluate performances and explain their reasoning, and experience music from diverse cultures, as well as learn how music interrelates with other arts and disciplines outside the arts.

For perhaps the first time in the history of music education, high school general music may be ready to assume a position of importance. For years, music educators have heard references to a monolithic group of students who do not elect to participate in performance classes. In truth, this diverse group— numbering perhaps 85 percent of the high school population—could be one of the major beneficiaries of the National Standards. The content of the high school publications in the *Strategies for Teaching* series and of the *Guide for Music Methods Classes* clearly targets the unique and diverse interests of high school students for students in methods classes. Strategies for high school general music include opportunities for students to participate in a variety of activities that range from simulating karaoke to improvising a 12-bar blues pattern on an electronic keyboard to comparing characteristics of Baroque music and painting.

Many music educators have combined their creativity, knowledge, and skills to contribute to the K–12 general music strategies for college methods classes. Through their considerable efforts, college methods teachers will have a means of preparing methods students for implementing the standards through a broad range of activities, materials, readings, and resources that can accommodate a variety of instructional approaches. The diversity and variety of the strategies in this publication may provide the key to music methods courses that do not infringe on individual philosophy and methodology.

—*Rosemary C. Watkins*

General Music
Grades K–4

STANDARD 1A

Singing, alone and with others, a varied repertoire of music: Students sing independently, on pitch
and in rhythm, with appropriate timbre, diction, and posture, and maintain a steady tempo.

Strategy

The instructor divides the methods class into groups to prepare activities for improving K–4 students'
ability to match pitch, sing with rhythmic accuracy, sing with appropriate timbre, and maintain a
steady tempo while singing a song.

Activities allowing singers to discover their vocal ranges could include imitating sirens and following
the teacher's conducting of an imaginary path of a bee by singing "zz" at the levels dictated by the contour of the path. Timbre could also be explored using the "zz" exercise. A sample activity to improve
rhythmic accuracy in a song and help K–4 students maintain a steady beat would be for the teacher to
have students speak or sing the text on one pitch while stepping the steady beat.

For a second activity, each methods student chooses one of the following exercise sets from the book
Teaching Kids to Sing to demonstrate and teach as an in-class activity: (1) muscle movers, set 1, pp.
153–54; (2) the slow sip, p. 201; and (3) pinwheels, p. 213. Students then view the *Teaching Kids to
Sing* video, vol. 1, and discuss the effectiveness of the techniques demonstrated.

Suggested Resources

Bertaux, Betty. "Teaching Children of All Ages to Use the Singing Voice, and How to Work with
Out-of-Tune Singers." In *Readings in Music Learning Theory,* edited by Darrel Walters and Cynthia
Taggart. Chicago: GIA Publications, 1989.

Feierabend, John M. *Music for Very Little People.* New York: Boosey & Hawkes, 1986.

Kemp, Helen. *Body, Mind, Spirit, Voice.* St. Louis: Concordia, 1985. Videocassette.

Phillips, Kenneth H. *Teaching Kids to Sing.* Old Tappan, NJ: Schirmer Books/Simon & Schuster, 1992.

Phillips, Kenneth H. *Teaching Kids to Sing.* Old Tappan, NJ: Schirmer Books/Simon & Schuster, 1992.
Six-videocassette series.

STANDARD 1B

Singing, alone and with others, a varied repertoire of music: Students sing
expressively, with appropriate dynamics, phrasing, and interpretation.

Strategy

After a discussion of the terms *espressivo* and *rubato,* methods students listen to a keyboard piece from
the Romantic period and move expressively to the music, paying particular attention to the phrasing.
Each student prepares a list of five appropriate, musical keyboard or other instrumental selections to
use for expressive movement activities in an elementary music class.

(continued)

Groups of four or five methods students each choose five expressions or emotions, and each group member draws a picture of the five emotions. The instructor asks each group to choose one picture to represent an emotion for their group. A member of each group holds up the group's chosen picture, and the class responds appropriately with body movements or poses.

Next, the class sings a simple folk tune, such as "Old McDonald," in unison. With groups taking turns, one student from each group holds up a picture of an emotion, and the class sings the folk tune expressively and moves appropriately. Finally, preserving the character and mood of the sound they have just produced, students sing the song again, but this time without expressive movement. Methods students discuss how they would use similar pictures of emotions in leading K–4 students in expressive singing.

Suggested Resource

Apfelstadt, Hilary. "What Makes Children Sing Well?" *Update: Applications of Research in Music Education* 7, no. 1 (1988): 27–32.

STANDARD 1C

Singing, alone and with others, a varied repertoire of music: Students sing from memory a varied repertoire of songs representing genres and styles from diverse cultures.

Strategy

The instructor shares with methods students the cultural meaning, function, and translation of four songs from East and Southeast Asian cultures, selected from *Roots and Branches*—Cambodia: "Leak Kanseng"; Japan: "Zui Zu Zukkorbashi"; Korea: "Achim Baram"; Vietnam: "Cum Num Cum Nui." (All are singing games popular with students at the K–4 level.)

The class then listens to recordings performed in the indigenous languages, learning the melodies, rhythms, and texts through continued listening. The instructor directs students' attention to performing in tune and in tempo, as well as to exhibiting the vocal nuances characteristic of the individual song traditions. After concentrated focus on the music, the instructor teaches the corresponding games.

The instructor then divides the class into four groups to design lessons for teaching an East or Southeast Asian song and its cultural context. Some groups design lessons in which K–4 students are taught to sing the song before learning the game, and others create lessons in which students are taught the game and informally learn the song by hearing numerous repetitions as they play. After all groups have taught their songs to the methods class, the class discusses which method they preferred and suggests situations in which one method might be more appropriate than the other.

Suggested Resources

Campbell, Patricia Shehan, Ellen McCullough-Brabson, and Judith Cook Tucker. *Roots and Branches: A Legacy of Multicultural Music for Children.* Danbury, CT: World Music Press, 1994. Book and recording.

Campbell, Patricia Shehan, and Carol Scott-Kassner. *Music in Childhood: From Preschool through the Elementary Grades.* Old Tappan, NJ: Schirmer Books/Simon & Schuster, 1995.

STANDARD 1D

Singing, alone and with others, a varied repertoire of music: Students sing ostinatos, partner songs, and rounds.

Strategy

The instructor introduces "Wilbert the Whale," from *Any Turkey Can Tango,* which uses three partner songs, or another piece of music that is constructed using partner songs. Methods students learn to sing each of the three "layers" independently. Then the instructor divides the class into three groups and assigns each group one of the three layers to choreograph. The groups perform and teach their choreography to the rest of the class.

Finally, the three groups perform "Wilbert the Whale" in three parts using motions. [*Note:* A similar strategy could be used with rounds or ostinatos, having students create motions for each phrase or each ostinato.] To conclude the lesson, methods students discuss the types of prior knowledge and skills that K–4 students would need in order to use movement to accompany partner songs such as those contained in elementary music series textbooks.

Suggested Resources

Campbell-Towell, Lee. *Any Turkey Can Tango.* Milwaukee: Hal Leonard Corporation, 1995.

Carlton, Elizabeth B., and Weikart, Phyllis S. *Foundations in Elementary Education: Music.* Ypsilanti, MI: High/Scope Press, 1994.

Lewis, Barbara. "The Effect of Movement-Based Instruction on First- and Third-Graders' Achievement in Selected Music Listening Skills." *Psychology of Music* 16, no. 2 (1988): 128–42.

STANDARD 1E

Singing, alone and with others, a varied repertoire of music: Students sing in groups, blending vocal timbres, matching dynamic levels, and responding to the cues of a conductor.

Strategy

The instructor asks methods students to focus on the sound of the consonant "p" while listening to a recording of the "Papagena/Papageno" duet from the second act finale of Mozart's *The Magic Flute.* Using listening selections that emphasize the consonants "v" and "m," the instructor introduces these consonants in a similar fashion.

Students then sing each of these consonants on "E" above Middle C while watching the instructor's conducting cues for attacks and releases. This accomplished, the class breaks into small groups and, using the consonants, devises descending five-note vocalises in easy rhythmic patterns using only quar-

(continued)

ter and eighth notes and having a vocal range of no more than a perfect fifth. As they practice the vocalises, members of each group pay particular attention to the blending of vocal timbres.

Students then substitute the words "popcorn" and "va-room" for the appropriate consonants in their vocalises. Next, each group teaches its exercises to the other groups and practices conducting them with the entire class. [*Note:* The "p" consonants in popcorn are useful for teaching ensemble attacks and releases, rhythmic accuracy, and careful attention to conducting cues. The consonants "v" and "m" in va-room are useful for teaching vocally healthy aspirate (breath) attacks, diaphragmatic breathing, and forward placement (resonance).]

Suggested Resource

Miller, Richard. *The Structure of Singing: System and Art in Vocal Technique.* Old Tappan, NJ: Schirmer Books/Simon & Schuster, 1986.

◆ ◆ ◆ ◆ ◆ ◆ ◆

STANDARD 2A

Performing on instruments, alone and with others, a varied repertoire of music: Students perform on pitch, in rhythm, with appropriate dynamics and timbre, and maintain a steady tempo.

Strategy

The instructor provides methods students with a variety of pitched and nonpitched percussion instruments and notates a simple rhythmic ostinato on the chalkboard. With the class working in groups of four or five students and one person in each group serving as a conductor, each group chooses an object that features motion as the basis of a simple composition. Each group then selects three or more instrumental sounds to fit the motion of its object and uses these sounds to play the given rhythmic ostinato. The groups then organize their ostinatos into a composition that maintains a steady beat and that includes tempo, dynamics, and timbre contrasts.

The class then reconvenes to perform its varied compositions on chosen instruments. Elements of steady beat, rhythm, tempo, and dynamics are featured in performance. Discussion follows based on the following questions: Would you describe the motion as a steady beat or pulse? What different timbres did you hear? What tempo was apparent? Did the initial dynamic level remain the same or did it change?

Summarizing by clarifying tempo as the speed of music and pulse as the underlying beat, the instructor asks students to consider how, as teachers, they may convey a given tempo to their K–4 students.

Suggested Resources

Atterbury, Betty W., and Carol P. Richardson. *The Experience of Teaching General Music.* New York: McGraw-Hill, 1995.

Campbell, Patricia Shehan, and Carol Scott-Kassner. *Music in Childhood: From Preschool through the Elementary Grades.* Old Tappan, NJ: Schirmer Books/Simon & Schuster, 1995.

Nye, Robert E., Vernice T. Nye, Gary M. Martin, and Mary Lou Van Rysselberghe. *Music in the Elementary School,* 6th ed. Englewood Cliffs, NJ: Prentice-Hall, 1992.

STANDARD 2B

Performing on instruments, alone and with others, a varied repertoire of music: Students perform easy rhythmic, melodic, and chordal patterns accurately and independently on rhythmic, melodic, and harmonic classroom instruments.

Strategy

Methods students view a portion of the video *Congos, Bongos, and Other Percussion*, which demonstrates proper techniques for playing claves, guiro, maracas, wood block, and temple blocks. The instructor then circulates these instruments among students for practice of playing technique.

On chart paper, the class creates a simple score of rhythmic ostinatos for the given instruments in 3/4 meter using stem notation. Students indicate markings for tempo and dynamics with colored felt pens on the oversized score.

The instructor asks a student to improvise on the alto metallophone a melody for the composition on a G pentatonic scale. The class then performs and records its composition.

Finally, the instructor reviews recognition of psychomotor developmental stages and corresponding levels of melodic and harmonic understanding in children. Methods students discuss how to impart to K–4 students the techniques of playing classroom percussion instruments. They consider to what degree lecture, demonstration, and hands-on experience should be used with students at that level.

Suggested Resources

Frazee, Jane. *Discovering Orff: A Curriculum for Music Teachers*. Paoli, PA: Schott/European American, 1987.

Solomon, Jim. *Congos, Bongos, and Other Percussion*. Crown Coast Productions, 155 Palm Valley Woods Drive, Ponte Vedra Beach, FL 32082. 1988. Videocassette.

STANDARD 2C

Performing on instruments, alone and with others, a varied repertoire of music: Students perform expressively a varied repertoire of music representing diverse genres and styles.

Strategy

The instructor plays two brief excerpts from the *Marsalis on Music* video *Why Toes Tap:* Tchaikovsky's "Waltz of the Flowers" and Ellington's "Waltz of the Flowers." Methods students discuss the style of each piece by identifying those common characteristics most easily heard and recognized by students at the K–4 level. These may include the presence of a steady beat or syncopation and the characteristic use of certain instruments for orchestral music versus jazz.

From each of the two excerpts, the students select and notate brief phrases to demonstrate a stylistic feature easily identified and imitated by K–4 students. The themes should be easy for K–4 students to learn and perform on choirchimes, resonator bells, or Orff mallet instruments. Methods students discuss their choices and other ways to provide students of various ages with opportunities to perform music of diverse styles and genres.

(continued)

Suggested Resources

Funes, Donald J. *Musical Involvement,* 2d ed. Orlando, FL: Harcourt Brace, 1992. Book and recording.

Marsalis, Wynton. *Marsalis on Music.* New York: Sony Classical Film & Video, 1995. Four-videocassette series.

STANDARD 2D

Performing on instruments, alone and with others, a varied repertoire of music:
Students echo short rhythms and melodic patterns.

Strategy

The instructor divides methods class into groups of four or five students and assigns a leader for each group. Student leaders then initiate the first two steps of the Music Learning Sequence prescribed by Froseth and Weikart in *Movement to Music,* as modeled by the instructor:

- *Listen-Watch-Move.* Leaders select taped music and direct students in synchronizing various movements to the music. Other students take turns leading this activity.

- *Lap-Pat, Listen, and Echo.* Leaders establish a steady lap-pat and ask students to echo verbal syllables (*du/de,* suggested by Froseth and Weikart) to the recorded selection. Other students take turns as the leader.

Student groups then perform repeating melodic and rhythmic patterns of a song (e.g., "Li'l 'Liza Jane") on classroom percussion instruments. They may create their own ostinatos to accompany the song.

Finally, each student group creates a composition made up of patterns using echo as the unifying feature. The instructor reconvenes the class, and each group invites the rest of the class to echo as it performs its ostinato piece. The class discusses the processes of introducing ostinatos to K–4 students and of adapting them as accompaniments on pitched and nonpitched classroom percussion instruments.

Suggested Resources

Froseth, James O., and Phyllis Weikart. *Movement to Music.* Chicago: GIA Publications, 1981.

Warner, Brigitte. *Orff-Schulwerk: Applications for the Classroom.* Englewood Cliffs, NJ: Prentice-Hall, 1991.

STANDARD 2E

Performing on instruments, alone and with others, a varied repertoire of music: Students perform in groups, blending instrumental timbres, matching dynamic levels, and responding to the cues of a conductor.

Strategy

The instructor initiates a class discussion of criteria to consider when choosing an instrumental musical arrangement for K–4 students to perform. They may include general age or grade level of the students; rhythmic perception; psychomotor skills; listening skills for ensemble; understanding of the music concepts involved; and previous musical experiences.

Methods students apply these criteria to each of three instrumental scores, determining the group of K–4 students for whom each would be a credible choice. The instructor leads a discussion of the conclusions, and the class selects one score to perform. A student conducts the performance of the score, drawing attention to dynamics and blend. The class discusses the methods they would use in teaching K–4 students to perform on instruments expressively in groups.

Suggested Resources

Choksy, Lois, Robert M. Abramson, Avon E. Gillespie, and David Woods. *Teaching Music in the Twentieth Century.* Englewood Cliffs, NJ: Prentice-Hall, 1986.

Frazee, Jane. *Discovering Orff: A Curriculum for Music Teachers.* Paoli, PA: Schott/European American, 1987.

Warner, Brigitte. Appendix to *Orff-Schulwerk: Applications for the Classroom.* Englewood Cliffs, NJ: Prentice-Hall, 1991.

STANDARD 2F

Performing on instruments, alone and with others, a varied repertoire of music: Students perform independent instrumental parts while other students sing or play contrasting parts.

Strategy

The instructor presents a method for introducing recorder playing to K–4 students who have already learned basic rhythmic notation. The staff and three pitches—B, A, and G—are included in the initial steps of the recorder sequence.

Methods students create ostinatos using the three given pitches on recorders, remembering that contrasting rhythmic patterns for these ostinatos provide variety. The class selects four ostinatos to put in order as a composition, making decisions about dynamics, rhythm, and form to keep it interesting. A student notates the composition on the chalkboard or on a transparency.

The class performs the composition in unison on recorders. The instructor then asks someone to suggest a possible harmonic structure (e.g., the primary chords I and V), and the class marks these chord changes on the score.

Together, on choirchimes, resonator bells, or Orff mallet instruments, methods students devise accompaniments that create the harmonic structure for the score. They then perform the composition on recorders and other instruments. Students discuss the possibilities for using these activities with K–4 students.

As an example of contemporary music that beginning recorder players could read and play, the instructor shows students the score for the prelude to Kenneth Simpson's "Suite on Three Notes."

(continued)

Suggested Resources

King, Carol. *Recorder Routes I,* rev. ed. Memphis: Musicraft, 1994.

Simpson, Kenneth. "Suite on Three Notes." Paoli, PA: Schott/European American, 1987.

◆ ◆ ◆ ◆ ◆ ◆ ◆

STANDARD 3A

Improvising melodies, variations, and accompaniments: Students improvise "answers" in the same style to given rhythmic and melodic phrases.

Strategy

The instructor introduces pitched and nonpitched percussion instruments to the methods class and models eight-beat rhythmic examples on a nonpitched percussion instrument, asking methods students to echo. Only quarter notes, half notes, paired-eighth notes, and quarter rests are initially used. After a discussion of the level of difficulty of various rhythmic patterns, the instructor introduces students to the idea of rhythmic "questions" and "answers" in the same style.

The instructor asks students to improvise simple eight-beat rhythmic answers to rhythmic questions in the same style. The students discuss and notate examples of varying levels of difficulty.

Finally, working in groups of three, students take turns improvising simple rhythmic questions and answers. They discuss the process and repeat it with pitched instruments set up in a pentatonic scale. The instructor videotapes the class for student evaluation. The class discusses the methods they would use in teaching K–4 students to improvise rhythmic questions and answers.

Suggested Resources

Atterbury, Betty W., and Carol P. Richardson. *The Experience of Teaching General Music.* New York: McGraw-Hill, 1995.

Campbell, Patricia Shehan, and Carol Scott-Kassner. *Music in Childhood: From Preschool through the Elementary Grades.* Old Tappan, NJ: Schirmer Books/Simon & Schuster, 1995.

Warner, Brigitte. *Orff-Schulwerk: Applications for the Classroom.* Englewood Cliffs, NJ: Prentice Hall, 1991.

Wiggins, Jackie. *Composition in the Classroom: A Tool for Teaching.* Reston, VA: Music Educators National Conference, 1990.

STANDARD 3B

Improvising melodies, variations, and accompaniments: Students improvise simple rhythmic and melodic ostinato accompaniments.

Strategy

The instructor leads the class in singing pentatonic songs and rounds. To accompany these songs, the instructor introduces appropriate ostinatos on nonpitched percussion instruments, pitched percussion instruments set up in a pentatonic scale, or keyboard instruments. The instructor encourages discussion and analysis of the songs and accompaniments. Methods students discuss the difference between the process of improvising an accompaniment and playing a composed accompaniment.

Working in groups of three, students improvise simple rhythmic or melodic ostinato accompaniments to simple pentatonic songs. The instructor reconvenes the class, and students share their improvisations. The class discusses the process and how to introduce this experience to K–4 students.

Suggested Resources

Campbell, Patricia Shehan, and Carol Scott-Kassner. *Music in Childhood: From Preschool through the Elementary Grades.* Old Tappan, NJ: Schirmer Books/Simon & Schuster, 1995.

Hamann, Donald L., ed. *Creativity in the Music Classroom: The Best of* MEJ. Reston, VA: Music Educators National Conference, 1991.

Wiggins, Jackie. *Composition in the Classroom: A Tool for Teaching.* Reston, VA: Music Educators National Conference, 1990.

STANDARD 3C

Improvising melodies, variations, and accompaniments: Students improvise simple rhythmic variations and simple melodic embellishments on familiar melodies.

Strategy

The instructor sings a familiar song to the methods class and asks them to identify it. Students listen for a rhythmic or melodic change as the instructor repeats the song with a simple variation. Discussion of rhythmic and melodic variation follows. The instructor transfers the melody in its original form to a keyboard instrument and encourages a student to demonstrate embellishment.

Working in three groups, students create improvisations on familiar songs of their choice (one song per group), singing or playing their group improvisations as follows: Group 1: rhythmic variation; Group 2: melodic variation; and Group 3: melodic embellishment.

The instructor reconvenes the class, and students share their improvisations. The class discusses the variations and how to engage K–4 students in improvisations based on familiar melodies.

(continued)

Suggested Resources

Caillet, Lucien. *Variations on the Theme "Pop! Goes the Weasel."* In *Share the Music,* Grade 3 (New York: Macmillan/McGraw-Hill, 1995); or *Music and You,* Grade 4 (New York: Macmillan/McGraw-Hill, 1991).

Ives, Charles, *Variations on "America."* In *Share the Music,* Grade 4; *The Music Connection,* Grades 4 and 6 (Parsippany, NJ: Silver Burdett Ginn, 1995); *Music and You,* Grade 8; or *World of Music,* Grades 5 and 6 (Parsippany, NJ: Silver Burdett Ginn, 1991).

Kratus, John. "Growing with Improvisation." *Music Educators Journal* 78, no. 4 (December 1991): 35–40.

Nye, Robert E., Vernice T. Nye, Gary M. Martin, and Mary Lou Van Rysselberghe. *Music in the Elementary School,* 6th ed. Englewood Cliffs, NJ: Prentice-Hall, 1992.

STANDARD 3D

Improvising melodies, variations, and accompaniments: *Students improvise short songs and instrumental pieces, using a variety of sound sources, including traditional sounds, nontraditional sounds available in the classroom, body sounds, and sounds produced by electronic means.*

Strategy

Singing or playing a recorder, the instructor teaches methods students several simple folk songs from non-Western cultures. Students improvise accompaniments to the songs using traditional or nontraditional sound sources. For some songs, a steady bordun may be created with the root and the fifth of the given key on a bass xylophone or metallophone.

Students discuss the elements that distinguish one melody from another, such as rhythmic character and intervallic patterns. The instructor encourages students to improvise new melodies using their voices or recorders. Students may choose to add words to their melodies.

The class discusses distinguishing elements of the melodies they have created. Students devise accompaniments for their improvised songs, using a variety of sound sources, including body sounds, environmental or found sounds, and synthesized sounds. Students may play individually or collectively. The instructor makes audio or video recordings of students' improvisations for assessment purposes. Finally, the class discusses how they would use a similar process in teaching K–4 students to improvise melodies and accompaniments and encourage them to incorporate many different sound sources.

Suggested Resources

Henry, Robert E. "Improvisation Through Guided Self-Study." *Music Educators Journal* 79, no. 8 (April 1993): 33–37.

Rudaitis, Cheryl, ed. "Jump Ahead and Take the Risk." *Teaching Music* 2, no. 5 (April 1995): 34–35.

Schafer, Andrea. "Playful Ideas for Teaching Beginning Recorder." *The Orff Echo* 26, no. 3 (Spring 1994): 27, 29.

◆ ◆ ◆ ◆ ◆ ◆ ◆

STANDARD 4A

Composing and arranging music within specified guidelines: Students create and arrange music to accompany readings or dramatizations.

Strategy

Methods students, working in groups, choose a short children's book, story, or poem to which they can add sounds. (Good choices might have counting, animals to imitate, expressive language, or a call-and-response structure.) Students may choose classroom instruments, body sounds, and/or vocal sounds to accompany their selection.

On chart paper, each group notates its score using iconic representation, for which the instructor has provided examples. Before the groups perform the pieces for the class, the instructor tapes the scores on the wall and has students spend some time silently looking at the scores to imagine how the pieces will sound.

Students then perform their pieces for the class and discuss how well their expectations were met. Discussion should focus on the effectiveness of the sounds chosen for expressive qualities as well as on how this activity might be taught in an elementary classroom. Each student could be assigned to write a lesson plan based on this strategy for the elementary grade of his or her choice.

Suggested Children's Literature

Berenstain, Stan and Jan. *Bears on Wheels.* New York: Random House, 1969.

Duke, Kate. *Seven Froggies Went to School.* New York: E. P. Dutton, 1985.

Mayer, Mercer. *I Was So Mad.* Racine, WI: Western Publishing Company, 1983.

Pomerantz, Charlotte. *The Piggy in the Puddle.* New York: Macmillan, 1974.

STANDARD 4B

Composing and arranging music within specified guidelines: Students create and arrange short songs and instrumental pieces within specified guidelines.

Strategy

In a field setting, the instructor pairs one methods student with one to three elementary students for the following procedure:

1. The methods student asks K–4 students to listen to a short musical example and, while listening, to mirror the methods student in a dance that reflects the composition's melodic contour and rhythm. After two hearings, the methods student asks the K–4 students to recall sections that were the same or different.

2. The methods student gives each K–4 student iconographic strips with line drawings of the melodic contour of the piece, asking the students to place the iconographic strips in the correct musical sequence as they listen to the musical excerpt again.

(continued)

3. Using the form of the musical example as a guide, the K–4 students create an original piece. The methods student guides the students in descriptions of the sound ideas (e.g., color, amplitude, range) so that they have the chance to reflect upon their perceptions and productions.

4. The methods student asks the K–4 students to "write the way the music sounds" on large sheets of paper. Then the methods student conducts from the visual representation while the K–4 students perform their composition for the entire elementary class.

In a journal entry, the methods student records his or her reflections concerning what worked well in the lesson plan and what changes should be made the next time the lesson is taught.

Suggested Resources

Davidson, Lyle, and Larry Scripp. "Young Children's Musical Representations: Windows on Music Cognition." In *Generative Processes in Music: The Psychology of Performance, Improvisation, and Composition,* edited by John A. Sloboda. Oxford, England: Clarendon Press, 1988.

Gromko, Joyce Eastlund. *In a Child's Voice: Interpretive Interactions with Young Composers.* Paper presented at the Qualitative Methodologies in Music Education Research Conference, The University of Illinois at Urbana–Champaign (May 19–21, 1994).

Upitis, Rena. *Can I Play You My Song?* Portsmouth, NH: Heinemann Educational Books, 1992.

Wolf Cohen, Veronika. *Explorations of Kinaesthetic Analogues for Musical Schemes.* Paper presented at the Qualitative Methodologies in Music Education Research Conference, The University of Illinois at Urbana–Champaign (May 19–21, 1994).

STANDARD 4C

Composing and arranging music within specified guidelines: Students use a variety of sound sources when composing.

Strategy

Methods students have completed assigned reading on composition with elementary students (Wiggins, 1990). The instructor divides students into groups and has each group develop a list of criteria for the evaluation of compositions.

The instructor assigns the groups the task of composing ABA instrumental pieces using a variety of pitched and nonpitched percussion instruments, instructing them to: (1) choose one instrument per person; (2) compose an A section using a fast tempo; (3) compose a B section using a slow tempo; (4) create a signal for changing from one section to another; (5) rehearse the entire piece without stopping; and (6) perform and tape the piece for class evaluations.

Before everyone starts the assignment, the instructor leads a small group in developing an A section as a model for the entire class. The instructor encourages the use of interesting rhythmic patterns for the compositions. After all compositions have been performed and taped, students listen to the tape and write a critique of the compositions. These evaluations should be guided by the list of criteria developed by students at the beginning of the lesson. The instructor notes that in teaching composition to K–4 students, teachers should encourage students to generate their own guidelines for evaluation.

Finally, the methods class discusses the effectiveness of both the compositions and the evaluation guidelines used in writing the critiques.

Suggested Resources

Lavender, Cheryl. *The Song Writing Kit.* Milwaukee, WI: Jenson Publishing, 1986.

Wiggins, Jackie. *Composition in the Classroom: A Tool for Teaching.* Reston, VA: Music Educators National Conference, 1990.

Wiggins, Jacqueline H. "Children's Strategies for Solving Compositional Problems with Peers." *Journal of Research in Music Education* 42, no. 3 (Fall 1994): 232–51.

Wilcox, Ella, ed. "How Do Children Compose?" *Teaching Music* 2, no. 3 (December 1994): 38–39.

❖ ❖ ❖ ❖ ❖ ❖ ❖

STANDARD 5A

Reading and notating music: *Students read whole, half, dotted half, quarter, and eighth notes and rests in 2/4, 3/4, and 4/4 meter signatures.*

Strategy

The instructor takes methods students through the Music Learning Sequence of Froseth and Weikart in *Movement to Music*:

- *Listen-Watch-Move.* The instructor leads students in synchronizing various movements to music. Recorded selection features a steady beat.

- *Lap-Pat, Listen, and Echo.* The instructor establishes a steady lap-pat and asks students to echo verbal syllables (*du/de*) to a recorded selection.

- *Lap-Pat, Listen, and Associate Rhythmic Syllables.* The instructor plays rhythmic patterns on recorder to a recorded selection. Students associate rhythmic syllables as selection is performed.

- *Listen, Echo, Look, and Associate.* The instructor establishes a steady lap-pat and chants a rhythmic pattern to the recorded selection while displaying the appropriate flash card just before and during the student echo.

- *Look and Say.* The instructor establishes a steady lap-pat and then displays a sequence of flash cards in 2/4 meter. Students respond to what they see. Successive flash cards of notes and rests in 3/4 and 4/4 meters are presented for student response and discussion. As a variation, flash cards could feature simple rhythmic patterns derived from familiar children's songs.

Students practice the process, take turns as leader, and discuss how to adapt this activity for teaching K–4 students of various ages to read notation.

Suggested Resource

Froseth, James O., and Phyllis Weikart. *Movement to Music.* Chicago: GIA Publications, 1981.

Reading and notating music: *Students use a system (that is, syllables, numbers, or letters)
to read simple pitch notation in the treble clef in major keys.*

Strategy

The instructor tells methods students that each student will take a turn teaching a choral piece written
for students at the K–4 level. The class chooses one choral piece from a set of masterworks for young
children and prepares an iconographic map for the students' part, eliminating all but the part the students are to sing and transforming the traditional symbol system into visual images that convey pitches
high and low in "paper-space." Colors may also be used to designate specific pitches on the scale.

The instructor asks students to do the following procedure.

- *Preparation.* Teaching student tells singers to listen as he or she sings the whole song while paint
  ing its melody in the air, following the melodic contour and shaping the dynamics and phrases
  with hand gestures.

- *Presentation.* Teaching student tells singers to refer to the iconographic notation and track the
  phrases with their fingers and eyes as he or she models each and they imitate each in return.

- *Practice.* As singers become comfortable with the scale and have a feeling for the piece, they
  sightread the next portions of the piece from the iconographic notation. They sing the entire
  song through to reinforce their sightreading skills. The class then discusses methods by which
  K–4 students begin to transfer from reading and writing iconic notation to using standard notation in the treble clef.

Suggested Resources

Bruner, Jerome. *Toward a Theory of Instruction.* Cambridge: Harvard University Press, 1966.

Gardner, Howard. *Frames of Mind.* New York: Basic Books, 1993.

Rao, Doreen, ed. *Choral Music for Children: An Annotated List.* Reston, VA: Music Educators National
Conference, 1990.

Winner, Ellen. *Invented Worlds: The Psychology of the Arts.* 1982. Reprint, Cambridge: Harvard
University Press, 1985.

Reading and notating music: *Students identify symbols and traditional terms referring to
dynamics, tempo, and articulation and interpret them correctly when performing.*

Strategy

During active listening to brief passages of several recordings that illustrate contrasting dynamics, tem-
pos, and articulations, methods students demonstrate these features through movements. Students consider nontraditional symbols that might be used by young composers to indicate the dynamic contrasts
and tempo changes in these examples. Students also indicate the traditional dynamic symbols and

terms for tempo that would be appropriate for the music they have heard.

The instructor projects a transparency of a familiar song with markings for dynamics, tempo, and articulation. The class discusses these features. Students plan the performance of the song, giving special attention to its markings for dynamics, tempo, and articulation.

Using the same familiar song, the instructor presents a score for classroom instruments that includes markings for dynamics, tempo, and articulation, and students plan, rehearse, and perform the piece. Their performance may be taped for review.

Reflecting on the class activities, the class discusses how to introduce K–4 students to these features of music notation through active listening and movement.

Suggested Resources

Atterbury, Betty W., and Carol P. Richardson. *The Experience of Teaching General Music.* New York: McGraw-Hill, 1995.

Campbell, Patricia Shehan, and Carol Scott-Kassner. *Music in Childhood: From Preschool through the Elementary Grades.* Old Tappan, NJ: Schirmer Books/Simon & Schuster, 1995.

Nye, Robert E., Vernice T. Nye, Gary M. Martin, and Mary Lou Van Rysselberghe. *Music in the Elementary School,* 6th ed. Englewood Cliffs, NJ: Prentice-Hall, 1992.

STANDARD 5D

Reading and notating music: Students use standard symbols to notate meter, rhythm, pitch, and dynamics in simple patterns presented by the teacher.

Strategy

Methods students consider the value of introducing recorder playing to fourth-grade students as a medium for having them learn to sightread and notate standard notation symbols. They identify the most common symbols of meter, rhythm, pitch, and dynamics that appear in standard notation.

As a model for teaching notation to fourth-grade students, the instructor first sings a brief melodic phrase using solfège, and methods students echo the phrase with Curwen hand signs. The instructor then plays the same phrase on recorder, and students echo the phrase on their recorders. The class determines the meter of the example. Each student transcribes the melodic phrase on manuscript paper as the instructor plays it repeatedly. One student then writes the melody on the chalkboard. Discussion follows regarding the melodic phrase's rhythmic characteristics, intervals of pitch, and dynamics, and students add appropriate symbols to their dictation. The instructor and class then perform the now-familiar melodic phrase with expression.

Methods students then hear, sing, play, and transcribe a new melodic phrase using standard notation symbols. They individually assign to their transcriptions symbols for rhythmic characteristics and dynamics.

Considering fourth-grade students' capabilities for reading and notating music, the class discusses any potential problems that they see in using these procedures with fourth-grade students.

(continued)

Suggested Resources

Bamberger, Jean. *The Mind behind the Musical Ear: How Children Develop Musical Intelligence.* Harvard University Press, 1991.

Upitis, Rena. "Fostering Children's Compositions." *General Music Today* 8, no. 3 (Spring 1995): 16–19.

◆ ◆ ◆ ◆ ◆ ◆ ◆

STANDARD 6A

Listening to, analyzing, and describing music: Students identify simple music forms when presented aurally.

Strategy

The instructor explains that the goal of this lesson is to understand how to teach the rondo form through work in four different disciplines. Methods students listen to Mozart's "Rondo alla Turca" and discuss its rondo form. The class then discusses variations of rondo form and they list characteristics for the simple rondo and five- and seven-part rondos.

With the class divided into three groups, each group must use the Mozart recording and a different assigned art medium to devise an activity for teaching the rondo form to K–4 students in an interdisciplinary way:

- The first group will use the recording and art materials.
- The second group will use the recording and dance.
- The third group will use the recording and poetry.

After all the planning has been completed, each group presents its part of the interdisciplinary whole to the class with the methods class students doing the given activities. As a summary activity, the instructor plays three different listening selections and the methods students determine whether each is in rondo form.

Suggested Resource

Citron, Marvin, and Margaret Gayle. *Educational Renaissance: Our Schools at the Turn of the 21st Century.* New York: St. Martin's Press, 1991.

STANDARD 6B

Listening to, analyzing, and describing music: Students demonstrate perceptual skills by moving, by answering questions about, and by describing aural examples of music of various styles representing diverse cultures.

Strategy

Methods students listen to the first sixteen measures of the second movement from Haydn's Symphony no. 94 ("Surprise") and identify its musical characteristics. The instructor and the class work together to outline a strategy for teaching this piece in an elementary general music class.

The instructor then divides the class into small groups and, including selections from several different styles and cultures, assigns each group another selection of music. After listening to the piece, each group identifies its prominent musical characteristics and writes a teaching strategy to be used in an elementary general music classroom. The strategies should include a movement response, discussion questions, and a call chart. After all groups have completed the strategies, each group gives a short presentation of its strategy to the class.

Suggested Resources

Harpole, Patricia. *Los Mariachis: An Introduction to Mexican Mariachi Music.* Danbury, CT: World Music Press, 1991.

Serwardda, W. Moses. *Songs and Stories from Uganda.* Edited by Hewitt Pantaleoni. Danbury, CT: World Music Press, 1987. Book and audiocassette.

Sims, Wendy. "Sound Approaches to Elementary Music Listening." *Music Educators Journal* 77, no. 4 (December 1990): 38–42.

STANDARD 6C

Listening to, analyzing, and describing music: Students use appropriate terminology in explaining music, music notation, instruments and voices, and music performances.

Strategy

The instructor divides the methods class into groups of two or three students and assigns each group the task of preparing a short interactive HyperCard or HyperStudio stack. [*Note:* At least one student in each group should be familiar with HyperCard or HyperStack programming.] Each stack should consist of at least three cards based upon one topic, such as tempo, rhythm, dynamics, form, instruments, or melody.

Using "Spring," from *The Four Seasons* by Antonio Vivaldi, each group focuses on the presentation of terminology used to describe the music according to its topic. Each stack should use a compact disc within it. Stacks should include one of the following: (1) an exercise in which K–4 students would identify whether examples from the piece are solo or tutti sections; (2) sections in which the group describes its topic, such as form (ritornello), in a narrative style while the music is being played; (3) a quiz to identify terms used within the topic, or; (4) a musical notation font to draw a section of the music for the explanation of ideas such as cadences. The groups exchange their stacks, work through them, and prepare written questions for the stack creators if any clarification is needed. Upon completion, all students should be given a copy of each stack for their personal libraries.

Alternative procedure: Presentation software such as Power Point may be used instead of HyperCard or HyperStudio. Students could narratively describe their musical sections and play the recording on a separate player or incorporate .wav files (format for the encoding of sound data) into their presentation. The quiz could be presented as simple questions asked through the computer and answered on paper.

(continued)

Suggested Resources

Goodman, Danny. *The Complete HyperCard 2.2 Handbook.* New York: Random House, 1993.

Salem, Julaine. "HyperCard: The Two-Dimensional Manipulative." *The Computing Teacher* 19, no. 6 (March 1992).

STANDARD 6D

Listening to, analyzing, and describing music: Students identify the sounds of a variety of instruments, including many orchestra and band instruments, and instruments from various cultures, as well as children's voices and male and female adult voices.

Strategy

After presenting one of the suggested introductory materials (see Suggested Readings) as an example of a basic overview of musical instruments, the instructor selects Tchaikovsky's *Nutcracker Suite* as a study piece and divides methods class into four groups. Each group listens to a recording of one of the following excerpts: "March of the Tin Soldiers," "Dance of the Sugar Plum Fairy," "Trepak," or "Waltz of the Flowers."

The instructor asks each group to identify as many instruments as it can in its excerpt. Then, each group describes to the class the musical sounds they discovered, making special note of any sounds that especially appealed to them.

After the group presentations, the instructor tells the specific story pertaining to each group's excerpt (from the ballet scenario—see program notes for any recording). Then each group discusses the implications of the story on the choices of instruments used and how its excerpt was different from the others.

The instructor then assigns each student to write a similar lesson plan for Prokofiev's *Peter and the Wolf,* Britten's *The Young Person's Guide to the Orchestra,* or another programmatic piece appropriate for K–4 students.

Suggested Resources

Kamien, Roger. *Music: An Appreciation,* 2d brief ed. New York: McGraw-Hill, 1994.

Machlis, Joseph, and Kristine Forney. *The Enjoyment of Music,* 7th ed. shorter. New York: W. W. Norton, 1995.

Musical Instruments: An Interactive Journey into the World of Musical Instruments. Seattle: Microsoft Corporation, 1993. Macintosh or IBM CD-ROM.

STANDARD 6E

Listening to, analyzing, and describing music: *Respond through purposeful movement to selected prominent music characteristics or to specific music events while listening to music.*

Strategy

While the instructor plays on a snare drum a series of improvisations that vary in dynamic level, tempo, and style, methods students walk around in a circle, keeping the steady beat in their feet or hands. Students also respond to changes in meter, dynamics, and tempo by adjusting their movements appropriately. They then perform movements expressive of the mood of the music being played by the teacher on the snare drum. To focus students' attention on sound and silence, musical chairs could be played using a snare drum.

The instructor then provides students with short musical selections that have simple changes in dynamic level, tempo, or style and asks them to create lesson plans that involve K–4 students in analyzing and describing music through movement. Students could be directed to read the sections on Eurhythmics in *Teaching Music in the Twentieth Century* before completing this assignment.

Suggested Resources

Choksy, Lois, Robert M. Abramson, Avon E. Gillespie, and David Woods. *Teaching Music in the Twentieth Century.* Englewood Cliffs, NJ: Prentice-Hall, 1986.

Weikart, Phyllis. *Teaching Movement and Dance: A Sequential Approach to Rhythmic Movement.* Ypsilanti, MI: High/Scope Press, 1982.

◆ ◆ ◆ ◆ ◆ ◆ ◆

STANDARD 7A

Evaluating music and music performances: *Students devise criteria for evaluating performances and compositions.*

Strategy

Methods students define criteria K–4 students might use to evaluate performances and compositions. They consider methods that would encourage K–4 students to generate their own criteria for evaluating music. Analyses by K–4 students might fall into three categories of questions:

- Analytical—What is happening in the music? How is it organized? What timbres are heard?
- Judicial—What kind of descriptive words best describe the different timbres? Is the way it was sung or played expressive and appropriate?
- Creative—Would you like to do something new with this music?

The instructor tells methods students that they would select a musical excerpt for listening related to one of the current musical experiences of the K–4 students they would be teaching. (For example,

(continued)

"Your composition had a very interesting ending. Now let's listen to a similar solution by Beethoven." Teacher plays the first movement of Beethoven's Symphony no. 5 to demonstrate.)

The instructor divides the class into groups and assigns each group a specific mode of analysis K–4 students might use, either orally in guided class discussion, in written responses, or by answering questions with a computer program. Each group creates a simple model for K–4 students within that mode. The class reconvenes to share these models.

Suggested Resources

Schafer, R. Murray. *Creative Music Education.* New York: Schirmer Books, 1976.

Upitis, Rena. "Fostering Children's Compositions." *General Music Today* 8, no. 3 (Spring 1995): 16–19.

Wiggins, Jackie. *Composition in the Classroom: A Tool for Teaching.* Reston, VA: Music Educators National Conference, 1990.

STANDARD 7B

Evaluating music and music performances: Students explain, using appropriate music terminology, their personal preferences for specific musical works and styles.

Strategy

The instructor asks methods students to name those musical terms easily understood and used by students at the K–4 level. The list may begin with the elements of melody, rhythm, harmony, and form, and should include simple terms for the expressive qualities of timbre, tempo, and dynamics, and for basic notation. These terms are listed on the chalkboard as the class agrees with their inclusion and their definitions.

Using colored flash cards (each listing a term on one side and its definition on the other), the instructor demonstrates visual focus on each musical term. Methods students consider ways to reinforce K–4 students' understanding and retention of appropriate musical terminology (e.g., posting terms on cards around the room, active listening, game playing).

The class discusses how K–4 students may be encouraged to use these terms to describe their personal preferences for specific works of music or appealing styles. For example, K–4 students may listen to two brief recordings of music of contrasting genres and be given the opportunity to express personal preferences for one or the other using appropriate musical terms. Familiarity with these terms will also be useful to K–4 students when they evaluate their own and others' compositions and performances.

Suggested Resource

Hackett, Patricia, and Carolynn A. Lindeman. *The Musical Classroom: Backgrounds, Models, and Skills for Elementary Teaching,* 4th ed. Englewood Cliffs, NJ: Prentice-Hall, 1997.

◆ ◆ ◆ ◆ ◆ ◆ ◆

Understanding relationships between music, the other arts, and disciplines outside the arts: Students identify similarities and differences in the meanings of common terms used in the various arts.

Strategy

The instructor plays a brief excerpt of music (e.g., first movement of Beethoven's Piano Concerto no. 5—"Emperor"). Methods students identify the historical period in which it was written and discuss features of form, line, and contrast that they heard.

Students view examples of visual art (prints or projected copies) painted during the same period. The class considers form, line, and contrast of these drawings or paintings.

The instructor then helps the class to note the physical features of the classroom as architectural examples of form, line, and contrast.

On videotape, students watch an excerpt of the children's chorus in Act I of the Bizet opera *Carmen,* a visual and aural art form performed by children.

All discuss the meaning of common terms for form, line, and contrast as they relate to each other in these music and visual art examples, identifying similarities and differences. Methods students consider thoughtful ways to provide K–4 students with visual and aural experiences that contribute to their understanding of relationships between music, the other arts, and disciplines outside the arts.

Suggested Resources

Fleming, William. *Arts and Ideas,* 9th ed. Orlando, FL: Harcourt Brace, 1995.

Funes, Donald J. *Musical Involvement,* 2d ed. Orlando, FL: Harcourt Brace, 1992. Book and recording.

Understanding relationships between music, the other arts, and disciplines outside the arts: Students identify ways in which the principles and subject matter of other disciplines taught in the school are interrelated with those of music.

Strategy

Methods students sing the folk song "Bought Me a Cat." The instructor divides the class into small groups and assigns each group a picture-book version of the song.

In their groups, students compare the book to the sung version, looking for similarities or differences in the text (order of animals, sounds, etc.) and ways in which the story is told through music. A recording of Aaron Copland's *Old American Songs, Part I:* "Bought Me a Cat," may also be used in this activity. Each group shares its information with the class. Then each group prepares a lesson plan for K–4 students involving the picture-book version of the song. The lesson plans should include a follow-up activity to be taught by the children's reading teacher.

(continued)

Other songs worthy of comparison with related books include "I Know an Old Lady Who Swallowed a Fly" and "Old McDonald Had a Farm."

Suggested Children's Literature

Galdone, Paul. *Cat Goes Fiddle-I-Fee*. New York: Clarion Books, 1985.

Manson, Christopher. *A Farmyard Song: An Old Rhyme with New Pictures*. New York: North-South Books, 1992.

Suggested Resources

McCoy, Claire. "Music and Children's Literature: Natural Partners." *General Music Today* 7, no. 3, (Spring 1994): 15–19.

Smale, Marcelyn. "Picture Books as Music Resources." *General Music Today* 8, no. 1 (Fall 1994): 24–25.

Will, Howard. *Teaching Music* 4, no. 5 (April 1997): 34–36.

◆ ◆ ◆ ◆ ◆ ◆ ◆

STANDARD 9A

Understanding music in relation to history and culture: Students identify by genre or style aural examples of music from various historical periods and cultures.

Strategy

The instructor first plays a selection of Gregorian chant and asks methods students to comment on how the piece sounded to them, how it made them feel, and what its genre and stylistic period are. Repeating the selection, the instructor asks students to indicate by raising their hands when the melodies start and stop.

In a second activity, the instructor teaches the class one of the standard psalm tones from the *Liber Usualis*. The students learn that these tones were originally applied to the psalms of the Christian Bible.

After learning to sing the half cadence in the middle and the full cadence at the end, the students are asked to take any two-phrase sentences (proverb, children's verse, famous saying) and sing them to the psalm tone, as groups or individually. Following this, students improvise their own sentences to sing to the psalm tone.

As a final activity, methods students prepare a listening guide for a Gregorian chant selection that could be used with K–4 students.

Suggested Resources

Apel, Willi. *Gregorian Chant*. Bloomington, IN: Indiana University Press, 1958: 179–245.

Choir of the Benedictine Monastery of Santo Domingo De Silos. *Gregorian Chant at the Monastery of Silos*. Francisco Lara. EMI Classics CDZ 62735.

Liber Usualis. Tournai, Belgium: Desclée and Company, 1934. See rules for chanting of psalms, xxxii–xxxv; psalms, 112–17, 128–207; common tones of the mass, 102–09. Later editions use modern notation.

Yudkin, Jeremy. *Music in Medieval Europe.* History of Music Series. Englewood Cliffs, NJ: Prentice-Hall, 1989.

STANDARD 9B

Understanding music in relation to history and culture: Students describe in simple terms how elements of music are used in music examples from various cultures of the world.

Strategy

The instructor has asked methods students to review a sequenced series of lessons on vocal tone color in *The Music Connection,* Grade 4 (teacher edition, part 1, pp. 100–109a), as impetus for class discussion of the following questions: What vocal tone colors were identified? What teaching strategies led to a greater awareness of vocal tone color? What musical traditions were represented in the examples? Does vocal tone color differ from culture to culture?

In class, the instructor introduces text and audio resources pertaining to a variety of musical traditions. Using these resources, students create lists of examples of vocal tone color from diverse musical traditions and subsequently construct "What Do You Hear?" charts for the examples (following the model from p. 109a in their reading), which they tape.

Students present their taped selections and "What Do You Hear?" charts to the class and put together a master list of examples. Class discussion follows as to how this strategy may be adapted and extended to provide a model for teaching other elements of music.

Suggested Resources

Booher, Jane, ed. *Maa-baa-hi Má-hac (We're Going Singing!): A Traditional Song Collection of the Mandan and Hidatsa Tribes.* New Town, ND: Fort Berthold Community College, 1992.

Mariachi Vargas de Tecalitlán. *Sones de Jalisco.* RCA Victor MKS 1653.

The Music Connection, Grade 4 (teacher edition, part 1). Parsippany, NJ: Silver Burdett Ginn, 1995.

Nguyen, Phong T., and Patricia Shehan Campbell. *From Rice Paddies to Temple Yards: Traditional Music of Vietnam.* Danbury, CT: World Music Press, 1989.

Understanding music in relation to history and culture: Students identify various uses of music in their daily experiences and describe characteristics that make certain music suitable for each use.

Strategy

The instructor describes to the methods students his or her first childhood experiences with music and illustrates with examples, such as photographs of the instructor as a child, a childhood instrument, or a brief example of recorded music created by the instructor as a child.

Next, the instructor reads brief examples from his or her own musical autobiography and then asks students to write their own musical autobiographies, as follows: Tell your own musical story. How were you introduced to music as a child? Describe the musical culture in which you grew up. What kind of music did your family listen to and/or perform? What does music mean to you? How have your knowledge, skills, and attitudes about music changed over the years? Students could also be asked to read a biography or autobiography of a composer and compare his or her musical story with their own.

Students share significant portions of their autobiographies with the class and discuss the meanings their earliest musical experiences had for them. They could also identify the functions of music in their lives and describe the characteristics that make certain music suitable for a particular function.

As a final activity, students discuss with the class ways in which music teachers can facilitate the exploration of K–4 students' own musical cultures and experiences.

Suggested Resources

Gardner, Howard. *To Open Minds: Chinese Clues to the Dilemma of Contemporary Education.* New York: Basic Books, 1989.

Holt, John. *Never Too Late.* New York: Delacorte Press, 1978.

Ledoux, Denis. *Turning Memories into Memoirs: A Handbook for Writing Lifestories.* Lisbon Falls, ME: Soleil Press, 1993.

Understanding music in relation to history and culture: Students identify and describe roles of musicians in various music settings and cultures.

Strategy

Methods students have completed assigned reading of two articles on careers and the article by Bennett Reimer (see Suggested Resources). In class, they discuss the importance of context in dealing with music of representative world cultures (Reimer); career settings; specific careers directly or indirectly related to music; personal musical roles of parents, peers, and students; and how musicians' roles might be similar or different in various cultures.

As a result of the discussion, the class generates a list of musical roles and careers to be explored with K–4 students. Then they brainstorm about how K–4 students could experience selected roles and careers (e.g., games involving role-playing, field trips, and exposure to instructional materials in music series textbooks) in several different settings and cultures.

Finally, methods students complete the following short in-class activity: The instructor assigns each student a particular role of a musician, making sure that several cultures are represented. Then each student creates a description for the role suitable for (1) a primary grade class and (2) an intermediate grade class. Students share their descriptions with other class members, and the class critiques each description.

Suggested Resources

Bjorneberg, Paul, ed. *Exploring Careers in Music.* Reston, VA: Music Educators National Conference, 1990.

Cowden, Robert, ed. "Careers in Music." Reston, VA: Music Educators National Conference, 1989. Brochure.

"Focus on Careers." *Teaching Music* 1, no. 3, (October 1993): 30–41. Six articles.

Reimer, Bennett. "Can We Understand the Music of Foreign Cultures?" In *Musical Connections: Tradition and Change.* Tampa, FL: International Society of Music Education, 1994.

Titon, Jeff Todd, ed. *Worlds of Music: An Introduction to the Music of the World's Peoples,* 3d ed. Old Tappan, NJ: Schirmer Books/Simon & Schuster, 1996. Book and recordings.

STANDARD 9E

Understanding music in relation to history and culture: *Students demonstrate audience behavior appropriate for the context and style of music performed.*

Strategy

The instructor initiates a class discussion about how various styles of music are performed (e.g., improvised or recreated from notation, performed in a formal or informal setting) and what the sociological implications are for the audience (e.g., dress, audience attentiveness, audience interaction).

Methods students are then assigned to attend a variety of performances and describe the audience behavior for each type of event. Students must also interview members of each audience to find out their reasons for attending.

Next, students compare and contrast audience behaviors for the different types of performances and present their findings to the class. They then discuss ways in which K–4 students can be taught to demonstrate appropriate audience behavior for various contexts and styles of musical performances.

Suggested Resource

Wilcox, Ella, and Gail Crum, eds. "No Bubblegum During Beethoven." *Teaching Music* 2, no. 6. (June 1995): 30–31.

General Music
Grades 5-8

STANDARD 1A

Singing, alone and with others, a varied repertoire of music: *Students sing accurately and with good breath control throughout their singing ranges, alone and in small and large ensembles.*

Strategy

The instructor has assigned readings and viewing of the video *Singing in General Music* in preparation for a class discussion concerning characteristics of and ways to develop unchanged and changing male and female voices. The class discusses techniques for identifying singing range and the stages of the changing voice, as well as ways to develop proper intonation and breath control.

Methods students then choose one of the following for an in-class activity: writing an instructional sequence that describes how to identify the singing range of students; or, devising vocal exercises to improve the singer's range, breath control, and intonation.

The instructor divides the class into pairs for microteaches. One student in each pair demonstrates identification of singing ranges; the other demonstrates a vocalise for proper singing. Each student critiques the other for content and presentation.

Microteaches can be videotaped as sources for implementation of a specific standard in a middle-level general music setting.

Suggested Resources

Cooksey, John M. *Working with the Adolescent Voice.* St. Louis: Concordia Publishing House, 1992.

Gackle, Lynne. "The Adolescent Female Voice: Characteristics of Change and Stages of Development." *Choral Journal* 31, no. 8 (March 1991): 17–25.

Gackle, Lynne. "Changing Voice." In *Music at the Middle Level: Building Strong Programs,* edited by June Hinckley. Reston, VA: Music Educators National Conference, 1994.

Thompson, Keith, ed. *Singing in General Music.* Reston, VA: Music Educators National Conference, 1994. Videocassette.

STANDARD 1B

Singing, alone and with others, a varied repertoire of music: *Students sing with expression and technical accuracy a repertoire of vocal literature with a level of difficulty of 2, on a scale of 1 to 6, including some songs performed from memory.*

Strategy

Prior to the class meeting, students in groups of four have located several songs, with a level of difficulty of 2, from middle-level music series textbooks. They have chosen one of the songs and have made two copies for use in class, one with all expressive markings deleted. In class, they develop a procedure for teaching one of the songs with (1) effective dynamics, (2) appropriate tempo, (3) rhythmic accuracy, and (4) pitch accuracy, all related to the meaning of the text.

(continued)

Each group teaches its song to the rest of the class. One student from each group is responsible for presenting one of the four components.

Suggested teaching procedures:

- *Dynamics and tempo:* Perform without expression; experiment to determine how sudden or gradual dynamic or tempo changes can affect meaning; determine appropriate dynamics and tempo.

- *Rhythmic accuracy:* Determine where varying rhythmic durations contribute to natural word rhythms; analyze for repetition and variety to aid in memorization.

- *Pitch accuracy:* Relate intervals to text meaning (i.e., disjunct intervals suggest accents, and conjunct intervals suggest continuity); analyze for repetition and variety to aid in memorization.

In writing, students critique presentations for content, preparation, and appropriateness for middle-level general music.

Suggested Resources

The Music Connection, Grades 5–8. Parsippany, NJ: Silver Burdett Ginn, 1995.

Music and You, Grades 5–8. New York: Macmillan/McGraw-Hill, 1991.

Share the Music, Grades 5–8. New York: Macmillan/McGraw-Hill, 1995, 1997.

The World of Music, Grades 5–8. Parsippany, NJ: Silver Burdett Ginn, 1991.

STANDARD 1C

Singing, alone and with others, a varied repertoire of music: *Students sing music representing diverse genres and cultures, with expression appropriate for the work being performed.*

Strategy

Methods class is divided into small groups to create teaching presentations of ten to fifteen minutes. The instructor has assigned selections representing cultural diversity from *Roots and Branches,* as well as readings in world music traditions that relate to the particular musical selection. Each group analyzes its selection and devises a warm-up including melodic and rhythmic motives from the piece or a solfège exercise based on the key of the piece.

Acting as a teaching team, each group leads the class in discovery of the music, using techniques and expression appropriate to the particular genre or style. For example, a song from Ghana could be learned by rote—in call and response—to be sung against a bell pattern, eventually incorporating walking and clapping in polyrhythmic layers; in contrast, a canon representing Western art music could be sung in unison with solfège based on the diatonic scale.

Teaching teams are encouraged to use a variety of approaches that have potential to engage middle-level students in active learning of each selection. The instructor videotapes the teaching presentations for the students for self-reflective journal entries.

Suggested Resources

Adzenyah, Abraham Kobena, Dumisani Maraire, and Judith Cook Tucker. *Let Your Voice Be Heard!: Songs from Ghana and Zimbabwe,* 2d ed. Danbury, CT: World Music Press, 1997. Book and recording.

Anderson, William M., and Patricia Shehan Campbell, eds. *Multicultural Perspectives in Music Education,* 2d ed. Reston, VA: Music Educators National Conference, 1996.

Campbell, Patricia Shehan, Ellen McCullough-Brabson, and Judith Cook Tucker. *Roots and Branches: A Legacy of Multicultural Music for Children.* Danbury, CT: World Music Press, 1994. Book and recording.

STANDARD 1D

Singing, alone and with others, a varied repertoire of music: Students sing music written in two and three parts.

Strategy

Methods students have collected canons/rounds, partner songs, and two- and three-part octavo selections from current music textbook series.

The instructor briefly reviews middle-level vocal characteristics and ranges as well as criteria for selecting appropriate music. Students then compare the levels of difficulty of the pieces they have collected.

The instructor divides the class into groups and assigns a different song form to each group. Groups are instructed to develop a teaching sequence for one of the selected pieces in that form, making certain to include the following: teaching the melody using solfège; and classifying the intervals between the beginning pitch and vocal entry points in the assigned music.

After the groups complete the teaching sequences, each group chooses one member to teach the song form to one other group, and the two groups evaluate the teaching sequences for potential effectiveness with middle-level students. After making suggested changes, they share the teaching procedures with the other groups.

Suggested Resources

Cooksey, John M. *Working with the Adolescent Voice.* St. Louis: Concordia Publishing House, 1992.

Gackle, Lynne. "Changing Voice." In *Music at the Middle Level: Building Strong Programs,* edited by June Hinckley. Reston, VA: Music Educators National Conference, 1994.

Thompson, Keith, ed. *Singing in General Music.* Reston, VA: Music Educators National Conference, 1994. Videocassette.

◆ ◆ ◆ ◆ ◆ ◆

STANDARD 2A

Performing on instruments, alone and with others, a varied repertoire of music: Students perform on at least one instrument accurately and independently, alone and in small and large ensembles, with good posture, good playing position, and good breath, bow, or stick control.

Strategy

Methods class has been divided into groups and each student has been assigned to present a five-minute microteaching demonstration for keyboard, focusing on good posture and good playing position. The microteaching demonstration should include the following criteria: instructional content based on one item from keyboard instruction for beginners, single-student or small-group format, and a means provided to use the newly learned skill to perform a melody or a harmonic accompaniment.

The teaching student may choose to direct instruction to a single student or a small ensemble, as long as there are examples of both formats in each group. Members of each group observe when the instruction is for a single student; they participate when the instruction is for a small ensemble.

Students write a description of each demonstration in their group, including a critique focusing on content, presentation, and learning outcome. Critiques are shared verbally within the group.

Suggested Resources

Chamberlin, Linda L. "Success with Keyboards in Middle School." *Music Educators Journal* 79, no. 9 (May 1993): 31–36.

Lancaster, E. L. "Teaching Piano Electronically." *Clavier* 33 (April 1994): 33–36.

Walczyk, Eugenia B. "Kids on Keyboards: Learning Music Concepts." *Music Educators Journal* 79, no. 2 (October 1991): 40–43.

STANDARD 2B

Performing on instruments, alone and with others, a varied repertoire of music: Students perform with expression and technical accuracy on at least one string, wind, percussion, or classroom instrument a repertoire of instrumental literature with a level of difficulty of 2, on a scale of 1 to 6.

Strategy

From middle-level music series textbooks, the instructor has selected two songs with a level of difficulty of 2 that can be performed on guitar. Methods students sing through both songs to decide the mood that should be expressed in the performance. They discuss whether any changes in expression should occur during the song.

Students select an appropriate strum, tempo, and dynamic level for the first song. Then they decide whether the second song should be performed with the same or different strum, tempo, and dynamics.

Finally, students break into small groups to perform the two songs, both alone and with a few other students. They take notes on the learning sequences, and then the class discusses whether the sequence can be used effectively with middle-level students. Students make any necessary changes in their notes.

Suggested Resources

The Music Connection, Grades 5–8. Parsippany, NJ: Silver Burdett Ginn, 1995.

Music and You, Grades 5–8. New York: Macmillan/McGraw-Hill, 1991.

Share the Music, Grades 5–8. New York: Macmillan/McGraw-Hill, 1995, 1997.

The World of Music, Grades 5–8. Parsippany, NJ: Silver Burdett Ginn, 1991.

STANDARD 2C

Performing on instruments, alone and with others, a varied repertoire of music: *Students perform music representing diverse genres and cultures, with expression appropriate for the work being performed.*

Strategy

Methods students engage in activities to become proficient in performing music of diverse cultures so that they can use this skill in teaching middle-level students. They perform a short Javanese gamelan composition as outlined in assigned readings from *Multicultural Perspectives in Music Education* (pp. 367–73). Then they discuss some of the salient features of this music: focus on percussion instruments, duple meter with cycles of beats outlined by gongs, and pentatonic melodies.

The entire class compares Javanese gamelan music with an African percussion ensemble of metal bells, rattle, and drums (as outlined in *Integrating Music into the Elementary Classroom,* pp. 410–12). The instructor tells students to pay particular attention to the polyrhythm in the African example. They discuss similarities and differences in instruments and rhythms of music from Indonesia and Africa. For their use in developing lessons for middle-level general music, they record in writing a summary of the newly learned performance and listening skills, the expressive loud and soft playing styles of Javanese gamelan compositions, and the percussive rhythmic style of much African music.

Suggested Resources

Anderson, William M., and Patricia Shehan Campbell, eds. *Multicultural Perspectives in Music Education,* 2d ed. Reston, VA: Music Educators National Conference, 1996.

Anderson, William M., and Joy E. Lawrence. *Integrating Music into the Elementary Classroom,* 3d ed. Belmont, CA: Wadsworth Publishing Company, 1995.

Sands, Rosita. "What Prospective Music Teachers Need to Know about Black Music." *Black Music Research Journal* 16, no. 2 (Fall 1996): 225–37.

STANDARD 2D

Performing on instruments, alone and with others, a varied repertoire of music: Students play by ear simple melodies on a melodic instrument and simple accompaniments on a harmonic instrument.

Strategy

The instructor has assigned methods students to locate several three-chord songs in middle-level music series textbooks. Working in small groups, each group selects two of the songs for another group to use for playing simple melodies and simple accompaniments by ear. The instructor checks the selected songs for each group in order to avoid duplication.

Groups choose the melodic and harmonic instruments from available classroom instruments. They practice and prepare the melody and chords for both songs that they have selected, before giving the songs to another group to play by ear.

Each group pairs with another group to form Groups 1 and 2. For the melodic activity, Group 1 starts by announcing the title of the song, the key, and the meter. As Group 1 plays the chord progression of the song, Group 2 plays the melody by ear; Groups 1 and 2 then reverse the process, Group 1 playing a melody selected by Group 2.

For the harmonic activity, Group 2 begins by announcing the title of the song, the key, and the meter. As Group 2 plays the melody, Group 1 accompanies on a selected harmonic instrument; both groups reverse the process.

The entire class analyzes the strategy, pinpointing strengths and possible problems. Students suggest ways to make the activity more effective in the middle-level general music classroom.

Suggested Resources

The Music Connection, Grades 5–8. Parsippany, NJ: Silver Burdett Ginn, 1995.

Music and You, Grades 5–8. New York: Macmillan/McGraw-Hill, 1991.

Share the Music, Grades 5–8. New York: Macmillan/McGraw-Hill, 1995, 1997.

The World of Music, Grades 5–8. Parsippany, NJ: Silver Burdett Ginn, 1991.

◆ ◆ ◆ ◆ ◆ ◆ ◆

STANDARD 3A

Improvising melodies, variations, and accompaniments: Students improvise simple harmonic accompaniments.

Strategy

The instructor has assigned methods students to select a two-chord folk song from middle-level music series textbooks. They have been asked to bring the book to class along with a soprano recorder.

Working in pairs, one student plays the melody on the recorder while the partner improvises a two-chord accompaniment using the auto-accompaniment feature of an electronic keyboard. The keyboard performer starts and ends the performance. The students then switch positions to give students who were playing recorders first an opportunity to improvise on the keyboards.

Each member of the pair critiques the other's playing and improvisation. They discuss how this activity can be adapted using other harmonic instruments available in a middle-level music classroom.

Suggested Resources

The Music Connection, Grades 5–8. Parsippany, NJ: Silver Burdett Ginn, 1995.

Music and You, Grades 5–8. New York: Macmillan/McGraw-Hill, 1991.

Share the Music, Grades 5–8. New York: Macmillan/McGraw-Hill, 1995, 1997.

The World of Music, Grades 5–8. Parsippany, NJ: Silver Burdett Ginn, 1991.

STANDARD 3B

Improvising melodies, variations, and accompaniments: Students improvise melodic embellishments and simple rhythmic and melodic variations on given pentatonic melodies and melodies in major keys.

Strategy

The instructor has assigned methods students readings that describe the ways that a composer can alter melody, rhythm, harmony, texture, tempo, dynamics, form, tone quality, and style to create variations in music. From middle-level music series textbooks, each student has selected one pentatonic song that would appeal to middle-level students.

Students work in groups of three, each person having an electronic keyboard. Group members compare the pentatonic songs brought to class for the activity and select one song as the source for improvisation. Students agree among themselves who will improvise melodic embellishments, rhythmic variations, and melodic variations. After practicing improvisations individually, members of the group decide the order and perform them in sequence.

The instructor evaluates the choice of song and the improvisations and discusses with the class whether modifications should be made to the activity for use with middle-level students.

Suggested Resources

Bergethon, Bjornar, Eunice Boardman, and Janet Montgomery. *Musical Growth in the Elementary School,* 6th ed. Orlando, FL: Harcourt Brace, 1996.

Hackett, Patricia, and Carolynn A. Lindeman. *The Musical Classroom: Backgrounds, Models, and Skills for Elementary Teaching,* 4th ed. Englewood Cliffs, NJ: Prentice-Hall, 1997.

The Music Connection, Grades 5–8. Parsippany, NJ: Silver Burdett Ginn, 1995.

Music and You, Grades 5–8. New York: Macmillan/McGraw-Hill, 1991.

(continued)

Nye, Robert E., Vernice T. Nye, Gary M. Martin, and Mary Lou Van Rysselberghe. *Music in the Elementary School,* 6th ed. Englewood Cliffs, NJ: Prentice-Hall, 1992.

Share the Music, Grades 5–8. New York: Macmillan/McGraw-Hill, 1995, 1997.

The World of Music, Grades 5–8. Parsippany, NJ: Silver Burdett Ginn, 1991.

STANDARD 3C

Improvising melodies, variations, and accompaniments: Students improvise short melodies, unaccompanied and over given rhythmic accompaniments, each in a consistent style, meter, and tonality.

Strategy

Each methods student selects a four-measure rhythmic accompaniment from the auto-accompaniment function of an electronic keyboard or records an accompaniment using classroom rhythm instruments. After listening to the rhythm pattern several times, each student decides whether to improvise a percussive, slurred, or smooth melody with scat or solfège syllables, making certain that the improvisation conforms to the meter of the accompaniment and maintains a consistent tonality.

Students perform for each other in small groups, and the groups evaluate the performances and quality of the improvisations. Students then write a learning sequence for middle-level students based on the activity.

Suggested Resources

Coker, Patty, and David Baker. *Vocal Improvisation—An Instrumental Approach.* Lebanon, IN: Studio P/R, 1981.

General Music Today 8, no. 3 (Spring 1995), entire issue.

◆ ◆ ◆ ◆ ◆ ◆ ◆

STANDARD 4A

Composing and arranging music within specified guidelines: Students compose short pieces within specified guidelines, demonstrating how the elements of music are used to achieve unity and variety, tension and release, and balance.

Strategy

Methods students have listened to at least three songs that are well known to middle-level students (e.g., "The Flintstones," "Camptown Races," and "It's a Small World," or other songs in AABA form or with antecedent/consequent phrases or sequences). The instructor has asked the students to analyze the listening selections.

The class engages in a brief discussion about the fundamental aspects of form—unity and variety, balance, tension and release. They identify basic compositional techniques used in each of the selected melodies—for example, antecedent/consequent phrases, AABA form, or sequence.

The instructor divides class into small groups and presents these suggested guidelines for a compositional activity: use of the C major scale; at least four two-measure phrases; a melody that exhibits at least one of the following: repetition of one phrase, antecedent/consequent phrase, one example of sequence.

Each group scores a composition for acoustic and electronic instruments likely to be found in the middle-level classroom. They rehearse and perform for the class. Following the performance, each group is asked to discuss and identify the compositional techniques that they used and explain how they can adapt the activity for a middle-level general music class.

Suggested Resources

Reese, Sam. "MIDI-Assisted Composing in Your Classroom." *Music Educators Journal* 8, no. 4 (January 1995): 37–40.

Wiggins, Jackie. "Composition as a Teaching Tool." *Music Educators Journal* 76, no. 8 (April 1990): 35–38.

Wilcox, Ella, ed. "How Do Children Compose?" *Teaching Music* 2, no. 3 (December 1994): 38–39.

STANDARD 4B

Composing and arranging music within specified guidelines: Students arrange simple pieces for voices or instruments other than those for which the pieces were written.

Strategy

Prior to the class meeting, methods students have each selected a folk melody from any national or ethnic source. Working alone or with another student, they use the melody for an in-class activity to create a simple arrangement for classroom instruments. Students can choose from these classroom instruments: pitched instruments (wind, barred, or stringed), any type of drum, wooden rhythm instruments, and metallic rhythm instruments.

Students' arrangements should have either two-part harmony and rhythmic accompaniment; a descant; or an arpeggiated accompaniment and rhythmic ostinato. If possible, the arrangements should be composed and printed using notation software.

Students write out the sequence of steps they used in creating the arrangements, and they adapt the strategy for use with middle-level students.

Suggested Resources

Hackett, Patricia. *The Melody Book: 300 Selections from the World of Music for Autoharp, Guitar, Piano, Recorder and Voice,* 2d ed. Englewood Cliffs, NJ: Prentice-Hall, 1992.

Warner, Anne, ed. *Traditional American Folk Songs.* Syracuse, NY: Syracuse University Press, 1984.

STANDARD 4C

Composing and arranging music within specified guidelines: *Students use a variety of traditional and nontraditional sound sources and electronic media when composing and arranging.*

Strategy

The instructor divides the methods class into groups A, B, and C in order to create a "sound composition." Students follow a sequence of steps that they can use for a general music lesson. In each group, each student selects sound sources in the classroom—traditional, nontraditional, acoustic, electronic—to use in the creation of a group composition. Each group is given fifteen minutes to compose a one- to two-minute piece using the following: instructor-selected rhythmic patterns; instructor-selected pitches; and a student-generated ostinato (rhythmic or melodic).

Each group performs its composition for the class. The instructor asks the groups to perform again, this time creating a rondo from the A, B, and C group compositions. Performances are videotaped for self-assessment.

Suggested Resources

Abeles, Harold F., Charles R. Hoffer, and Robert H. Klotman. *Foundations of Music Education,* 2d ed. Old Tappan, NJ: Schirmer Books/Simon & Schuster, 1994.

Rudaitis, Cheryl, ed. "Jump Ahead and Take the Risk." *Teaching Music* 2, no. 5 (April 1995): 34–35.

Upitis, Rena. "Fostering Children's Compositions." *General Music Today* 8, no. 3 (Spring 1995): 16–19.

◆ ◆ ◆ ◆ ◆ ◆

STANDARD 5A

Reading and notating music: *Students read whole, half, quarter, eighth, sixteenth, and dotted notes and rests in 2/4, 3/4, 4/4, 6/8, 3/8, and alla breve meter signatures.*

Strategy

Methods students have examined a variety of music series textbooks and music methods books that explain how to read whole, half, quarter, eighth, sixteenth, and dotted notes and rests in 2/4, 3/4, 4/4, 6/8, 3/8, and alla breve meter signatures. Their assignment was to select a method of instructing middle-level students in reading and notating music that could be presented in three different learning modalities: aural, visual, and kinesthetic.

In class, students work in groups to discuss instructional strategies that are most effective for middle-level students. After a selection of the instructional method has been made, each group develops a sequence that could be used with a different emphasis for each of the three learning modalities. Students also write a rationale for their choice of methods and sequence.

Each group chooses one of the three sequences to present to the class. The instructor ensures that each modality is represented. Students discuss whether instruction in reading and notating music should employ all three learning modalities or whether one of the three may be more appropriate for the middle level.

Suggested Resources

Choksy, Lois, Robert M. Abramson, Avon E. Gillespie, and David Woods. *Teaching Music in the Twentieth Century.* Englewood Cliffs, NJ: Prentice-Hall, 1986.

Lindeman, Carolynn A. *PianoLab: An Introduction to Class Piano,* 3d ed. Belmont, CA: Wadsworth Publishing Company, 1996.

Uszler, Marienne. *The Well-Tempered Keyboard Teacher.* Old Tappan, NJ: Schirmer Books/Simon & Schuster, 1990.

STANDARD 5B

Reading and notating music: Students read at sight simple melodies in both the treble and bass clefs.

Strategy

The instructor divides methods class into pairs. Each pair of students has one electronic keyboard and two short melodies with a treble clef "call" (antecedent) and a bass clef "response" (consequent). (See middle-level music series textbooks for call-and-response melodies.)

Assuming that middle-level students will have had experience reading pitch notation from treble and bass clefs as well as reading simple rhythmic patterns, methods students write a plan for a sightreading activity. The instructor tells them to include directions for performing the melodies on the keyboard with one middle-level student sightreading and playing the treble clef call, and the other sightreading and playing the bass clef response.

After students perform the treble clef call and the bass clef response, they switch clefs. Each member of the pair critiques the lesson plan of the other as well as his or her own lesson plan.

Suggested Resources

The Music Connection, Grades 5–8. Parsippany, NJ: Silver Burdett Ginn, 1995.

Music and You, Grades 5–8. New York: Macmillan/McGraw-Hill, 1991.

Share the Music, Grades 5–8. New York: Macmillan/McGraw-Hill, 1995, 1997.

The World of Music, Grades 5–8. Parsippany, NJ: Silver Burdett Ginn, 1991.

STANDARD 5C

Reading and notating music: *Students identify and define standard notation symbols for pitch, rhythm, dynamics, tempo, articulation, and expression.*

Strategy

Methods students have each selected one folk song from middle-level music series textbooks. Working in groups of four separated into pairs, each pair selects one song to analyze for melody, rhythmic patterns, and expression.

When the analysis is complete, the pairs come together in their groups for a microteaching demonstration. The first pair serves as "teachers" to explain information about the melody and rhythmic patterns of their selected song. Both pairs of students then sing the song, carefully observing all expressive markings. The "students" pair is asked to define the symbols for dynamics, tempo, articulation, and expression.

Pairs reverse teacher/student roles and repeat the activity using the song selected by the second pair in each group. Each group verbally critiques the effectiveness of its pairs' teaching demonstrations for identifying and defining standard notation symbols in middle-level general music classes.

Suggested Resources

The Music Connection, Grades 5–8. Parsippany, NJ: Silver Burdett Ginn, 1995.

Music and You, Grades 5–8. New York: Macmillan/McGraw-Hill, 1991.

Share the Music, Grades 5–8. New York: Macmillan/McGraw-Hill, 1995, 1997.

The World of Music, Grades 5–8. Parsippany, NJ: Silver Burdett Ginn, 1991.

STANDARD 5D

Reading and notating music: *Students use standard notation to record their musical ideas and the musical ideas of others.*

Strategy

The instructor notates a chromatic scale on the chalkboard and then asks methods students to volunteer to play the chromatic scale using a full set of resonator bells. Students, organized in small groups, are assigned to develop a learning activity whereby middle-level students can discover how Schoenberg used all of the notes of a twelve-tone scale before repeating any note in a composition. The learning activity should include an opportunity for each middle-level student to perform the twelve-tone row for Schoenberg's String Quartet no. 4, first movement, on resonator bells or Orff mallet instruments.

In their small groups, students rearrange the resonator bells to compose their own tone row. They may use whole notes to notate the tone row composition on manuscript paper. Groups record their own compositions for a future listening lesson.

Suggested Resource

Schoenberg, Arnold. String Quartet no. 4, first movement. In *The World of Music*, Grade 8. Parsippany, NJ: Silver Burdett Ginn, 1991.

◆ ◆ ◆ ◆ ◆ ◆ ◆

STANDARD 6A

Listening to, analyzing, and describing music: Students describe specific music events in a given aural example, using appropriate terminology.

Strategy

For a demonstration of a discovery lesson on basso ostinato, the instructor begins by playing a recording of "Fifty-Ninth Street Bridge Song," from Simon and Garfunkel's *Greatest Hits*. Then the instructor asks methods students to hum and "draw" the contour of the lowest sounds of the music with one arm outstretched, palm down.

The instructor questions students about the direction of the lowest pitches, asking whether these pitches are one long melody or one short melodic pattern that is repeated. Students are asked to define basso ostinato. They decide whether the listening example fits the definition; that is, whether the lowest notes are in a pattern that is "obstinate" and that does not change.

The instructor plays a recording of Chopin's Polonaise in A♭ Major. Students identify the repeated bass melody in Chopin's piano composition and compare it with the basso ostinato in "Fifty-Ninth Street Bridge Song" in terms of melodic shape and duration of pitches. They discuss how the use of repeated patterns contributes to unity in a musical composition.

As an outline for a middle-level listening lesson, students write down the steps used to discover basso ostinato.

Suggested Resources

Simon and Garfunkel. *Greatest Hits*. Columbia 31350.

Watkins, Rosemary C. "A Music Listening Project for Classroom and Home." *General Music Today* 1, no. 3 (Spring 1988): 8–10.

STANDARD 6B

Listening to, analyzing, and describing music: Students analyze the uses of elements of music in aural examples representing diverse genres and cultures.

Strategy

Methods students sing "America" and use their hands to outline the Euro-American major scale on which it is based. They sing the scale on a neutral syllable or play it on an instrument, then verbally describe its distinctive quality.

(continued)

Students sing or listen to the Korean song "Arirang" (from *Sounds of the World*). They use their hands to outline the pentatonic scale on which "Arirang" is based—C, D, F, G, A—and sing the scale on a neutral syllable, listening to its distinctive quality. They listen to the recording again, particularly noting the "wavering" tones.

Finally, students listen to the African composition "Lost Your Head Blues," sung by blues singer Bessie Smith. They follow the AAB form, outlining the melody with their hands in the air, particularly noticing the characteristic "scoops" and "slides" between notes and the descending melodic contours.

The instructor directs a class discussion to compare similarities and differences in melodies from these three cultures. Students are encouraged to locate many listening examples from various cultures for purposes of comparison.

Students record information derived from the analysis for use in planning listening strategies for middle-level students.

Suggested Resources

Anderson, William M., and Joy E. Lawrence. *Integrating Music into the Elementary Classroom*, 3d. ed. Belmont, CA: Wadsworth Publishing Company, 1995.

"Lost Your Head Blues," performed by Bessie Smith, on *The Smithsonian Collection of Classic Jazz*. Vol. 1 of Smithsonian Collection of Classic Jazz RD 033-1.

Sounds of the World: East Asia—Chinese, Korean, and Japanese Traditions in the United States. Teacher's guide by William M. Anderson. Reston, VA: Music Educators National Conference, 1989. Audiocassettes and teacher's guide.

STANDARD 6C

Listening to, analyzing, and describing music: Students demonstrate knowledge of the basic principles of meter, rhythm, tonality, intervals, chords, and harmonic progressions in their analyses of music.

Strategy

Methods students are familiar with the song "When Johnny Comes Marching Home." Working in small groups, they listen to and analyze each of the variations in a recording of Morton Gould's "American Salute."

The instructor asks each group to create a rough draft of a music map (see Suggested Resources) for each variation, using icons as well as words to represent meter, rhythmic patterns, tempo, melodic contour, major or minor tonality, instrumentation, and harmonic progressions.

When groups have completed the music maps, students attach them in sequence and roll them to unfold from the first to the last variation. Groups exchange maps and listen again to a recording of "American Salute," critiquing the maps and making additions and corrections directly on the map they are following.

Finally, groups retrieve their original maps, edit for clarity and information, and copy for future use with middle-level students.

Suggested Resources

Elrod, Pamela, and David Doss. *Music Memory Bulletin: Bass Clef Book.* Austin, TX: University Interscholastic League, 1989–90.

The Music Connection, Grades 5–8. Parsippany, NJ: Silver Burdett Ginn, 1995.

Music and You, Grades 5–8. New York: Macmillan/McGraw-Hill, 1991.

Share the Music, Grades 5–8. New York: Macmillan/McGraw-Hill, 1995, 1997.

University Interscholastic League. *Music Memory Bulletin: Treble Clef Book.* Austin, TX: University Interscholastic League, 1990–91.

The World of Music, Grades 5–8. Parsippany, NJ: Silver Burdett Ginn, 1991.

◆ ◆ ◆ ◆ ◆ ◆

STANDARD 7A

Evaluating music and music performances: Students develop criteria for evaluating the quality and effectiveness of music performances and compositions and apply the criteria in their personal listening and performing.

Strategy

Each methods student has interviewed a middle-level student to obtain information about a preferred recorded piece by using questions similar to the following:

(1) What is the best recorded piece of music that you own? (2) Did you like it the first time you listened to it? (3) What are some words that you would use to describe it to a friend? (4) What feeling does the music seem to express? Why? Give at least two reasons. (5) What instruments are used? Can you describe the underlying beat? Is the singer's voice pretty? Are the words important? Is the music fast, medium, or slow? Is it loud, medium, or soft? Do the tempo and dynamics change during the music? (6) Does liking a piece of music mean that it is good music? Why or why not? Give at least two reasons.

In class, small groups of methods students work together to process the information from the interviews. They create a thesaurus of vocabulary used by the students interviewed and look for similarities and differences in descriptions of the music. Finally, they plan a strategy to help middle-level students use the questions asked in the interview as a basis for not only developing criteria for evaluation of musical performance and composition but also applying the criteria to their own performances and listening.

Suggested Resource

Fowler, Charles. Chapter 1 in *Music! Its Role and Importance in Our Lives.* Mission Hills, CA: Glencoe/McGraw-Hill, 1994. Book and recordings.

Evaluating music and music performances: Students evaluate the quality and effectiveness of their own and others' performances, compositions, arrangements, and improvisations by applying specific criteria appropriate for the style of the music and offer constructive suggestions for improvement.

Strategy

Methods students have been assigned to view the video *The World's Greatest Music,* read the accompanying teacher's guide, and view the video *Singing in General Music.* In class, small groups of students work together to use information from the videos and the guide to develop a "judging sheet" that middle-level students can use for evaluating classroom vocal and instrumental performances.

Each group then designs a strategy for the middle-level classroom that involves use of the judging sheet by a panel of three "judges" for all performances in the general music class, making certain that the panel rotates to eventually include all middle-level students.

Suggested Resources

May, William V., Vanissa B. Murphy, Cecile Johnson, and Bonnie B. Williams, eds. *The World's Greatest Music.* Reston, VA: Music Educators National Conference, 1988. Videocassette and teacher's guide.

Thompson, Keith, ed. *Singing in General Music.* Reston, VA: Music Educators National Conference, 1994. Videocassette.

◆ ◆ ◆ ◆ ◆ ◆

Understanding relationships between music, the other arts, and disciplines outside the arts: Students compare in two or more arts how the characteristic materials of each art can be used to transform similar events, scenes, emotions, or ideas into works of art.

Strategy

The instructor has assigned methods students to study one of Monet's paintings of Rouen Cathedral, West Facade (color plate 42 in *Manet/Monet/Degas*), to prepare for a class discussion concerning Monet's use of color, intensity, line, and space to suggest the idea of a cathedral in diffused morning light.

After a discussion of Monet's painting, students listen to any recording of Debussy's "La Cathedrale engloutie," an impressionistic piano composition. The instructor leads students to discuss, using terminology that middle-level students will understand, how Debussy changed the traditional ways that scales, melodies, and chords were used. They also discuss how Debussy's avoidance of cadences suggested, rather than stated, musical ideas.

Students form small groups to discuss similarities and differences in the way the visual artist and the composer dealt with a common underlying principle—an impression or suggestion of an idea. The instructor and class discuss how these similarities and differences could be taught to middle-level students.

Suggested Resources

Manet/Monet/Degas. Master of Art Series. Orlando, FL: Harcourt Brace, 1971.

Wold, Milo, and Edmund Cykler. *An Introduction to Music and Art in the Western World,* 10th ed. Columbus, OH: Wm. C. Brown Communications/McGraw-Hill, 1995.

STANDARD 8B

Understanding relationships between music, the other arts, and disciplines outside the arts:
Students describe ways in which the principles and subject matter of other disciplines taught in the school are interrelated with those of music.

Strategy

Methods students have read one of three versions of *The Firebird* (Isadora, Rosenberg, Zvorykin) and listed ways that one can "know" a representational work (e.g., through musical themes and motives, the story, scenic design and costuming, choreography, the creators and performers, performance reviews, the score of the work, and details of its origin).

During class, the instructor asks students to imagine that they have been commissioned to write music for a ballet for this Russian folk tale. Noting the most striking events in the story, each student selects one event and develops a list of musical characteristics a composer might choose to portray that event (i.e., decisions about rhythm, timbre, dynamics, etc.).

The instructor then displays Zvorykin's brilliant illustrations of the Firebird and Isadora's vibrant watercolors and asks: How does the illustrator choose visual characteristics that are brilliant or sumptuous or exciting to enhance the event? After discussion, students return to their list of characteristics, adding expressive words or musical ideas as inspired by the illustrations. Then the class discusses how sounds, images, and story combine to make the Russian folk tale "come alive."

The instructor introduces Stravinsky's musical "solution" to events that students selected. Students identify ways to experience Stravinsky's music firsthand (e.g., sing and label themes, improvise stylistic movements, conduct, follow simplified scores, or create graphic representations).

Finally, students write down the steps in this activity for use as a model in developing middle-level lesson plans.

Suggested Children's Literature

Isadora, Rachel. *The Firebird.* New York: G. P. Putnam's Sons, 1994.

Rosenberg, Jane. *Dance Me a Story: Twelve Tales from the Classic Ballets.* New York: Thames and Hudson, 1985.

(continued)

Zvorykin, Boris Vasil'evich. *The Firebird and Other Russian Fairy Tales.* New York: Viking Press, 1978.

Suggested Resource

Upitis, Rena. "Music and Story." In *This Too Is Music.* Portsmouth, NH: Heinemann Educational Books, 1990.

◆ ◆ ◆ ◆ ◆ ◆ ◆

STANDARD 9A

Understanding music in relation to history and culture: Students describe distinguishing characteristics of representative music genres and styles from a variety of cultures.

Strategy

Methods students have watched the video *Bringing Multicultural Music to Children.* Working in small groups, they have been assigned to use middle-level music series textbooks to locate children's songs from three different cultures.

Students analyze and come to agreement on similarities and differences in the three songs their group has chosen. They use an analysis sheet prepared by the instructor to compare melodies, rhythmic patterns, text, expressive markings, intervallic range, and difficulty.

Each group prepares a short presentation to demonstrate the similarities and differences in their three selected songs from different cultures. The groups sing their three songs and give an analysis of the similarities and differences among the songs. They discuss the potential use of the songs in a middle-school general music class for teaching students to describe distinguishing characteristics of music from a variety of cultures.

Suggested Resources

Bringing Multicultural Music to Children. Reston, VA: Music Educators National Conference, 1992. Videocassette.

The Music Connection, Grades 5–8. Parsippany, NJ: Silver Burdett Ginn, 1995.

Music and You, Grades 5–8. New York: Macmillan/McGraw-Hill, 1991.

Share the Music, Grades 5–8. New York: Macmillan/McGraw-Hill, 1995, 1997.

The World of Music, Grades 5–8. Parsippany, NJ: Silver Burdett Ginn, 1991.

STANDARD 9B

Understanding music in relation to history and culture: Students classify by genre and style (and, if applicable, by historical period, composer, and title) a varied body of exemplary (that is, high-quality and characteristic) musical works and explain the characteristics that cause each work to be considered exemplary.

Strategy

Methods students have been assigned to watch two instructor-selected musical compositions on the video *The World's Greatest Music*. They have also been assigned to read chapters 6 and 7 from *Music! Its Role and Importance in Our Lives* so that they can discuss how repertoire becomes identified as "good."

In class, students listen to at least one of the selected examples, identify its salient characteristics, and describe the characteristics using terminology appropriate for middle-level students. The class then discusses the issues of personal preference, the role of the music critic, how often a work is performed by respected ensembles, widespread acceptance of the quality of a work, number of years a work has been a part of standard orchestral repertoire, and stylistic characteristics that make a work exemplary. Based on this activity, students are assigned to develop a model lesson plan that can be used with a variety of musical genres and styles.

Suggested Resources

Fowler, Charles. Chapters 6 and 7 in *Music! Its Role and Importance in Our Lives*. Mission Hills, CA: Glencoe/McGraw-Hill, 1994. Book and recordings.

May, William V., Vanissa B. Murphy, Cecile Johnson, and Bonnie B. Williams, eds. *The World's Greatest Music*. Reston, VA: Music Educators National Conference, 1988. Videocassette and teacher's guide.

STANDARD 9C

Understanding music in relation to history and culture: Students compare, in several cultures of the world, functions music serves, roles of musicians, and conditions under which music is typically performed.

Strategy

Methods students have been assigned readings concerning music in the wedding rituals of Bulgaria and Zimbabwe. In class, the instructor plays recorded selections of wedding music from Bulgaria ("Potajno Rada godiya," from *Village Music of Bulgaria*) and Zimbabwe ("Wai bamba" or "Chiro chacho," from *Let Your Voice Be Heard*). Students answer the following questions to compare the function of music in the wedding celebrations, roles of the musicians, and conditions for performance of the wedding music:

- Compare the role of the two songs in the wedding rituals of the two cultures.

- What was the underlying feeling of each music example? Energetic? Anxious? Sad? Happy?

(continued)

- Describe the setting for performance of the wedding music.

- How would people from each culture probably react to the wedding music of the other culture?

- Are there any similarities (or differences) in the role of wedding music in the United States and Bulgaria? The United States and Zimbabwe?

Methods students devise a model for middle-level general music students to use for comparing the function of music, role of musicians, and conditions of performance in world cultures using a variety of ceremonies and celebrations.

Suggested Resources

Adzenyah, Abraham Kobena, Dumisani Maraire, and Judith Cook Tucker. *Let Your Voice Be Heard!: Songs from Ghana and Zimbabwe,* 2d ed. Danbury, CT: World Music Press, 1997. Book and recording.

Village Music of Bulgaria. Collected and produced by Ethel Raim and Martin Koenig. Elektra/ Nonesuch 79195-2.

GENERAL MUSIC
GRADES 9–12

STANDARD 1A
Proficient

Singing, alone and with others, a varied repertoire of music: Students sing with expression and technical accuracy a large and varied repertoire of vocal literature with a level of difficulty of 4, on a scale of 1 to 6, including some songs performed from memory.

Strategy

Methods students have read about characteristics of and ways to develop male and female voices. The instructor has asked them to suggest songs from karaoke and recording studio catalogs to use for an activity to build vocal confidence and has selected one of these recordings with sheet music with a level of difficulty of 4 (on a scale of 1 to 6).

Using the sheet music, the class sings one of the songs along with a recording of the soloist and then minus the soloist. [*Note:* The recording is a special cassette tape with the soloist on a separate channel that can be faded in or out. It is played on a stereo cassette recorder that has separate channel volume controls.] The instructor divides the class into groups of four to simulate a karaoke or recording studio experience.

In their groups, students sing the song first with the recording of a professional soloist. Then, using the volume control of the soloist channel, they gradually withdraw the support of the soloist. Each group selects a leader who listens to the instrumental lead-in and cues the other performers, and each group practices at the microphones as high school students would before the final performance. Using a rating sheet developed by the instructor, each student evaluates the performance of each group on the basis of appropriate expression and technical accuracy.

Finally, students write a lesson plan for use in high school general music classes, making certain to follow closely the steps they carried out in the lesson.

Suggested Resources

Cooksey, John M. *Working with the Adolescent Voice.* St. Louis: Concordia Publishing House, 1992.

Edwin, Robert. "Karaoke: Everybody Sing," in "The Bach to Rock Connection" column. *Journal of Singing* 52, no. 2: 63–64.

Karaoke Singing Source Catalog. Bridgeview, IL: ProSing, 1995. Source for both equipment and accompaniment tracks.

Thompson, Keith, ed. *Singing in General Music.* Reston, VA: Music Educators National Conference, 1994. Videocassette.

STANDARD 1B

Proficient

Singing, alone and with others, a varied repertoire of music: *Students sing music written in four parts, with and without accompaniment.*

Strategy

The instructor selects repertoire that will provide high school general music students with ensemble experience but that is within the range of their musical skills. (Suggested octavo selections are Brahms' "Six Folk Songs," arranged for four voices.) The instructor notes to methods students that for high school general music students, they may need to create a cambiata part consisting of notes taken from alto and tenor parts.

All methods students sing the bass part in their own registers; then just the baritones sing the part as a section. This procedure is repeated for the other parts, with the melody last. The instructor asks basses and sopranos to sing their parts together, and then altos and tenors to sing their parts together. The emphasis should be on balancing within the parts and between the parts. As a last step, students sing all four parts in ensemble, both with piano accompaniment and a cappella.

Students review the class activities and make any necessary revisions for use with high school general music.

Suggested Resources

Brahms, Johannes. "Six Folk Songs." In *Something to Sing About,* Level I, edited by Will Schmid. Mission Hills, CA: Glencoe/McGraw-Hill, 1989.

Cooksey, John M. *Working with the Adolescent Voice.* St. Louis: Concordia Publishing House, 1992.

STANDARD 1C

Proficient

Singing, alone and with others, a varied repertoire of music: *Students demonstrate well-developed ensemble skills.*

Strategy

The instructor selects a ballad or dance tune (from Jacobean, Restoration, Elizabethan, or Shakespearean England), arranged for soprano, alto, and tenor recorders. Methods students choose the soprano, alto, or tenor part to vocalize using "doo."

As students sing, they should attempt to tune to each other and produce a uniform "doo" vowel. Students critique their sound after each performance.

Using questions, the instructor leads the students to describe how the strategy can be used with high school general music students to help them develop ensemble skills.

Suggested Resources

Burakoff, Gerald, and Willy Strickland, arr. *Musicke from Olde England.* Levittown, NY: Sweet Pipes, 1981.

Cooksey, John M. *Working with the Adolescent Voice.* St. Louis: Concordia Publishing House, 1992.

STANDARD 1D
Advanced

Singing, alone and with others, a varied repertoire of music: Students sing with expression and technical accuracy a large and varied repertoire of vocal literature with a level of difficulty of 5, on a scale of 1 to 6.

Strategy

Methods students have been assigned to look through music series textbooks for grades 7 and 8 (possible source for appropriate level 5 songs) to locate several songs and spirituals associated with the history of African Americans and with the Civil Rights movement.

In class, students plan a Martin Luther King Day presentation that would feature advanced students in a high school general music class performing for social studies classes. The class shares titles of songs and spirituals they have located and selects songs to be performed solo and in ensemble.

Methods students work in groups to analyze one solo work and one vocal ensemble piece each. They design a learning sequence whereby advanced general music students can not only learn the music efficiently and accurately but also sing expressively. The plans should include instructions for general music students to determine and interpret expressive markings as suggested by texts of the songs and spirituals.

Suggested Resources

The Music Connection, Grades 5–8. Parsippany, NJ: Silver Burdett Ginn, 1995.

Music and You, Grades 5–8. New York: Macmillan/McGraw-Hill, 1991.

Share the Music, Grades 5–8. New York: Macmillan/McGraw-Hill, 1995, 1997.

Southern, Eileen. *The Music of Black Americans,* 3d ed. New York: W. W. Norton, 1997.

The World of Music, Grades 5–8. Parsippany, NJ: Silver Burdett Ginn, 1991.

Standard 1E

Advanced

Singing, alone and with others, a varied repertoire of music: *Students sing music written in more than four parts.*

Strategy

The instructor introduces methods students to the song "Wonfa Nyem," an easy a cappella song for SATB with divisi bass for most of the selection (or to another song with more than four parts but within the range of the musical skills of advanced students in high school general music classes). "Wonfa Nyem" is from Ghana and is traditionally sung at festivals or funerals. The Akan text reminds listeners that participation in the community is important.

The instructor chooses the appropriate key to accommodate the ranges of high school students. As written, the tenor part could be sung easily by cambiatas. To teach the octavo parts, the instructor pairs parts so that students learn their parts in relation to another vocal line. Upper male and female parts are paired; students sing each other's parts and then their own parts alone. The process is repeated for other combinations of upper and lower voices until all parts have been sung together and alone. Emphasis should be on balancing within the parts and between the parts. As a last step, students sing their vocal parts in ensemble a cappella.

Methods students follow the procedure used to learn "Wonfa Nyem" as a model for constructing a lesson plan for high school general music. Students use the guide included with the octavo selection to add suggestions for translation, pronunciation, and performance to their lesson plans.

Suggested Resource

Adzenyah, Abraham Kobena, arr. "Wonfa Nyem." Danbury, CT: World Music Press, 1992. Includes translation and pronunciation guide.

Standard 1F

Advanced

Singing, alone and with others, a varied repertoire of music: *Students sing in small ensembles with one student on a part.*

Strategy

Using a song of medium difficulty arranged for SATB, SAB, or SSA, the instructor models for methods students a procedure for developing the skill of singing with one student on a part. [*Note:* This procedure could be adapted for any voice combination in a high school general music class.]

As an initial step, the entire ensemble sings each individual part successively; then they sing the selection in parts. As they sing in parts in ensemble again, the instructor randomly points to one student, who continues singing while the other students continue their parts using a hum.

Students divide into ensembles (quartets or trios) with one student on a part, and rehearse until they are prepared to perform for another ensemble. Students evaluate the overall procedure in terms of its applicability for advanced students in a high school general music class and discuss any suggestions for modification.

Suggested Resources

Choral Connections, Levels 3 and 4. Mission Hills, CA: Glencoe/McGraw-Hill, 1997.

Hausmann, Charles S., Hunter C. March, Samuel D. Miller, and Betty G. Roe, eds. *World of Choral Music.* Parsippany, NJ: Silver Burdett Ginn, 1988.

Schmid, Will, ed. *Something to Sing About,* Level I. Mission Hills, CA: Glencoe/McGraw-Hill, 1989.

◆ ◆ ◆ ◆ ◆ ◆ ◆

STANDARD 2A
Proficient

Performing on instruments, alone and with others, a varied repertoire of music: *Students perform with expression and technical accuracy a large and varied repertoire of instrumental literature with a level of difficulty of 4, on a scale of 1 to 6.*

Strategy

Methods students form small recorder groups. Each student within the group should perform on soprano recorder and choose alto or tenor recorder as a second instrument. From *Musicke from Old England,* the instructor selects ballads and dance tunes (from Jacobean, Restoration, Elizabethan, and Shakespearean England) with a level of difficulty of 4.

Each student learns to play melody as well as harmony parts in the selected pieces, and then the groups perform for the class. The instructor and students listen to performances and evaluate for correct playing technique and expression. Finally, students analyze the melody, harmony, and rhythmic motives to determine potential problems when using these selections with high school general music classes.

Suggested Resource

Burakoff, Gerald, and Willy Strickland, arr. *Musicke from Olde England.* Levittown, NY: Sweet Pipes, 1981.

Proficient

Performing on instruments, alone and with others, a varied repertoire of music: *Students perform an appropriate part in an ensemble, demonstrating well-developed ensemble skills.*

Strategy

The instructor has assigned methods students readings concerning hand-drum techniques and exercises to develop skills. At the beginning of class, students prepare for a performance with hand drums and recorders by working in pairs on one of the hand-drum exercises.

Students select a sopranino, soprano, alto, or tenor recorder and sightread "Pavane," by Jean Tabouret (*For Hand Drums and Recorders,* p. 38). (Students playing F instruments—sopranino and alto—transpose up an octave.) Working in two groups, students rehearse "Pavane," using hand drums and recorders and making certain to switch parts so that they have ensemble experience with both parts.

As students perform for each other, they critique the performance of the other ensemble as well as their own performance using a proficiency checklist for ensemble rehearsals. The checklist, provided by the instructor, includes items related to precise entrances and cutoffs, accurate rhythmic and melodic patterns, and blend.

Students use information from the readings and class activities to structure a plan for use in high school general music.

Suggested Resource

Carley, Isabel McNeill. *For Hand Drums and Recorders.* Allison Park, PA: Music Innovations, 1982.

Proficient

Performing on instruments, alone and with others, a varied repertoire of music: *Students perform in small ensembles with one student on a part.*

Strategy

Methods students form small ensembles composed of at least three different instruments for melody, harmony, and rhythmic accompaniment (e.g., keyboard, guitar, and percussion; recorder, keyboard, and percussion; or recorder, guitar, and percussion). They select a repertoire of several types of music (rock, country, folk songs, ballads) that have a lyrical melody and chord symbols (see Suggested Resources).

Students takes turns playing each instrument within their ensembles. They play the melody with proper expression for the genre, a harmonic accompaniment pattern, and a rhythmic accompaniment pattern or ostinato.

The instructor critiques at least one performance by each group. Criteria for evaluation are based on the individual contribution of each performer to the successful blend of the ensemble and the ensemble's interpretation of the appropriate style of the song. Methods students evaluate the overall procedure in terms of its applicability for advanced students in a high school general music class.

Suggested Resources

Award Winning Songs of the Country Music Association. Vol 2. Milwaukee, WI: Hal Leonard Corporation, 1992.

History of Rock: Late 60's. Milwaukee, WI: Hal Leonard Corporation, 1992.

McNeil, William K., compiler. *Southern Folk Ballads.* Little Rock: August House, 1987.

Warner, Anne, ed. *Traditional American Folk Songs.* Syracuse, NY: Syracuse University Press, 1984.

Wright, Roger, ed. *Spanish Ballads.* Warminster, England: Aris & Phillips, 1987.

◆ ◆ ◆ ◆ ◆ ◆

STANDARD 3A
Proficient
Improvising melodies, variations, and accompaniments: Students improvise stylistically appropriate harmonizing parts.

Strategy

Methods students have been assigned to analyze the harmonic progressions of a few soft rock songs with guitar accompaniments that follow standard chord progressions of the 1950s. The instructor has digitized the melodies of songs that follow harmonic sequences of I-vi-IV-V or I-vi-ii-V.

After giving students the meter for each song, the instructor plays back the digitized melodies on the electronic keyboard and students improvise strumming and/or picking accompaniments on the guitar. Performing for each other in pairs over the digitized melody, students evaluate each other based on the following criteria: pacing the tempo of the digitized melodies with harmonic accompaniments, changing chords at the appropriate times, and using a strumming/fingerpicking style that has vitality.

Students discuss necessary adaptations to this process so that it can be used in a high school general music class.

Suggested Resources

The Doo-Wop Song Book. Milwaukee, WI: Hal Leonard Corporation, 1989.

Save the Last Dance for Me. Secaucus, NJ: Warner Bros. Publications, 1990.

Stuessy, Joe. Chapter 4 in *Rock and Roll: Its History and Stylistic Development,* 2d ed. Englewood Cliffs, NJ: Prentice-Hall, 1994.

STANDARD 3B

Proficient

Improvising melodies, variations, and accompaniments: *Students improvise rhythmic and melodic variations on given pentatonic melodies and melodies in major and minor keys.*

Strategy

Methods students have been assigned to select one song—pentatonic, major, or minor—as source material for unaccompanied rhythmic and melodic improvisation. Song selection criteria include limited intervallic range, absence of melodic embellishment, absence of intense rhythmic patterns, short to medium length, and a narrative-type text.

The instructor plays "It Don't Mean a Thing if It Ain't Got That Swing," from *Duke Ellington and Friends,* as an example of melodic and rhythmic improvisation.

The instructor then presents a model instructional sequence for students to follow individually: (1) Decide whether improvisation will be instrumental or vocal. (2) If instrumental, select a melody instrument. (3) Sing or play melody several times to internalize tonality and melodic contour. (4) Read text aloud to determine where "word painting," vocal inflections (see Anderson, chapter 8), and dynamic changes would help express meaning and mood. (5) Read text aloud again to explore whether meter could be changed and whether duration of rhythmic patterns could be augmented or diminished. (6) Audiotape improvisation or enter it into memory of an electronic keyboard. (7) Perform improvisation for class. (8) Solicit verbal evaluations from class. (9) Record in log most effective techniques from other class members.

After all students have performed, the class discusses how these techniques could be taught to high school general music students.

Suggested Resources

Anderson, Doug. Chapters 8–10 in *Jazz and Show Choir Handbook.* Chapel Hill, NC: Hinshaw Music Textbook, 1978.

Ellington, Duke. *Duke Ellington and Friends.* Verve Records 833291.

Hackett, Patricia. *The Melody Book: 300 Selections from the World of Music for Autoharp, Guitar, Piano, Recorder, and Voice,* 2d ed. Englewood Cliffs, NJ: Prentice-Hall, 1992.

STANDARD 3C

Proficient

Improvising melodies, variations, and accompaniments: *Students improvise original melodies over given chord progressions, each in a consistent style, meter, and tonality.*

Strategy

Methods students have been assigned readings describing characteristics of classic blues melodies: blue notes (flatted third and seventh, and sometimes flatted fifth scale degrees), occurrence of *do, mi,* or *sol* on the last word of a line of lyrics, and two-and-a-half-bar melodies in each four-bar phrase (allowing "resting" time for singers to create new verses).

The instructor and students sing a classic blues scale several times, beginning on the roots of I, IV, and V chords, to become aware of the sound of the blue notes against the three major chords. [*Note:* The major chord accompaniment, together with the blues scale, approximates an African melodic idiom that is not possible in traditional European tonal singing.]

The instructor encourages students to imitate the sliding or wailing sounds of jazz instruments using scat syllables (free choice) as they improvise original melodies over a standard 12-bar blues harmonic progression—I, IV, and V.

Working in small groups, students listen to a standard 12-bar blues harmonic progression—played on electronic keyboards, on a recording, or on guitars by group members. Students take turns singing original blues melodies as time allows. They critique the improvised melodies by comparing them with characteristics of blues melodies.

Methods students evaluate the procedure in terms of its applicability for students in a high school general music class.

Suggested Resources

Anderson, Doug. Chapter 9 in *Jazz and Show Choir Handbook*. Chapel Hill, NC: Hinshaw Music Textbook, 1978.

Coker, Patty, and David Baker. *Vocal Improvisation—An Instrumental Approach*. Lebanon, IN: Studio P/R, 1981.

Fowler, Charles. Chapter 16 in *Music! Its Role and Importance in Our Lives*. Mission Hills, CA: Glencoe/McGraw-Hill, 1994. Book and recordings.

Stuessy, Joe. Chapter 2 in *Rock and Roll: Its History and Stylistic Development*, 2d ed. Englewood Cliffs, NJ: Prentice-Hall, 1994.

STANDARD 3D

Advanced

Improvising melodies, variations, and accompaniments: *Students improvise stylistically appropriate harmonizing parts in a variety of styles.*

Strategy

Methods students have been assigned to analyze a Kabalevsky piano selection (Scherzo, op. 39, no. 12), identifying the use of pattern, repetition, sequence, and rhythmic variations. In class, they work in small groups to record the Scherzo as written, and they save the best performance from each group on the sequencer. They then devise a learning sequence for discovery of the following:

- The melodic pattern in the first measure is treated sequentially throughout the composition.

- All triads are on white keys in root position.

(continued)

- There are two triads per measure that could be performed as either block chords or arpeggios.

To improvise a new harmonic accompaniment for the Scherzo, each group creates a one-measure harmonic figure using block and/or arpeggiated triads as a model. Using the lead sheet chord symbols as a guide, students perform a harmonic accompaniment in a duet with the sequencer, observing articulations and dynamic contrasts. The instructor initiates a discussion of which harmonizations were most effective and why.

Students review the learning sequence, from the recording of the Scherzo to evaluation of the improvised harmonizations. They create a brief sketch of steps to use for future lesson plans for high school general music.

Suggested Resource

Kabalevsky, Dimitri. Scherzo, op. 39, no. 12. In *Easiest Kabalevsky*. Van Nuys, CA: Alfred Publishing Company, 1976.

STANDARD 3E

Advanced

Improvising melodies, variations, and accompaniments: *Students improvise original melodies in a variety of styles, over given chord progressions, each in a consistent style, meter, and tonality.*

Strategy

Methods students have been assigned to listen to folk hymns sung in a gospel style. The instructor has provided an example of the Southern folk hymn with notated melody and chordal accompaniment and a recorded version in the gospel style.

Working alone or with one other person, students improvise on the melody of a Southern folk hymn, such as "Amazing Grace," in a gospel style. The instructor then directs students to improvise an original melody over the chord progression of the selected hymn, using the following criteria:

- More pitches per beat than the notated original.
- Blue notes (flatted third, fifth, and seventh scale degrees) to emphasize specific words.
- Repetition of selected words.
- Insertion of short vocal phrases for expressive effect.
- Melisma that extends one syllable over two or more pitches.

Students evaluate their own performance based on assigned criteria, and the instructor critiques the self-evaluations. With direction from the instructor, the class decides whether adaptations need to be made for use in high school general music.

Suggested Resources

Fowler, Charles. Chapter 12 in *Music! Its Role and Importance in Our Lives*. Mission Hills, CA: Glencoe/McGraw-Hill, 1994. Book and recordings.

Franklin, Aretha. "Amazing Grace," from *Amazing Grace*. Atlantic CD-906-2.

Stuessy, Joe. Chapter 9 in *Rock and Roll: Its History and Stylistic Development,* 2d ed. Englewood Cliffs, NJ: Prentice-Hall, 1994.

◆ ◆ ◆ ◆ ◆ ◆

STANDARD 4A
Proficient

Composing and arranging music within specified guidelines: *Students compose music in several distinct styles, demonstrating creativity in using the elements of music for expressive effect.*

Strategy

Methods students have been assigned to listen to "Finale" from Stravinsky's *The Firebird Suite* and to list the different ways in which the composer varies the theme (e.g., dynamics, tempo, timbre, registration, texture).

In class, students discuss the creative means Stravinsky used to vary the theme. The instructor leads students to see how the manipulation of a theme generates certain kinds of responses in the listener. After the discussion, the instructor divides the class into several small groups for an in-class compositional activity requiring fifteen to twenty minutes. Using available instruments (acoustic and/or electronic), the groups collaborate to vary the theme of "Finale" in a number of ways to create specific effects (e.g., build excitement, establish serenity, surprise the listener).

Students perform their compositions for at least one other group. The instructor suggests that a student from each group assume a leadership role and encourages the groups to engage in active discussion of each work. Discussion could focus on whether the group carried out the assignment, whether they included anything not specified by the instructor, whether the final product was successful, and whether there are ways to improve the composition.

The group discussions serve as evaluation for both the composition and adaptability of the strategy for high school general music.

Suggested Resources

General Music Today 8, no. 3 (Spring 1995), entire issue.

Paynter, John J. *Sound and Structure.* New York: Cambridge University Press, 1992.

Upitis, Rena. *This Too Is Music.* Portsmouth, NH: Heinemann Educational Books, 1990.

Wiggins, Jackie. *Composition in the Classroom: A Tool for Teaching.* Reston, VA: Music Educators National Conference, 1990.

STANDARD 4B

Proficient

Composing and arranging music within specified guidelines: Students arrange pieces for voices or instruments other than those for which the pieces were written in ways that preserve or enhance the expressive effect of the music.

Strategy

Prior to the class meeting, methods students have selected a simple ballad or folk melody from any national or ethnic source, analyzed the underlying harmonic progression, and notated the melody on manuscript paper. The instructor gives students the following criteria for an in-class activity to arrange the song for guitar and recorder ensemble:

- Write four guitar parts for at least four different skill levels: level 1—ostinato part consisting of root and alternate, marking the underlying beat or divisions of the beat; level 2—strumming pattern; level 3—fingerpicking pattern, using the root, alternate, and three highest strings; and level 4—melody.

- Write recorder parts using one of the following: (1) a melody or countermelody for soprano, alto, or tenor recorders; (2) a duet for soprano/alto or alto/tenor; or, (3) a solo and descant for soprano/alto or alto/tenor.

The instructor evaluates the arrangements. Students discuss how their arrangements preserve or enhance the expressive effect of the original melody. Finally, students decide whether changes need to be made in the procedure before using it in a high school general music class.

Suggested Resources

Hackett, Patricia. *The Melody Book: 300 Selections from the World of Music for Autoharp, Guitar, Piano, Recorder, and Voice,* 2d ed. Englewood Cliffs, NJ: Prentice-Hall, 1992.

McNeil, William K., compiler. *Southern Folk Ballads.* Little Rock: August House, 1987.

Warner, Anne, ed. *Traditional American Folk Songs.* Syracuse, NY: Syracuse University Press, 1984.

STANDARD 4C

Proficient

Composing and arranging music within specified guidelines: Students compose and arrange music for voices and various acoustic and electronic instruments, demonstrating knowledge of the ranges and traditional usages of the sound sources.

Strategy

The instructor has assigned readings to methods students for review of written examples of African polyrhythms (see Jessup and Adzenyah, Maraire, and Tucker). Readings also include polyrhythmic writing (see Nketia).

In class, students listen to line-by-line performance instructions for polyrhythmic writing on the companion tape to *Let Your Voice Be Heard!* The instructor then divides the class into small groups to write simple pieces for a polyrhythmic ensemble.

In their groups, students experiment with available African percussion instruments or appropriate classroom instrument substitutes and compose their group piece. Students should keep in mind the following traditional practices of African drum music: (1) each instrument plays a one- or two-measure pattern that is repeated throughout the piece; (2) frequently in performances, instruments enter one at a time until the entire ensemble is playing; (3) pitch and timbre of different instruments are often used to create a "melody" that may be discerned when the full ensemble plays; (4) often one instrument, such as bell or "master drum," is designated as "leader" of the ensemble and sets tempo, etc.

Each small group performs for at least one other group. Students make any adaptations to the recorded instructions that would be necessary for use in high school general music.

Suggested Resources

Adzenyah, Abraham Kobena, Dumisani Maraire, and Judith Cook Tucker. *Let Your Voice Be Heard! Songs from Ghana and Zimbabwe,* 2d ed. Danbury, CT: World Music Press, 1997. Book and recording.

Jessup, Lynne E. *All Hands On.* Danbury, CT: World Music Press, 1996.

Nketia, Joseph H. K. *Music of Africa.* New York: W. W. Norton, 1974.

STANDARD 4D

Advanced

Composing and arranging music within specified guidelines: *Students compose music, demonstrating imagination and technical skill in applying the principles of composition.*

Strategy

Working alone, methods students use sequencer/notation software to create a composition of at least twenty-four measures divided into three eight-measure sections. The sections can be ABA or ABC, but the primary compositional goal is for the middle section to have maximum contrast.

The instructor assigns one unifying device to be used throughout the composition (e.g., melodic or rhythmic ostinato, melodic variations). As students work on their compositions, they make notes as to how the activity could be adapted for acoustic instruments. When the compositions are completed, each student prints out his or her composition and presents it to a few other students who listen to it and critique it, looking particularly for evidence of imagination and skill in applying the principles of composition.

Students discuss how the sequence of steps used in the composition activity can serve as a lesson plan for use with high school general music.

(continued)

Suggested Resources

General Music Today 8, no. 3 (Spring 1995), entire issue.

Wiggins, Jackie. *Composition in the Classroom: A Tool for Teaching*. Reston, VA: Music Educators National Conference, 1990.

◆ ◆ ◆ ◆ ◆ ◆ ◆

STANDARD 5A

Proficient

Reading and notating music: *Students demonstrate the ability to read an instrumental or vocal score of up to four staves by describing how the elements of music are used.*

Strategy

The instructor asks methods students a series of questions about Jones's "Whist Hist," a four-part setting of an e. e. cummings poem (in *World of Choral Music*). Students describe how the elements of music are used in the piece by answering questions such as the following:

Harmony—How many vocal parts are there? Which of the vocal parts are paired? Are they exact imitations throughout the selection?

Melody—Are parts written on precise pitches? Explain. Which clef (unlabeled) is used for notation in all four parts? Locate examples of vocalizations not associated with singing and chromaticism in the voice parts.

Rhythm—What meter is used throughout the piece? Besides the percussion part, can you find examples of rhythmic patterns other than simple divisions of the beat?

Expressive qualities—Is there a peak of excitement in the piece? A release of tension? Explain. How do dynamic markings contribute to the interpretation of the text?

Text—Do you find repetition of initial and internal consonants, consonance, and assonance? Specify.

After students have responded to the questions, the instructor leads the class in sightreading "Whist Hist." Following their reading, the class discusses the value of such an analysis as a preparation for sightreading.

Suggested Resource

Jones, R. W. "Whist Hist." In *World of Choral Music,* edited by Charles S. Hausmann, Hunter C. March, Samuel D. Miller, and Betty G. Roe. Parsippany, NJ: Silver Burdett Ginn, 1988.

STANDARD 5D

Advanced

Reading and notating music: *Students interpret nonstandard notation symbols used by some 20th-century composers.*

Strategy

At the beginning of class, methods students are asked to list the elements of music that could be used in a composition (*sound:* pitch, duration, timbre, dynamics, tempo, texture; *silence:* duration).

Students then experiment with the strings inside a piano to determine differences in the various registers of strings. Having students refer to copies of the composition "Middle, Bottom, and Top," from *32 Piano Games,* the instructor asks students to determine the meaning for *p, sfz, f, pp, mf, 15ma* (two octaves higher than written), and *8va* in the piano composition; read the composer's explanation for V marks; note that there is no meter signature or bar lines; and discuss the element of duration in the piece.

Students then follow the nonstandard notation as student volunteers perform the piece. The instructor leads a discussion about how personal interpretation can influence the nonstandard notation. The class lists steps of the learning sequence used to interpret nonstandard notation symbols so that they can adapt the strategy for high school general music classes.

Suggested Resource

Finney, Ross L. *32 Piano Games.* New York: C. F. Peters Corporation, 1969.

◆ ◆ ◆ ◆ ◆ ◆ ◆

STANDARD 6B

Proficient

Listening to, analyzing, and describing music: *Students demonstrate extensive knowledge of the technical vocabulary of music.*

Strategy

In class, methods students randomly choose one of the following from repertoire that could be performed in a high school general music class: vocal solos, instrumental solos, choral ensembles, and instrumental ensembles.

Students list examples of music terminology found in the selected composition. Using music dictionaries provided by the instructor, they create a music dictionary to be used as a resource for high school general music activities. For each word in their music dictionary, students write out a formal definition as well as a definition using ordinary language that can be used later in general music classes. The class discusses their definitions and comes to a consensus on the best definitions.

(continued)

The instructor directs methods students to design a lesson plan in which general music students would demonstrate their knowledge of a technical vocabulary of music. Learning activities could include:

- Assigning tempo, dynamics, and accent marks, with an additional sentence explaining the choice of terminology or markings, given a short musical excerpt without expressive markings.

- Identifying in writing the meaning of music terminology as it is used in a selected piece of music.

- Performing a short musical excerpt by singing or playing an instrument and properly observing the expressive markings; then performing the same musical excerpt with different expressive markings.

- Describing vocal and instrumental performances using terminology for vocal production and techniques.

Each student exchanges his or her plan with one other person, and students critique the adaptability of the plans for high school general music.

Suggested Resources

Baker, Theodore, ed. *Dictionary of Musical Terms.* New York: AMS Press, 1970.

Randel, Don Michael, ed. *The New Harvard Dictionary of Music.* Cambridge: Belknap Press of Harvard University Press, 1986.

STANDARD 6C

Proficient

Listening to, analyzing, and describing music: Students identify and explain compositional devices and techniques used to provide unity and variety and tension and release in a musical work and give examples of other works that make similar uses of these devices and techniques.

Strategy

Methods students have been assigned to read about meters in mariachi music. The class discusses three types of meters that are prevalent in the music of the mariachi: sesquiáltera or additive meter, an alternation of musical passages between 6/8 and 3/4; ritmo colonial or bimeter, with 6/8 and 3/4 occurring simultaneously; and waltz rhythm, with a slight delay of the offbeats.

Students are able to recognize hemiola and correctly clap alternating meters. The instructor plays recorded examples of "El Caporal," a mariachi song (on *Sounds of the World: Music of Latin America*); and "America," from Bernstein's *West Side Story.* As students listen to "El Caporal," they clap in two when they hear 6/8 and in three when they hear 3/4. Then they identify the type of mariachi meter present in "El Caporal." Students then clap the beat of "America," alternating meters of two and three for every other measure.

The instructor initiates a class discussion including the following questions: Does alternating meters for every measure create more or less tension than alternating meter changes over more than one measure? Does the use of hemiola provide unity or variety or both? Why?

Based on the class activities, methods students design a lesson plan for teaching high school general music students to identify and explain meters used in mariachi music.

Suggested Resources

Anderson, William M., ed. *Teaching Music with a Multicultural Approach.* Reston, VA: Music Educators National Conference, 1991. 65–68. Book and videocassettes.

Kilpatrick, David. *El Mariachi: Traditional Music of Mexico.* Vol. 2. Pico Rivera, CA: Fiesta Publications, 1989.

Sounds of the World: Music of Latin America—Mexico, Ecuador, Brazil. Teacher's guide by Dale Olsen, Charles Perrone, and Daniel Sheehy. Reston, VA: Music Educators National Conference, 1987. Audiocassettes and teacher's guide.

STANDARD 6E
Advanced

Listening to, analyzing, and describing music: Students compare ways in which musical materials are used in a given example relative to ways in which they are used in other works of the same genre or style.

Strategy

Students have been assigned to listen to three Native American songs—"Prairie Chicken Dance," "Hello Song," and "Axawire Imilla"—from the compact disc *Creation's Journey.* In class, the instructor plays the three recordings, directing students to analyze each song by responding to the following:

- Are the singers male, female, or mixed? Describe the tone quality and style of the singers.

- What kinds of instruments, if any, are used?

- Describe the rhythmic patterns in the melody and accompaniments.

- Describe the tempo and dynamics.

- What is the form?

Students discuss their responses and reach a consensus. They develop a lesson plan to help advanced general music students in grades 9–12 recognize and describe Native American music.

Suggested Resource

Creation's Journey. Smithsonian Folkways SF 40410. Recording and book.

◆ ◆ ◆ ◆ ◆ ◆ ◆

Evaluating music and music performances: *Students evolve specific criteria for making informed, critical evaluations of the quality and effectiveness of performances, compositions, arrangements, and improvisations and apply the criteria in their personal participation in music.*

Strategy

The instructor divides the class into small working groups and provides four or five copies of music reviews, chart paper, and markers for each group. The reviews of performances are from the *New York Times*. Reviews of new recordings are from *Hi-Fi Review, Rolling Stone,* or similar sources. Students are familiar with the role of the music critic in evaluating music, music performances, and recordings.

Each group selects a discussion leader and a recorder. Members of each group carefully go over the reviews written by professional music critics. With suggestions from the group, the recorder lists comments about performances that critics considered crucial to the evaluation.

After each group has delineated the critics' criteria for evaluation, the instructor reassembles the class and plays a recording that has been critiqued in one of the reviews. Then, the discussion leaders take turns leading a general class discussion of the criteria listed for that recording. The instructor frequently replays excerpts of the recording to illustrate specific items that have been denoted by critics.

The class discusses how this activity can be used to help high school general music students develop criteria for making informed critical evaluations of music and music performances and applying the criteria.

Suggested Resources

Hi-Fi Review (any issue). Reviews of new recordings.

New York Times (any edition). Reviews of music performances.

Rolling Stone (any issue). Reviews of new recordings.

Evaluating music and music performances: *Students evaluate a performance, composition, arrangement, or improvisation by comparing it to similar or exemplary models.*

Strategy

Methods students are given an in-class assignment to listen to a musical composition, selected by the instructor, that is a superior example of a particular period, both in terms of composition and performance. The instructor has prepared an analysis sheet to be used with high school students, listing the elements, concepts, and expressive qualities of music. Each of the basic musical elements and concepts and expressive qualities on the analysis sheet is followed by a list of descriptors for students to choose; for example: *melody*—lyrical, twelve-tone row, embellished tonal melody, many disjunct intervals, pentatonic.

As the instructor plays a music example, students circle a descriptor for each element, concept, or expressive quality. After students have chosen descriptors for the music example, the instructor plays at least three excerpts of music examples from the same period of music history. Students listen and select the excerpt that most nearly matches the exemplary model in composition and performance.

Students engage in a class discussion to explain their choices and how they can structure a similar activity for high school general music.

Suggested Resource

Grout, Donald J., and Claude V. Palisca. *A History of Western Music,* 5th ed. New York: W. W. Norton, 1996.

STANDARD 7C
Advanced

Evaluating music and music performances: *Students evaluate a given musical work in terms of its aesthetic qualities and explain the musical means it uses to evoke feelings and emotions.*

Strategy

Methods students watch two video clips of scenes from Oliver Stone's film *Platoon* (scene of burning of the village; and scene that depicts the intensity of the "good" sergeant futilely struggling to escape the Viet Cong). Both scenes use Barber's *Adagio for Strings* as a musical background. Based on a similar idea from *Music! Its Role and Importance in Our Lives* (p. 416), students work in groups to analyze why the composition was chosen as the background for two intense scenes in the film and how musical elements were used to add to the emotional effect.

Students come back together to discuss in which scene the *Adagio* is more effective as background music. The instructor emphasizes that students must be specific as to how the interrelationship of musical elements and expressive qualities contributes to the dynamic shape (tension and release) in the composition and to the emotions the video clips evoke. The class discusses whether the procedure needs any further adaptation before use in high school general music.

Suggested Resources

Fowler, Charles. *Music! Its Role and Importance in Our Lives.* Mission Hills, CA: Glencoe/McGraw-Hill, 1994. Book and recordings.

Meyer, Leonard. Chapter 1 in *Emotion and Meaning in Music.* Chicago: University of Chicago Press, 1961.

Platoon. Produced by Arnold Kopelson. Directed by Oliver Stone. Herndale Film Corporation, 1986. Videocassette.

Reimer, Bennett. Chapter 7 in *A Philosophy of Music Education,* 2d ed. Englewood Cliffs, NJ: Prentice-Hall, 1989.

◆ ◆ ◆ ◆ ◆ ◆ ◆

Proficient

Understanding relationships between music, the other arts, and disciplines outside the arts:
Students explain how elements, artistic processes, and organizational principles are used in similar and distinctive ways in the various arts and cite examples.

Strategy

Methods students have completed assigned readings to derive a list of jazz characteristics that George Gershwin incorporated in traditional forms of concert music. They have also looked at works of Pablo Picasso to derive a list of unique characteristics.

In class, the instructor asks students to assume the following statement as a basis for discussion: In order to create unique examples of art, both Gershwin and Picasso used the elements, processes, and principles of form in their respective arts to challenge the prevailing European models.

The instructor plays excerpts from Gershwin's *An American in Paris* and the opening of *Rhapsody in Blue*. Students list the characteristics that are related to classical music and those related to jazz.

The instructor then shows a couple early Picasso works and a couple from a period when the artist was influenced by the art of primitive African tribes and ancient Iberian sculptures. Students discuss their distinctive characteristics and list those related to traditional painting styles.

Students compare the similarities and differences in the means used in the two arts to challenge tradition. They devise a plan to present their ideas in high school general music.

Suggested Resources

Fowler, Charles. Chapter 26 in *Music! Its Role and Importance in Our Lives*. Mission Hills, CA: Glencoe/McGraw-Hill, 1994. Book and recordings.

Neret, Gilles. *Picasso*. Westminster, MD: Taschen/Random House. 1996.

Warncke, C. P., and I. F. Walther. *Picasso*. Westminster, MD: Taschen/Random House, 1996.

Wold, Milo, and Edmund Cykler. *An Introduction to Music and Art in the Western World*, 10th ed. Columbus, OH: Wm. C. Brown Communications/McGraw-Hill, 1995.

Proficient

Understanding relationships between music, the other arts, and disciplines outside the arts:
Students compare characteristics of two or more arts within a particular historical period or style and cite examples from various cultures.

Strategy

Methods students were assigned to listen to one movement of a concerto grosso (by Bach, Corelli, or Vivaldi) that clearly demonstrates contrast in dynamic levels, tonal color, and virtuosic writing between the ripieno sections (full sections of a small string orchestra) and the concertino sections (small group of soloists). They were also asked to locate one example of a Baroque painting (by El Greco, Rembrandt, or Velázquez) that clearly demonstrates the use of contrast in light and shade.

Using the materials they have chosen, students work in small groups to prepare a presentation on the use of contrast in Baroque music and painting. The instructor explains that the presentation should include excerpts from contrasting sections of a concerto grosso, with verbal descriptions and icons to describe how contrast is achieved through the composer's use of melody, rhythm, harmony, dynamics, tempo, and timbre.

Additionally, the instructor asks that slides, posters, or reproductions of Baroque paintings be included, along with descriptions of how contrast—light and shade—is achieved through use of line, color, form, organization, and space. Each small group critiques its presentation and makes any necessary adaptations for use in high school general music.

Suggested Resources

Fowler, Charles. Chapter 23 in *Music! Its Role and Importance in Our Lives.* Mission Hills, CA: Glencoe/McGraw-Hill, 1994. Book and recordings.

Wold, Milo, and Edmund Cykler. *An Introduction to Music and Art in the Western World,* 10th ed. Columbus, OH: Wm. C. Brown Communications/McGraw-Hill, 1995.

STANDARD 8C

Proficient
Understanding relationships between music, the other arts, and disciplines outside the arts:
Students explain ways in which the principles and subject matter of various disciplines outside the arts are interrelated with those of music.

Strategy

Beginning a discussion of the relationship between principles of Baroque architecture and of Baroque music, the instructor shows cruciforms representing the shapes (see a dictionary under "cross") of a traditional Latin cross church and a Greek cross church. Methods students discuss how they think a choir would sound positioned together at the front of the church in comparison with a choir divided at the sides of the church.

The following questions guide the discussion:

- What is the difference between homophonic and polyphonic texture?

- Which positioning of the choir—small space or split—would be more likely to produce a homophonic texture or a polyphonic texture? Why?

- Does a composer need to consider where a work will be performed?

- Are there special considerations for performing choral music in a large marble or stone building?

(continued)

The instructor shows a photograph of St. Mark's Basilica in Venice, Italy, explaining that the separation of two or more choir lofts led to the development of "broken choruses" (*chori spezzati*). Students listen to an excerpt from Giovanni Gabrieli's *Symphoniae Sacrae,* focusing attention on the alternation of contrasting bodies of sound. They then discuss how they could present these procedures to high school general music students.

Suggested Resources

Empire Brass. *Symphoniae Sacrae.* On *Music of Gabrieli.* TELARC CD-80204.

Fleming, William. Chapter 12 in *Arts and Ideas,* 9th ed. Orlando, FL: Harcourt Brace, 1995.

Grout, Donald J., and Claude V. Palisca. *A History of Western Music,* 5th ed. New York: W. W. Norton, 1996.

STANDARD 8E

Advanced

Understanding relationships between music, the other arts, and disciplines outside the arts:
Students explain how the roles of creators, performers, and others involved in the production and presentation of the arts are similar to and different from one another in the various arts.

Strategy

Methods students have been assigned to analyze the roles of a creator and a re-creator in music and in visual art. Previous to the class meeting, the instructor has given them the following statement (Munro, p. 438), or a paraphrase of the statement, to use in their analysis: "An art always involves doing something to (a process) and with something (a medium) in order to make or do something (a product or performance)."

In class, students work in groups to discuss the following in language easily understood by high school general music students:

- What are the raw materials that the creator of music (composer) uses? The raw materials for the creator of visual art (either painter or sculptor)? How does the medium (sound, shapes, color) affect the creative process?

- What does the composer "do" with the medium? The visual artist?

- Describe the products produced by the composer and the visual artist.

- Point out the differences in the creators and the products of both arts; the similarities.

- Discuss the following philosophical principle: Re-creation in music is the fine art of performance. Re-creation in visual and space art, if not clearly identified, is plagiarism. Why?

Each group develops a plan for using the information gained from the discussion in a high school general music class.

Suggested Resources

Becker, Howard. *Art Worlds.* Chicago: University of California Press, 1982.

Munro, Thomas. *The Arts and Their Interrelations.* Cleveland: The Press of Case Western Reserve, 1967.

◆ ◆ ◆ ◆ ◆ ◆ ◆

STANDARD 9A
Proficient

Understanding music in relation to history and culture: *Students classify by genre or style and by historical period or culture unfamiliar but representative aural examples of music and explain the reasoning behind their classifications.*

Strategy

In preparation for class, methods students have read excerpts discussing the rationale for using music that represents a variety of cultures. Students discuss the value of its inclusion and establish the basis on which music from different cultures will be used with high school general music students.

The instructor plays authentic recordings of musical excerpts from three contrasting cultures: Yoruba (Africa), China, and Scotland. The students classify examples according to their country of origin. The students then identify at least five aural indicators that led them to the classifications they made. (Suggested indicators: instrumentation, melodic and/or harmonic structure, rhythmic structure, form, language, vocal timbre)

Students then identify aural skills necessary for this discriminative listening. They develop a learning sequence that directs the aural skills of students toward the specific musical characteristics of the culture being studied. They suggest ways to relate the music from these three cultures to music that is familiar to the high school students.

Suggested Resources

Campbell, Patricia Shehan. *Music in Cultural Context: Eight Views on World Music Education.* Reston, VA: Music Educators National Conference, 1996.

Collinson, Francis M. *The Traditional and National Music of Scotland.* London: Routledge Chapman & Hall, 1966.

Fung, C. Victor. "Rationales for Teaching World Musics." *Music Educators Journal* 82, no. 1 (July 1995): 36–40.

"Jà Fún Mi." On *King Sunnyadé: Ju Ju Music.* Island Records/Mango 162-539712.

Maccoll, Ewan, and Peggy Seeger. *The Long Harvest.* Records 1 and 2, with pamphlet giving text and origin of songs. Argo ZDA 67 (115 Fulham Road, London SW). Presents traditional children's ballads in English, Scottish, and North American variants.

A Musical Anthology of the Orient: China. UNESCO Collection: Muscaphon BM30 SL2032.

STANDARD 9B
Proficient

Understanding music in relation to history and culture: *Students identify sources of American music genres, trace the evolution of those genres, and cite well-known musicians associated with them.*

Strategy

Methods students have been assigned readings about Dixieland Jazz and its origins, musical and cultural influences, salient musical characteristics, repertoire, and distinguished performers. The instructor leads students through the following learning sequence that can be used with high school general music students.

Working in small groups, methods students develop a time line to illustrate the roots of Dixieland Jazz, making sure to identify specific historical and cultural influences. They also list instruments used, the most important musical characteristics, and distinguishing stylistic characteristics.

The instructor asks students to sing "When the Saints Go Marching In" (in *Music! Its Role and Importance in Our Lives*). As suggested in the text (p. 466), they are instructed to decide where short improvisations or "licks" would be appropriate musically. Then they tap out the rhythmic patterns of their improvisations and assign scat syllables (nonsense words). Students then listen to the Preservation Hall Jazz Band instrumental version of the song, from *Music!*, and compare their own improvisation with it.

Finally, students discuss how they would use this learning sequence with high school general music students.

Suggested Resource

Fowler, Charles. Chapter 24 in *Music! Its Role and Importance in Our Lives*. Mission Hills, CA: Glencoe/McGraw-Hill, 1994. Book and recordings.

STANDARD 9C
Proficient

Understanding music in relation to history and culture: *Students identify various roles that musicians perform, cite representative individuals who have functioned in each role, and describe their activities and achievements.*

Strategy

Each methods student has researched the role of one of the following types of musicians in the culture of the United States: composer, song arranger, studio musician, studio teacher, public school music teacher (ensemble and general music at elementary, middle school, and high school levels), college music educator, virtuoso performer, rock musician, musicologist, jazz musician, church musician, or professional accompanist. As part of their research, the students were directed to include information concerning training, money-making potential, duties, well-known role models, advantages and disadvantages, and a brief history of the position.

Assuming the role of the musician researched, each student presents information to the class. Students explain their roles and take questions from the floor. Roles presented to the class afford methods students information for creating activities to help high school students understand the contemporary roles of musicians.

Suggested Resources

Bjorneberg, Paul, ed. *Exploring Careers in Music.* Reston: Music Educators National Conference, 1990.

Cowden, Robert, ed. "Careers in Music." Reston: Music Educators National Conference, 1989. Brochure.

Hopke, William E. *Encyclopedia of Careers and Vocational Guidance,* 10th ed. Chicago: J. G. Ferguson Publishing Company, 1996–97.

National Academy of Recording Arts & Sciences. *The Careers in Music Video.* Santa Monica, CA: NARAS, 1991. Available from Music Educators National Conference, Reston, VA.

STANDARD 9E
Advanced

Understanding music in relation to history and culture: *Students identify and describe music genres or styles that show the influence of two or more cultural traditions, identify the cultural source of each influence, and trace the historical conditions that produced the synthesis of influences.*

Strategy

Methods students have been assigned readings about the origins, cultural influences, and musical characteristics of *conjunto,* dance music of the Southwest created by Texas-Mexican *tejano* musicians. The instructor plays a recording of Texas-Mexican music ("Ay te dejo en San Antonio," on recording accompanying *Music! Its Role and Importance in Our Lives*); students identify instruments used, meter, and the type of dance.

Working in small groups, students use material in chapter 4 of *Music!* to develop a flow chart showing the synthesis of Mexican and European influences leading to the creation of *conjunto* by Texas-Mexicans. They trace how dances came from Europe to Texas, not only by way of Mexico, but also by immigration of Europeans and Eastern Europeans to south Texas. The cultural influences include types of dances, types of instruments, lyrics, accompaniment styles, and musical characteristics of harmony, texture, and meter.

Students discuss how the information gained from the readings and in-class activities will help them develop lessons for high school general music.

(continued)

Suggested Resources

Casey, Betty. *Dance Across Texas.* Austin, TX: University of Texas Press, 1985.

Fowler, Charles. Chapter 24 in *Music! Its Role and Importance in Our Lives.* Mission Hills, CA: Glencoe/McGraw-Hill, 1994. Book and recordings.

Pena, Manuel T. *The Texas-Mexican Conjunto: History of a Working Class Music.* Austin: University of Texas Press, 1985.

Books

Abeles, Harold F., Charles R. Hoffer, and Robert H. Klotman. *Foundations of Music Education,* 2d ed. Old Tappan, NJ: Schirmer Books/Simon & Schuster, 1994.

Adzenyah, Abraham Kobena, Dumisani Maraire, and Judith Cook Tucker. *Let Your Voice Be Heard! Songs from Ghana and Zimbabwe,* 2d ed. Danbury, CT: World Music Press, 1997. Book and recording.

Anderson, Doug. *Jazz and Show Choir Handbook.* Chapel Hill, NC: Hinshaw Music Textbook, 1978.

*Anderson, William M., ed. *Teaching Music with a Multicultural Approach.* Reston, VA: Music Educators National Conference, 1991. Book and videocassettes.

*Anderson, William M., and Patricia Shehan Campbell, eds. *Multicultural Perspectives in Music Education,* 2d ed. Reston, VA: Music Educators National Conference, 1996.

Anderson, William M., and Joy E. Lawrence. *Integrating Music into the Elementary Classroom,* 3d ed. Belmont, CA: Wadsworth Publishing Company, 1995.

Apel, Willi. *Gregorian Chant.* Bloomington, IN: Indiana University Press, 1958.

Atterbury, Betty W., and Carol P. Richardson. *The Experience of Teaching General Music.* New York: McGraw-Hill, 1995.

Award Winning Songs of the Country Music Association. Vol 2. Milwaukee, WI: Hal Leonard Corporation, 1992.

Baker, Theodore, ed. *Dictionary of Musical Terms.* New York: AMS Press, 1970.

Bamberger, Jean. *The Mind behind the Musical Ear: How Children Develop Musical Intelligence.* Harvard University Press, 1991.

Becker, Howard. *Art Worlds.* Chicago: University of California Press, 1982.

Bergethon, Bjornar, Eunice Boardman, and Janet Montgomery. *Musical Growth in the Elementary School,* 6th ed. Orlando, FL: Harcourt Brace, 1996.

*Bjorneberg, Paul, ed. *Exploring Careers in Music.* Reston, VA: Music Educators National Conference, 1990.

Booher, Jane, ed. *Maa-baa-hi Má-hac (We're Going Singing!): A Traditional Song Collection of the Mandan and Hidatsa Tribes.* New Town, ND: Fort Berthold Community College, 1992.

Bruner, Jerome. *Toward a Theory of Instruction.* Cambridge: Harvard University Press, 1966.

Burakoff, Gerald, and Willy Strickland, arr. *Musicke from Olde England.* Levittown, NY: Sweet Pipes, 1981.

*Campbell, Patricia Shehan. *Music in Cultural Context: Eight Views on World Music Education.* Reston, VA: Music Educators National Conference, 1996.

Campbell, Patricia Shehan, Ellen McCullough-Brabson, and Judith Cook Tucker. *Roots and Branches: A Legacy of Multicultural Music for Children.* Danbury, CT: World Music Press, 1994. Book and recording.

Campbell, Patricia Shehan, and Carol Scott-Kassner. *Music in Childhood: From Preschool through the Elementary Grades.* Old Tappan, NJ: Schirmer Books/Simon & Schuster, 1995.

Campbell-Towell, Lee. *Any Turkey Can Tango.* Milwaukee: Hal Leonard Corporation, 1995.

Carley, Isabel McNeill. *For Hand Drums and Recorders.* Allison Park, PA: Music Innovations, 1982.

Carlton, Elizabeth B., and Weikart, Phyllis S. *Foundations in Elementary Education: Music.* Ypsilanti, MI: High/Scope Press, 1994.

Casey, Betty. *Dance Across Texas.* Austin, TX: University of Texas Press, 1985.

Choksy, Lois, Robert M. Abramson, Avon E. Gillespie, and David Woods. *Teaching Music in the Twentieth Century.* Englewood Cliffs, NJ: Prentice-Hall, 1986.

Choral Connections. Mission Hills, CA: Glencoe/McGraw-Hill, 1997. Eight-book series in four levels.

Citron, Marvin, and Margaret Gayle. *Educational Renaissance: Our Schools at the Turn of the 21st Century.* New York: St. Martin's Press, 1991.

Coker, Patty, and David Baker. *Vocal Improvisation—An Instrumental Approach.* Lebanon, IN: Studio P/R, 1981.

Collinson, Francis M. *The Traditional and National Music of Scotland.* London: Routledge Chapman & Hall, 1966.

Cooksey, John M. *Working with the Adolescent Voice.* St. Louis: Concordia Publishing House, 1992.

The Doo-Wop Song Book. Milwaukee, WI: Hal Leonard Corporation, 1989.

Elrod, Pamela, and David Doss. *Music Memory Bulletin: Bass Clef Book.* Austin, TX: University Interscholastic League, 1989–90.

Feierabend, John M. *Music for Very Little People.* New York: Boosey & Hawkes, 1986.

Finney, Ross L. *32 Piano Games.* New York: C. F. Peters Corporation, 1969.

Fleming, William. *Arts and Ideas,* 9th ed. Orlando, FL: Harcourt Brace, 1995.

Fowler, Charles. *Music! Its Role and Importance in Our Lives.* Mission Hills, CA: Glencoe/McGraw-Hill, 1994. Book and recordings.

Frazee, Jane. *Discovering Orff: A Curriculum for Music Teachers.* Paoli, PA: Schott/European American, 1987.

Froseth, James O., and Phyllis Weikart. *Movement to Music.* Chicago: GIA Publications, 1981.

Funes, Donald J. *Musical Involvement,* 2d ed. Orlando, FL: Harcourt Brace, 1992. Book and recording.

Gardner, Howard. *Frames of Mind.* New York: Basic Books, 1993.

———. *To Open Minds: Chinese Clues to the Dilemma of Contemporary Education.* New York: Basic Books, 1989.

Goodman, Danny. *The Complete HyperCard 2.2 Handbook.* New York: Random House, 1993.

Grout, Donald J., and Claude V. Palisca. *A History of Western Music,* 5th ed. New York: W. W. Norton, 1996.

Hackett, Patricia. *The Melody Book: 300 Selections from the World of Music for Autoharp, Guitar, Piano, Recorder and Voice,* 2d ed. Englewood Cliffs, NJ: Prentice-Hall, 1992.

Hackett, Patricia, and Carolynn A. Lindeman. *The Musical Classroom: Backgrounds, Models, and Skills for Elementary Teaching,* 4th ed. Englewood Cliffs, NJ: Prentice-Hall, 1997.

*Hamann, Donald L., ed. *Creativity in the Music Classroom: The Best of MEJ.* Reston, VA: Music Educators National Conference, 1991.

Harpole, Patricia. *Los Mariachis: An Introduction to Mexican Mariachi Music.* Danbury, CT: World Music Press, 1991.

Hausmann, Charles S., Hunter C. March, Samuel D. Miller, and Betty G. Roe, eds. *World of Choral Music.* Parsippany, NJ: Silver Burdett Ginn, 1988.

*Hinckley, June, ed. *Music at the Middle Level: Building Strong Programs.* Reston, VA: Music Educators National Conference, 1994.

History of Rock: Late 60's. Milwaukee, WI: Hal Leonard Corporation, 1992.

Holt, John. *Never Too Late.* New York: Delacorte Press, 1978.

Hopke, William E. *Encyclopedia of Careers and Vocational Guidance,* 10th ed. Chicago: J. G. Ferguson Publishing Company, 1996–97.

Jessup, Lynn. *All Hands On.* Danbury, CT: World Music Press, 1996.

Kabalevsky, Dimitri. *Easiest Kabalevsky.* Van Nuys, CA: Alfred Publishing Company, 1976.

Kamien, Roger. *Music: An Appreciation,* 2d brief ed. New York: McGraw-Hill, 1994.

Kilpatrick, David. *El Mariachi: Traditional Music of Mexico.* Vol. 2. Pico Rivera, CA: Fiesta Publications, 1989.

King, Carol. *Recorder Routes I,* rev. ed. Memphis: Musicraft, 1994.

Lavender, Cheryl. *The Song Writing Kit.* Milwaukee, WI: Jenson Publishing, 1986.

Ledoux, Denis. *Turning Memories into Memoirs: A Handbook for Writing Lifestories.* Lisbon Falls, ME: Soleil Press, 1993.

Liber Usualis. Tournai, Belgium: Desclée and Company, 1934.

Lindeman, Carolynn A. *PianoLab: An Introduction to Class Piano,* 3d ed. Belmont CA: Wadsworth Publishing Company, 1996.

Machlis, Joseph, and Kristine Forney. *The Enjoyment of Music,* 7th ed. shorter. New York: W. W. Norton, 1995.

Manet/Monet/Degas. Master of Art Series. Orlando, FL: Harcourt Brace, 1971.

McNeil, William K., compiler. *Southern Folk Ballads.* Little Rock: August House, 1987.

Meyer, Leonard. *Emotion and Meaning in Music.* Chicago: University of Chicago Press, 1961.

Miller, Richard. *The Structure of Singing: System and Art in Vocal Technique.* Old Tappan, NJ: Schirmer Books/Simon & Schuster, 1986.

Munro, Thomas. *The Arts and Their Interrelations.* Cleveland: The Press of Case Western Reserve, 1967.

Music and You, Grades K–8. New York: Macmillan/McGraw-Hill, 1991.

The Music Connection, Grades K–8. Parsippany, NJ: Silver Burdett Ginn, 1995.

Musical Connections: Tradition and Change. Tampa, FL: International Society of Music Education, 1994.

Neret, Gilles. *Picasso.* Westminster, MD: Taschen/Random House. 1996.

Nguyen, Phong T., and Patricia Shehan Campbell. *From Rice Paddies to Temple Yards: Traditional Music of Vietnam.* Danbury, CT: World Music Press, 1989.

Nketia, Joseph H. K. *Music of Africa.* New York: W. W. Norton, 1974.

Nye, Robert E., Vernice T. Nye, Gary M. Martin, and Mary Lou Van Rysselberghe. *Music in the Elementary School,* 6th ed. Englewood Cliffs, NJ: Prentice Hall, 1992.

Paynter, John J. *Sound and Structure.* New York: Cambridge University Press, 1992.

Pena, Manuel T. *The Texas-Mexican Conjunto: History of a Working Class Music.* Austin: University of Texas Press, 1985.

Phillips, Kenneth H. *Teaching Kids to Sing.* Old Tappan, NJ: Schirmer Books/Simon & Schuster, 1992.

Randel, Don Michael, ed. *The New Harvard Dictionary of Music.* Cambridge: Belknap Press of Harvard University Press, 1986.

*Rao, Doreen, ed. *Choral Music for Children: An Annotated List.* Reston, VA: Music Educators National Conference, 1990.

Reimer, Bennett. *A Philosophy of Music Education,* 2d ed. Englewood Cliffs, NJ: Prentice-Hall, 1989.

Save the Last Dance for Me. Secaucus, NJ: Warner Bros. Publications, 1990.

Schafer, R. Murray. *Creative Music Education.* New York: Schirmer Books, 1976.

Schmid, Will, ed. *Something to Sing About,* Level I. Mission Hills, CA: Glencoe/McGraw-Hill, 1989.

Serwardda, W. Moses. *Songs and Stories from Uganda.* Edited by Hewitt Pantaleoni. Danbury, CT: World Music Press, 1987. Book and audiocassette.

Share the Music, Grades K–8. New York: Macmillan/McGraw-Hill, 1995, 1997.

Sloboda, John A., ed. *Generative Processes in Music: The Psychology of Performance, Improvisation, and Composition.* Oxford, England: Clarendon Press, 1988.

Southern, Eileen. *The Music of Black Americans,* 3d ed. New York: W. W. Norton, 1997.

Stuessy, Joe. *Rock and Roll: Its History and Stylistic Development,* 2d ed. Englewood Cliffs, NJ: Prentice-Hall, 1994.

Titon, Jeff Todd, ed. *Worlds of Music: An Introduction to the Music of the World's Peoples,* 3d ed. Old Tappan, NJ: Schirmer Books/Simon & Schuster, 1996. Book and recordings.

University Interscholastic League. *Music Memory Bulletin: Treble Clef Book.* Austin, TX: University Interscholastic League, 1990–91.

Upitis, Rena. *Can I Play You My Song?* Portsmouth, NH: Heinemann Educational Books, 1992.

———. *This Too Is Music.* Portsmouth, NH: Heinemann Educational Books, 1990.

Uszler, Marienne. *The Well-Tempered Keyboard Teacher.* Old Tappan, NJ: Schirmer Books/Simon & Schuster, 1990.

Walters, Darrel, and Cynthia Taggart, eds. *Readings in Music Learning Theory.* Chicago: GIA Publications, 1989.

Warncke, C. P., and I. F. Walther. *Picasso.* Westminster, MD: Taschen/Random House, 1996.

Warner, Anne, ed. *Traditional American Folk Songs.* Syracuse, NY: Syracuse University Press, 1984.

Warner, Brigitte. *Orff-Schulwerk: Applications for the Classroom.* Englewood Cliffs, NJ: Prentice-Hall, 1991.

Weikart, Phyllis. *Teaching Movement and Dance: A Sequential Approach to Rhythmic Movement.* Ypsilanti, MI: High/Scope Press, 1982.

*Wiggins, Jackie. *Composition in the Classroom: A Tool for Teaching.* Reston, VA: Music Educators National Conference, 1990.

Winner, Ellen. *Invented Worlds: The Psychology of the Arts.* 1982. Reprint, Cambridge: Harvard University Press, 1985.

Wold, Milo, and Edmund Cykler. *An Introduction to Music and Art in the Western World,* 10th ed. Columbus, OH: Wm. C. Brown Communications/McGraw-Hill, 1995.

World of Music, Grades K–8. Parsippany, NJ: Silver Burdett Ginn, 1991.

Wright, Roger, ed. *Spanish Ballads.* Warminster, England: Aris & Phillips, 1987.

Yudkin, Jeremy. *Music in Medieval Europe.* History of Music Series. Englewood Cliffs, NJ: Prentice-Hall, 1989.

Children's Literature

Berenstain, Stan and Jan. *Bears on Wheels.* New York: Random House, 1969.

Duke, Kate. *Seven Froggies Went to School.* New York: E. P. Dutton, 1985.

Galdone, Paul. *Cat Goes Fiddle-I-Fee.* New York: Clarion Books, 1985.

Isadora, Rachel. *The Firebird.* New York: G. P. Putnam's Sons, 1994.

Manson, Christopher. *A Farmyard Song: An Old Rhyme with New Pictures.* New York: North-South Books, 1992.

Mayer, Mercer. *I Was So Mad.* Racine, WI: Western Publishing Company, 1983.

Pomerantz, Charlotte. *The Piggy in the Puddle.* New York: Macmillan, 1974.

Rosenberg, Jane. *Dance Me a Story: Twelve Tales from the Classic Ballets.* New York: Thames and Hudson, 1985.

Zvorykin, Boris Vasil'evich. *The Firebird and Other Russian Fairy Tales.* New York: Viking Press, 1978.

Periodicals

Black Music Research Journal, Center for Black Music Research, Columbia College Chicago, 600 South Michigan Avenue, Chicago, IL 60605-1996.

Choral Journal, American Choral Directors Association, PO Box 6310, Lawton, OK 73506.

Clavier, The Instrumentalist Publishing Company, 200 Northfield Road, Northfield, IL 60093.

The Computing Teacher. See *Learning and Leading with Technology.*

*General Music Today, Music Educators National Conference, 1806 Robert Fulton Drive, Reston, VA 20191.

*Journal of Research in Music Education, Music Educators National Conference, 1806 Robert Fulton Drive, Reston, VA 20191.

Journal of Singing, National Association of Teachers of Singing, 2800 University Boulevard N., JU Station, Jacksonville, FL 33221.

Learning and Leading with Technology (formerly *The Computing Teacher*), International Society for Technology in Education, University of Oregon, 1787 Agate St., Eugene, OR 97403-1923.

*Music Educators Journal, Music Educators National Conference, 1806 Robert Fulton Drive, Reston, VA 20191.

The Orff Echo, American Orff-Schulwerk Organization, PO Box 391089, Cleveland, OH 44139.

Psychology of Music, Society for Research in Psychology of Music and Music Education, Department of Psychology, The University, Leicester LE1 7RH England.

*Teaching Music, Music Educators National Conference, 1806 Robert Fulton Drive, Reston, VA 20191.

*Update: Applications of Research in Music Education, Music Educators National Conference, 1806 Robert Fulton Drive, Reston, VA 20191.

Recordings

Choir of the Benedictine Monastery of Santo Domingo De Silos. *Gregorian Chant at the Monastery of Silos.* Francisco Lara. EMI Classics CDZ 62735.

Creation's Journey. Smithsonian Folkways SF 40410. Recording and book.

Ellington, Duke. *Duke Ellington and Friends.* Verve Records 833291.

Empire Brass. *Music of Gabrieli.* TELARC CD-80204.

Franklin, Aretha. *Amazing Grace.* Atlantic CD-906-2.

King Sunnyadé: Ju Ju Music. Island Records/Mango 162-539712.

Maccoll, Ewan, and Peggy Seeger. *The Long Harvest.* Records 1 and 2, with pamphlet giving text and origin of songs. Argo ZDA 67 (115 Fulham Road, London SW). Presents traditional children's ballads in English, Scottish, and North American variants.

Mariachi Vargas de Tecalitlán. *Sones de Jalisco.* RCA Victor MKS 1653.

A Musical Anthology of the Orient: China. UNESCO Collection: Muscaphon BM30 SL2032.

Simon and Garfunkel. *Greatest Hits.* Columbia 31350.

The Smithsonian Collection of Classic Jazz. Vol. 1 of Smithsonian Collection of Classic Jazz RD 033-1.

*Sounds of the World: East Asia—Chinese, Korean, and Japanese Traditions in the United States. Teacher's guide by William M. Anderson. Reston, VA: Music Educators National Conference, 1989. Audiocassettes and teacher's guide.

*Sounds of the World: Music of Latin America—Mexico, Ecuador, Brazil. Teacher's guide by Dale Olsen, Charles Perrone, and Daniel Sheehy. Reston, VA: Music Educators National Conference, 1987. Audiocassettes and teacher's guide.

Village Music of Bulgaria. Collected and produced by Ethel Raim and Martin Koenig. Elektra/Nonesuch 79195-2.

Videotapes

*Bringing Multicultural Music to Children. Reston, VA: Music Educators National Conference, 1992.

Kemp, Helen. *Body, Mind, Spirit, Voice.* St. Louis: Concordia, 1985.

Marsalis, Wynton. *Marsalis on Music.* New York: Sony Classical Film & Video. Four-videocassette series. 1995.

**May, William V., Vanissa B. Murphy, Cecile Johnson, and Bonnie B. Williams, eds. *The World's Greatest Music.* Reston VA: Music Educators National Conference, 1988. Videocassette and teacher's guide.

*National Academy of Recording Arts & Sciences. *The Careers in Music Video.* Santa Monica, CA: NARAS, 1991.

Phillips, Kenneth H. *Teaching Kids to Sing.* Old Tappan, NJ: Schirmer Books/Simon & Schuster, 1992. Six-videocassette series.

Platoon. Produced by Arnold Kopelson. Directed by Oliver Stone. Herndale Film Corporation, 1986.

Solomon, Jim. *Congos, Bongos, and Other Percussion.* Crown Coast Productions, 155 Palm Valley Woods Drive, Ponte Vedra Beach, FL 32082. 1988.

*Thompson, Keith, ed. *Singing in General Music.* Reston, VA: Music Educators National Conference, 1994.

Other Resources

Adzenyah, Abraham Kobena, arr. "Wonfa Nyem." Danbury, CT: World Music Press, 1992. Includes translation and pronunciation guide.

*Cowden, Robert, ed. "Careers in Music." Reston, VA: Music Educators National Conference, 1989. Brochure.

Gromko, Joyce Eastlund. *In a Child's Voice: Interpretive Interactions with Young Composers.* Paper presented at the Qualitative Methodologies in Music Education Research Conference, The University of Illinois at Urbana–Champaign (May 19–21, 1994).

Musical Instruments: An Interactive Journey into the World of Musical Instruments. Seattle: Microsoft Corporation, 1993. Macintosh or IBM CD-ROM.

Simpson, Kenneth. "Suite on Three Notes." Paoli, PA: Schott/European American, 1987.

Wolf Cohen, Veronika. *Explorations of Kinaesthetic Analogues for Musical Schemes.* Paper presented at the Qualitative Methodologies in Music Education Research Conference, The University of Illinois at Urbana–Champaign (May 19–21, 1994).

---

*Available from MENC.

Choral Music

Section compiled and edited by:

Nancy R. Boone, Joe W. Grant, Joyce Eastlund Gromko, and Diane C. Persellin

INTRODUCTION

The choral strategies that follow suggest activities and experiences that will help students in all choral methods courses become acquainted with the content of the National Standards for Music Education and incorporate them into their rehearsal planning. It is assumed that methods students have a broad base of musical knowledge and skills that includes music theory, aural skills, sightsinging, music history and literature of Western and non-Western musics, conducting, and educational psychology.

The National Standards are consistent with the course of study that college music education students receive in private studio lessons, rehearsals, performances, conducting classes, listening, and analysis in music history and theory. The total undergraduate music faculty should be encouraged to address the standards in all classes, ensembles, and seminars. Through relating their own music learning experiences to the National Standards, students will be able to draw upon a wide variety of experiences as they shape their personal repertoire of teaching strategies.

The choral methods strategies have been written by a diverse group of college music teacher educators. As with most issues in education, specific interpretation of a standard and its most appropriate application are open to debate. The strategies presented here can be used intact or be modified as the situation demands. The editors encourage methods teachers to use fewer single-activity lessons and more chains of related activities to meet learning outcomes. Although each strategy focuses on one achievement standard, the editors do not wish to promote the notion that methods classes are a series of single, unrelated activities. The strategies are not all-inclusive of literature, listening possibilities, types of choirs, or kinds of schools. In most cases, methods students will need more experiences than can be included in one class period's worth of discussion, examination, and elucidation. Essential components of the methods student's preparation are field experiences in school music programs in which the standards are being implemented and opportunities to apply the standards in preparatory teaching experiences with peers and with students in schools.

The editors of this guide hope that these strategies and the list of resources will help choral methods teachers in their ongoing attempts to prepare tomorrow's teachers. A critical responsibility for the implementation and eventual effectiveness of the National Standards rests with those who educate tomorrow's music specialists. Music teacher educators must incorporate the standards into their methods courses if these proficiencies are to become an integral part of the student's approach to teaching. Within their careers, these preservice teachers will bring the standards into full practice, and, in doing so, they will provide models for future generations of teachers.

—Nancy R. Boone

CHORAL MUSIC
GRADES K–4

STANDARD 1B

Singing, alone and with others, a varied repertoire of music: Students sing expressively, with appropriate dynamics, phrasing, and interpretation.

Strategy

The methods class becomes a chorus and the instructor asks one student to teach them a selected song, such as Michael Praetorius's "Jubilate Deo," arr. Doreen Rao (New York: Boosey & Hawkes), OCTB6350, unison and round, Level 1. The teaching student translates the text for the other methods students, discusses its meaning, and asks students to speak the text expressively and in rhythm.

The teaching student then shapes the phrases in the air with his or her conducting hand, moving from the students' left to right. He or she models phrasing and dynamics with the voice as well as with hand movement.

Methods students listen to themselves as they sing, and the instructor videotapes their performance. Students review the tape and, after reflection, discuss how their singing might be more expressive with greater attention to dynamics, phrasing, and interpretation. They then try their ideas and evaluate them for effectiveness. Finally, the class considers techniques they would use to evoke expressive singing from K–4 students.

Suggested Resources

Bartle, Jean Ashworth. *Lifeline for Children's Choir Directors,* rev. ed. Miami: Gordon V. Thompson Music/Warner Bros. Publications, 1993.

Choksy, Lois. *Teaching Music Effectively in the Elementary School.* Englewood Cliffs, NJ: Prentice-Hall, 1991.

Tacka, Philip, and Michael Houlahan. *Sound Thinking.* Vol. 1. New York: Boosey & Hawkes, 1995.

STANDARD 1C

Singing, alone and with others, a varied repertoire of music: Students sing from memory a varied repertoire of songs representing genres and styles from diverse cultures.

Strategy

Methods students have completed assigned readings about selecting a repertoire of songs, for the K–4 level, representing genres and styles from diverse cultures. Using music series textbooks for grades K–4, students work in small groups to select songs that represent a variety of genres and styles. Each group member selects one song for a particular grade level to teach to the class. Working in pairs, students peer-coach each other, and then each student takes a turn teaching his or her song to the entire group while being videotaped. After reviewing the videotape, students take time for self-reflection and peer evaluation, considering how they might need to adapt their techniques in teaching K–4 students.

To broaden their knowledge of multicultural literature appropriate for young singers, students examine current catalogues from various music publishers.

(continued)

Suggested Resources

Anderson, William M., and Joy E. Lawrence. *Integrating Music into the Elementary Classroom,* 3d ed. Belmont, CA: Wadsworth Publishing Company, 1995.

Campbell, Patricia Shehan, Ellen McCullough-Brabson, and Judith Cook Tucker. *Roots and Branches: A Legacy of Multicultural Music for Children.* Danbury, CT: World Music Press, 1994. Book and recording.

The Music Connection, Grades K–4. Parsippany, NJ: Silver Burdett Ginn, 1995.

Music and You, Grades K–4. New York: Macmillan/McGraw-Hill, 1991.

O'Brien, James P. *Teaching Music.* Fort Worth, TX: Holt, Rinehart & Winston, 1983.

Rao, Doreen. "Children's Choirs: A Revolution from Within." *Music Educators Journal* 81, no. 3 (November 1994): 44–49.

Share the Music, Grades K–4. New York: Macmillan/McGraw-Hill, 1995.

The World of Music, Grades K–4. Parsippany, NJ: Silver Burdett Ginn, 1991.

STANDARD 1D

Singing, alone and with others, a varied repertoire of music: Students sing ostinatos, partner songs, and rounds.

Strategy

Methods students meet in small groups to discuss the meaning of the following statement:

> In domains, such as the performing arts, thinking effectively in action is what counts. Many students grasp principles nonverbally in the process of music making and in the course of seeing and hearing models. . . of how to perform artistically. (Elliott, 1995, p. 60)

The instructor then distributes to each group audio-playback equipment, compact discs or audiocassettes, and fourth-grade music series textbooks. Students find and listen to songs with ostinatos, partner songs, and rounds, and then make a list of these songs. Each student selects one exemplar to teach to the methods class.

Taking turns as the teacher, students ask the class to articulate the structural features that create harmonies when singing ostinatos, partner songs, and rounds. The class decides on the most effective sequence for teaching fourth-grade students ostinatos, partner songs, and rounds, based on the developmental demands of each (e.g., Which ostinatos fit in conjunction with the melody? Which create a polyrhythmic texture that is more difficult to perceive and perform?).

Suggested Resources

Campbell, Patricia Shehan, and Carol Scott-Kassner. *Music in Childhood: From Preschool through the Elementary Grades.* Old Tappan, NJ: Schirmer Books/Simon & Schuster, 1995.

Elliott, David J. *Music Matters: A New Philosophy of Music Education.* New York: Oxford University Press, 1995.

The Music Connection, Grade 4. Parsippany, NJ: Silver Burdett Ginn, 1995.

Music and You, Grade 4. New York: Macmillan/McGraw-Hill, 1991.

Rozmajzl, Michon, and Rene Boyer-White. *Music Fundamentals, Methods and Materials for the Elementary Classroom Teacher,* 2d ed. White Plains, NY: Longman Publishing Group, 1995.

Share the Music, Grade 4. New York: Macmillan/McGraw-Hill, 1995.

Winslow, Robert W., and Leon Dallin. *Music Skills for the Classroom Teacher,* 8th ed. Columbus, OH: Wm. C. Brown Communications/McGraw-Hill, 1991.

The World of Music, Grade 4. Parsippany, NJ: Silver Burdett Ginn, 1991.

STANDARD 1E

Singing, alone and with others, a varied repertoire of music: *Students sing in groups, blending vocal timbres, matching dynamic levels, and responding to the cues of a conductor.*

Strategy

The instructor divides the methods class into small groups to generate vocal warm-ups, appropriate for K–4 choirs, for blending vocal timbres and matching dynamic levels. The groups write their warm-ups on the chalkboard, transparencies, or charts.

The class then becomes a chorus, with each class member taking a turn as teacher. The chorus listens as the teaching student models one of the warm-up examples, accompanied by hand gestures that convey the tone quality and dynamics desired. After listening to and watching the teaching student's demonstration, the choir sings the warm-up in its entirety, imitating the teaching student's gestures, tone quality, and dynamics.

After singing all the warm-ups, and after all students have had the opportunity to conduct, students return to their small groups for reflection on the effectiveness of each warm-up. Each group considers the following questions: Did the warm-up help the choir to blend their vocal timbres? Were dynamics a part of the warm-up? Was the warm-up appropriate for a young choir? Was teacher feedback incorporated into the warm-ups? Were the warm-ups metrically consistent? Were the keyboard cues clear for higher and lower pitch levels?

Suggested Resources

Heffernan, Charles W. *Choral Music.* Englewood Cliffs, NJ: Prentice-Hall, 1982.

Kemp, Helen. *Of Primary Importance.* Dayton, OH: The Lorenz Corporation, 1989.

Rao, Doreen. *The Artist in Every Child.* New York: Boosey & Hawkes, 1987.

Rao, Doreen. *The Young Singing Voice.* New York: Boosey & Hawkes, 1987.

◆ ◆ ◆ ◆ ◆ ◆ ◆

STANDARD 2A

Performing on instruments, alone and with others, a varied repertoire of music: Students perform on pitch, in rhythm, with appropriate dynamics and timbre, and maintain a steady tempo.

Strategy

As a class, methods students select a choral piece appropriate for a third- and fourth-grade chorus—for example, "Cock-a-doodle-doo!" arr. Betty Bertaux (New York: Boosey & Hawkes), OCTB6480, two-part treble, Level 2. Working in small groups, students study the choral piece to find a rhythmic motive that presents an appropriate rhythmic challenge. Using a nonpitched percussion instrument, a student in each group plays the motive, and methods students imitate by clapping or playing on a similar instrument. The teaching student then sings the motive, and students imitate by singing on a neutral syllable such as "loo." The teaching student next sings the motive with text and dynamics, and the students imitate by singing the motive on pitch and in rhythm, with appropriate dynamics and at a steady tempo. Finally, students sing and play the motive together.

The teaching students from each group then justify their choices of rhythmic motives and lead a class discussion and assessment of the effectiveness of their teaching approaches.

Suggested Resources

Bartle, Jean Ashworth. *Lifeline for Children's Choir Directors,* rev. ed. Miami: Gordon V. Thompson Music/Warner Bros. Publications, 1993.

McRae, Shirley W. *Directing the Children's Choir.* Old Tappan, NJ: Schirmer Books/Simon & Schuster, 1991.

Swears, Linda. *Teaching the Elementary School Chorus.* Old Tappan, NJ: Prentice-Hall, 1985.

STANDARD 2D

Performing on instruments, alone and with others, a varied repertoire of music: Students echo short rhythms and melodic patterns.

Strategy

The instructor gives methods students a series of melodic patterns, in duple or triple meters, derived from specific K–4 literature. Methods students take turns leading these as echo-patterns with appropriate counting language or with one or two levels of body percussion and then with soprano recorders or tuned mallet percussion instruments.

Students then discuss the process and how it would lead to teaching K–4 students songs that embody the imitated patterns or motives.

Suggested Resources

American Odyssey. Cleveland, OH: American Orff-Schulwerk Association, 1979. Videocassette.

Regner, Hermann, ed. *Music for Children: Orff-Schulwerk, American Edition.* Vol. 1, *Preschool;* vol. 2,

Primary, 2d ed. Paoli, PA: Schott/European American. 1982; 1991.

Warner, Brigitte. *Orff-Schulwerk: Applications for the Classroom.* Englewood Cliffs, NJ: Prentice-Hall, 1991.

STANDARD 2F

Performing on instruments, alone and with others, a varied repertoire of music: *Students perform independent instrumental parts while other students sing or play contrasting parts.*

Strategy

The instructor divides the methods class into small groups and gives each group songs—selected from third- and fourth-grade music series textbooks—in contrasting meters with instrumental accompaniments.

Each group selects one of the songs to teach the entire class, analyzes its form or the pattern of its accompaniment, chooses appropriate instruments, and plans ways to teach the accompaniment patterns most efficiently and effectively. Each student teaches his or her group's selected song, teaches the accompaniment, and conducts a performance of the song and its accompaniment. The instructor videotapes each student's teaching.

After all have taken a turn teaching, the class views the videotapes and discusses and evaluates the teaching process, the balance between singing and accompaniment, the pacing, and the overall effectiveness of the performances. They consider any changes that would need to be made in teaching the instrumental accompaniments to K–4 students.

Suggested Resources

Frazee, Jane. *Discovering Orff: A Curriculum for Music Teachers.* Paoli, PA: Schott/European American, 1987.

The Music Connection, Grades 3 and 4. Parsippany, NJ: Silver Burdett Ginn, 1995.

Music and You, Grades 3 and 4. New York: Macmillan/McGraw-Hill, 1991.

Saliba, Konnie K. *Accent on Orff: An Introductory Approach.* Englewood Cliffs, NJ: Prentice-Hall, 1991.

Shamrock, Mary. "Orff Schulwerk: An Integrated Foundation." *Music Educators Journal* 71, no. 6 (February 1986): 51–55.

Share the Music, Grades 3 and 4. New York: Macmillan/McGraw-Hill, 1995.

The World of Music, Grades 3 and 4. Parsippany, NJ: Silver Burdett Ginn, 1991.

◆ ◆ ◆ ◆ ◆ ◆ ◆

STANDARD 3A

Improvising melodies, variations, and accompaniments: Students improvise "answers" in the same style to given rhythmic and melodic phrases.

Strategy

The instructor arranges resonator bells or Orff mallet instruments, set up in an F pentatonic scale, in a circle. Each methods student sits behind an instrument to play the following two games:

Game 1: On an instrument, the first person in the circle "asks," or creates, a musical question that begins on F and ends on a note other than F. The next person in the circle creates an answer of the same length, beginning on a note other than F and ending on F home tone. The musical conversation continues around the circle as each methods student takes a turn improvising.

Game 2: Instead of playing instruments, students sing questions and answers according to the same rules as in game 1.

The class then discusses suggestions for preparing a young chorus to improvise musical answers in this manner, according to the chorus's experience with such an activity, and for promoting quality in the improvised musical examples. For example, a K–4 student may provide a stronger sense of tonality by playing a simple accompaniment pattern on F bordun (an open fifth on F and C) or a simple chordal accompaniment on keyboard, moving from tonic to dominant and back.

Suggested Resources

Hamann, Donald L., ed. *Creativity in the Music Classroom: The Best of* MEJ. Reston, VA: Music Educators National Conference, 1991.

Kenney, Susan. "The Voice Within." *Teaching Music* 2, no. 5 (April 1995): 36–37.

Wiggins, Jackie. "Composition as a Teaching Tool." *Music Educators Journal* 25, no. 8 (April 1989): 36–38.

STANDARD 3B

Improvising melodies, variations, and accompaniments: Students improvise simple rhythmic and melodic ostinato accompaniments.

Strategy

Methods students list names of favorite candy bars on the chalkboard and write the rhythm pattern of each above the name in traditional symbols. Working in small groups, students create several four-beat ostinatos from "candy bar rhythms." Students then transfer their candy bar ostinatos to nonpitched percussion instruments. From third- or fourth-grade music series textbooks, the groups then select songs that they can accompany with their ostinatos.

Each group leads a performance of its song, with the entire class singing the song and group members playing the ostinatos. Students then extend the activity to create an ABA form, using melodic ostinatos for the B section.

After the ABA performance, class members discuss the effectiveness of this approach for encouragement of rhythmic and melodic improvisation at the K–4 level.

Suggested Resources

The Music Connection, Grades 3 and 4. Parsippany, NJ: Silver Burdett Ginn, 1995.

Music and You, Grades 3 and 4. New York: Macmillan/McGraw-Hill, 1991.

Rudaitis, Cheryl, ed. "Jump Ahead and Take the Risk." *Teaching Music* 2, no. 5 (April 1995): 34–35.

Share the Music, Grades 3 and 4. New York: Macmillan/McGraw-Hill, 1995.

Upitis, Rena. "Fostering Children's Compositions: Activities for the Classroom." *General Music Today* 8, no. 3 (Spring 1995): 16–19.

Wiggins, Jackie. *Composition in the Classroom: A Tool for Teaching.* Reston, VA: Music Educators National Conference, 1990.

The World of Music, Grades 3 and 4. Parsippany, NJ: Silver Burdett Ginn, 1991.

STANDARD 3D

Improvising melodies, variations, and accompaniments: Students improvise short songs and instrumental pieces, using a variety of sound sources, including traditional sounds, nontraditional sounds available in the classroom, body sounds, and sounds produced by electronic means.

Strategy

Methods students experiment with a variety of improvised vocal sounds (e.g., sirens, swoops, flutters, clicks, hums, whispers). The instructor then assigns them to small groups at one of four composition stations: traditional (e.g., classroom percussion instruments), nontraditional (e.g., paper crunching, pencils tapping), body percussion (e.g., clapping, snapping, patsching, stamping), and electronic (e.g., computers or electronic keyboards).

Using their voices and the instruments located within their composition stations, the groups are assigned to create a sound composition based on a poem or rhyme from a collection (e.g., Mother Goose or Ogden Nash). Groups consider the following questions: What is the mood of this poem? What vocal sounds are appropriate to accompany the poem? Will the poem be spoken or sung? Will a melody be improvised on instruments? How will each instrument be played? Who will play each instrument?

After groups discuss a general plan, each group performs an improvisation. Then, as a class, students discuss the following questions about each performance: How did the sounds heighten the perception of the poem's text? How did the text suggest melodic contours? How did the rhythm of the text suggest rhythmic patterns? Students then consider how this procedure would work with K–4 students.

(continued)

Suggested Resources

Biasini, Americole, and Lenore Pogonowski. *MMCP Interaction.* Bellingham, WA: Americole, 1979.

Bridges, Madeline. "The Benefits of Vocal Exploration." *General Music Today* 6, no. 2 (Winter 1993): 30–34.

Tait, Malcolm J. "Whispers, Growls, Screams and Puffs . . . Lead to Composition." In *Elementary General Music: The Best of* MEJ, edited by Betty W. Atterbury. Reston, VA: Music Educators National Conference, 1992.

◆ ◆ ◆ ◆ ◆ ◆ ◆

STANDARD 4A

Composing and arranging music within specified guidelines: Students create and arrange music to accompany readings or dramatizations.

Strategy

The instructor divides the methods class into groups of three or four students. Each group selects a children's book in which the visual images inspire aural images or the text is rhythmic. Then, each team prepares a choral reading embellished with sound effects and performs the reading for the other teams.

Following each performance, the group members lead the class in a discussion using the following questions: What sounds, in particular, were effective in creating an atmosphere or mood? Which sounds heightened the meaning of a word or phrase? What instruments could be used to more effectively communicate the mood or meaning of the poem? How could the performance be refined or improved? What chants or songs could be added to increase the dramatic effects?

After all groups have performed, the class discusses any changes they would need to make to the procedure in using it with K–4 students.

Suggested Children's Literature

Martin, Bill, and John Archambault. *Chicka Chicka Boom Boom.* New York: Simon & Schuster Books for Young Readers, 1989.

Servozo, Mary. *Rain Talk.* New York: Margaret K. McElderry Books, 1990.

Showers, Paul. *The Listening Walk.* New York: Crowell, 1961.

Vozar, David. *Yo, Hungry Wolf!* New York: Doubleday Books for Young Readers, 1993.

Suggested Resources

Durland, Frances Caldwell. *Creative Dramatics for Children.* Kent, OH: Kent State University Press, 1975.

Sawyer, Ruth. *The Way of the Storyteller.* New York: Viking Press, 1962.

STANDARD 4B

Composing and arranging music within specified guidelines: *Students create and arrange short songs and instrumental pieces within specified guidelines.*

Strategy

Dividing the methods class into groups of three to six students, the instructor asks each group to arrange the same folk song selected from a collection of folk songs for children. Groups may choose to arrange the song for singing or a combination of singing and playing instruments. The groups that choose to arrange for voices may add a sung melodic ostinato, vocalized animal sounds, and changes in dynamics or articulations. If they choose to arrange for a combination of voices and instruments, the groups may create an instrumental rhythmic ostinato based on one of the rhythmic motives within the song.

Each group performs its arrangement for the entire class. Following the performances, the class discusses similarities and differences among the arrangements and discusses each in terms of its developmental appropriateness for students from kindergarten through fourth grade.

Suggested Resources

Erdei, Peter. *150 American Folk Songs to Sing, Read and Play.* New York: Boosey & Hawkes, 1974.

Jones, Bessie, and Bess Lomax Hawes. *Step It Down: Games, Plays, Songs, and Stories from the Afro-American Heritage.* Athens, GA: University of Georgia Press, 1987.

Locke, Eleanor. *Sail Away: 155 American Folk Songs.* New York: Boosey & Hawkes, 1989.

Wilson, Sarah J., and Roger J. Wales. "An Exploration of Children's Musical Compositions." *Journal of Research in Music Education* 43, no. 2 (Summer 1995): 94–111.

STANDARD 4C

Composing and arranging music within specified guidelines: *Students use a variety of sound sources when composing.*

Strategy

The instructor divides the methods class into groups of three or four students. Each team is asked to compose a soundscape, based on children's literature and organized according to environmental events (e.g., wind, rain, drought, hurricane) or an environmental place (e.g., underwater, rain forest, space). Working in groups, students compose their pieces, using vocal and instrumental sounds and a variety of metered and unmetered sounds.

Each group performs its soundscape for the class. Based on a list of possibilities (as above), the class guesses the environmental event or place for each team's soundscape.

(continued)

Class members then take turns miming inside the "magic square" (an area of about five square feet bounded by masking tape) while each group performs its composed soundscape again. As the vocalists and instrumentalists express various articulations, dynamics, and durations, the mimers reflect these musical events. Following the performances, the class discusses how this composition procedure could be used most effectively with K–4 students.

Suggested Children's Literature

Bulla, Clyde Robert. *What Makes a Shadow?* New York: Crowell, 1962.

Cowcher, Helen. *Rain Forest.* New York: Farrar, Strauss, and Giroux, 1988.

Freeman, Don. *A Rainbow of My Own.* New York: Viking Press, 1966.

Keats, Ezra Jack. *Regards to the Man in the Moon.* New York: Four Winds Press, 1981.

McNulty, Faith. *How to Dig a Hole to the Other Side of the World.* New York: HarperCollins Publishers, 1990.

Suggested Resources

Biasini, Americole, and Lenore Pogonowski. *MMCP Interaction.* Bellingham, WA: Americole, 1979.

Schafer, R. Murray. *Creative Music Education.* New York: Schirmer Books, 1976.

◆ ◆ ◆ ◆ ◆ ◆ ◆

STANDARD 5A

Reading and notating music: *Students read whole, half, dotted half, quarter, and eighth notes and rests in 2/4, 3/4, and 4/4 meter signatures.*

Strategy

Methods students prepare a listening map on a transparency with graphic notation of the children's part in a K–4 choral piece in 2/4, 3/4, or 4/4 meter. The map eliminates from children's perceptual fields all but the part they are to sing and transforms the traditional symbol system into visual images that convey pitches and rhythms. While the class acts as the elementary chorus, each student takes a turn as the teacher and first sings the entire song.

The teaching student then sings one phrase at a time in rhythmic syllables. The singers echo each phrase in rhythmic syllables while patsching the beat with the teaching student. When one verse is learned, the singers hum the melody while clapping the rhythm of the words as the teaching student continues to patsch the beat.

Singers refer to the listening map and track the phrases with their eyes as they hum. The instructor notes that K–4 students would track the phrase with their fingers, as well, on copies of the listening maps. One singer then converts the listening map's graphic notation to traditional notation by writing quarter, eighth, or half notes above the graphic notation.

After each student has had a turn as teacher, the class offers suggestions and comments to the teaching students. Discussion centers on strengths and weaknesses of the teaching presentation, the effectiveness of the graphic map, the choral performance, and the level of the singers' understanding based on their performance. The class considers any adaptations that would need to be made in teaching K–4 students to read notation through a similar procedure.

Suggested Resources

Goodman, Nelson. *Languages of Art: An Approach to a Theory of Symbols.* Indianapolis: Hackett Publishing Company, 1976.

Gordon, Edwin. *Learning Sequences in Music: Skill, Content, and Patterns.* Chicago, IL: GIA Publications, 1993.

Winner, Ellen. *Invented Worlds: The Psychology of the Arts.* 1982. Reprint, Cambridge: Harvard University Press, 1985.

STANDARD 5C

Reading and notating music: Students identify symbols and traditional terms referring to dynamics, tempo, and articulation and interpret them correctly when performing.

Strategy

Methods students choose one choral reading from a list of children's literature and prepare the text in "picture-print," as follows, on a transparency or chart.

- Dynamics: loud, large print; soft, small print; crescendo, small to large print; decrescendo, large to small print.

- Tempo: fast, print very close together; slow, print far apart.

- Articulation: Staccato, in jagged, angular print; legato, in cursive script.

With methods students acting as an elementary chorus, each student takes a turn acting as teacher. Singers listen as the teaching student recites the entire verse of the choral reading. Then as they read the text with the teaching student, they refer to the picture-print text and track the phrases with their eyes. The instructor notes that K–4 students would track the phrases with their fingers, as well, on their copies of the text in picture-print.

As the singers become comfortable with the picture-print and have a feeling for the text, they sightread the next portions of the text from the picture-print notation. When they have learned the piece, they place the traditional symbols for piano, forte, crescendo, and decrescendo below the print, as appropriate. They may also add the symbols for the tempo and articulation. The instructor notes that in the K–4 classroom, they would plan and have students perform a choral reading of the text from traditional print and symbols.

Methods students offer suggestions and comments to the teaching students. They discuss the teaching presentation, the picture-print, the choral reading performance, the level of the singers' understanding based on their performance, and any changes they would make in using the procedure with K–4 students.

(continued)

Suggested Children's Literature

Martin, Bill, and John Archambault. *Chicka Chicka Boom Boom.* New York: Simon & Schuster Books for Young Readers, 1989.

Vozar, David. *Yo, Hungry Wolf!* New York: Doubleday Books for Young Readers, 1993.

STANDARD 5D

Reading and notating music: Students use standard symbols to notate meter, rhythm, pitch, and dynamics in simple patterns presented by the teacher.

Strategy

Methods students choose a choral piece (in the key of C, F, or G) from a set of folk songs for young children and write out the children's part in standard notation (using treble clef), leaving out one short motive.

The students act as an elementary chorus and take turns acting as teacher, as the instructor videotapes each teaching student so that they can reflect later on their presentations. The chorus listens as the teaching student sings the entire song with words. The teaching student then sings one phrase at a time in rhythmic syllables, patsching the steady beat, while students echo each phrase and patsch the beat. Then the teaching student sings the words while patsching an eighth-note ostinato. The singers echo the words and patsch.

When the singers have learned the song, they refer to the children's part (with the missing motive). They tap the phrases with their fingers and track them with their eyes as they sing. When they discover the missing motive's rhythm, they place rhythmic stems on the staff of their music.

The teaching student plays the missing motive on a recorder as the singers paint the melody in the air. With the teacher guiding, singers make ovals on the staff and connect the stems to complete the notation of the missing motive.

The class offers suggestions and comments to the teaching student. They discuss each presentation, the choral reading performance, the level of the singers' understanding based on their performance, and any changes they would make in using the procedure with K–4 students.

Suggested Resources

Erdei, Peter. *150 American Folk Songs to Sing, Read and Play.* New York: Boosey & Hawkes, 1974.

Locke, Eleanor. *Sail Away: 155 American Folk Songs.* New York: Boosey & Hawkes, 1989.

◆ ◆ ◆ ◆ ◆ ◆ ◆

STANDARD 6C

Listening to, analyzing, and describing music: Students use appropriate terminology in explaining music, music notation, music instruments and voices, and music performances.

Strategy

The instructor asks methods students to select one choral piece appropriate for third- and fourth-grade choirs, to analyze the piece (paying particular attention to expressive qualities), and to assemble a list of musical terms that describe those qualities.

Acting as the teacher, one student models the teaching of a segment of the piece by drawing attention to one or more of its expressive qualities and describing those qualities in colloquial or everyday terms (e.g., howling sound), gradually introducing the musical term (e.g., a tone that rises in intensity while staying on the same pitch), and finally asking students to use only musical terminology (e.g., a sustained pitch that grows in intensity).

Students prepare peer-teaching segments for their selected choral pieces. Also, they design listening guides for their musical examples, including musical terminology.

Suggested Resources

Haack, Paul. "The Acquisition of Music Listening Skills." In *Handbook of Research on Music Teaching and Learning,* edited by Richard Colwell. Old Tappan, NJ: Schirmer Books/Simon & Schuster, 1992.

Masterson, Michael L. "Moving Beyond 'It's Got a Good Beat.'" *Music Educators Journal* 80, no. 6 (May 1994): 24–28.

STANDARD 6D

Listening to, analyzing, and describing music: Students identify the sounds of a variety of instruments, including many orchestra and band instruments, and instruments from various cultures as well as children's voices and male and female adult voices.

Strategy

Prior to class, methods students have selected a favorite folk or traditional song, such as "Shenandoah," that has been arranged, set, or otherwise treated in a variety of ways. They have researched the treatments, looking for recordings by both singers and instrumentalists, performing alone or in ensembles.

For a third- and fourth-grade chorus, students design listening strategies in which the chorus's attention is drawn to the timbral qualities of the selected songs. They must present at least three versions of their selected songs and design listening maps for each version.

(continued)

While the focus of the listening strategies should be the identification of voices and instruments used, students should formulate questions that will guide the chorus in discussion of the effects of timbral choices on the mood/quality of the song (e.g., What mood was the arranger trying to create? What instrumental timbres were especially soothing? Can you play your recorder in a soothing way and then in a not-soothing way? What was the difference in the way you played your recorder to create that effect? Did you play the recorder low or high? Does highness or lowness matter for creating that effect?).

Students create their own arrangement of the folk song, considering timbral qualities.

Suggested Resources

Campbell, Patricia Shehan, and Carol Scott-Kassner. "The Listening Child." Chapter 7 in *Music in Childhood: From Preschool through the Elementary Grades.* Old Tappan, NJ: Schirmer Books/Simon & Schuster, 1995. (See especially Table 7.1, "Active Listening to Tone Color," p. 163.)

Sims, Wendy. "Sound Approaches to Elementary Music Listening." *Music Educators Journal* 77, no. 4. (December 1990): 38–42.

STANDARD 6E

Listening to, analyzing, and describing music: *Students respond through purposeful movement to selected prominent music characteristics or to specific music events while listening to music.*

Strategy

Methods students listen to recorded music examples and suggest ways to move that reinforce changes in the music. Musical examples might include Haydn's Symphony no. 94 ("Surprise"), Second Movement, Andante (change in dynamics in the theme); Grieg's "In the Hall of the Mountain King," from *Peer Gynt Suite* (accelerando); or Bizet's "Farandole," from *L'arlésienne,* Suite no. 1 (contrasting themes/sections).

The instructor asks students to reflect on the following: For every musical event, there is at least one physical movement that can express it.

Students then create movements for one of the musical examples and assess the effectiveness of their movements for assisting perception of musical characteristics or specific musical events, perhaps by having other students guess what characteristics or events they are expressing.

From an array of octavos provided by the instructor, each student then selects a choral piece to teach and prepares an activity that would encourage K–4 students to respond with movements reflecting musical changes in the piece. After leading the class in a performance of his or her selected piece, each student then leads a discussion of the movement activity's effectiveness for assisting children with perception of musical characteristics.

After each student has led the class in this movement exercise, the class discusses benefits of movement for improving musical perception with a chorus of K–4 students.

Suggested Resources

Abramson, Robert M. *Dalcroze Eurhythmics*. Chicago: GIA Publications, 1992. Videocassette.

Choksy, Lois, Robert M. Abramson, Avon E. Gillespie, and David Woods. *Teaching Music in the Twentieth Century*. Englewood Cliffs, NJ: Prentice-Hall, 1986.

Hackett, Patricia, and Carolynn A. Lindeman. *The Musical Classroom: Backgrounds, Models, and Skills for Elementary Teaching*, 4th ed. Englewood Cliffs, NJ: Prentice-Hall, 1997.

Sing! Move! Listen! Music and Young Children. Reston, VA: Music Educators National Conference, 1993. Videocassette.

◆ ◆ ◆ ◆ ◆ ◆ ◆

STANDARD 7A

Evaluating music and music performances: Students devise criteria for evaluating performances and compositions.

Strategy

Prior to class, three or four methods students, working as a team, have selected a choral piece from a set of masterworks for young children and have prepared a videotape with two performances in which they have sung the same choral work. The performances should differ in the number of singers, the type(s) of accompaniment, or the tempo of the work.

One student, acting as the teacher, begins by playing one videotaped performance and then soliciting from the class a nonjudgmental description of the visual and sound images the students remember. The student then plays the second tape, and the class describes the performance.

Finally, the class listens to and watches both examples again and describe similarities and differences between them. The teaching student helps methods students devise criteria, listing the similarities and differences on the chalkboard as they are mentioned and asking students to categorize the differences. After listening to and watching both examples a third time, students describe which performance they believe is the better interpretation of the music and explain their reasoning based on the criteria they devised. The activity is repeated with other students acting as teacher as time allows.

Students discuss the appropriateness of the process for K–4 students, based on musical and language development.

Suggested Resources

Chuska, Kenneth R. *Teaching the Process of Thinking, K–12*. Bloomington, IN: Phi Delta Kappa Educational Foundation, 1986.

Johnson, Tony. *Philosophy for Children: An Approach to Critical Thinking*. Bloomington, IN: Phi Delta Kappa Educational Foundation, 1984.

Evaluating music and music performances: Students explain, using appropriate music terminology, their personal preferences for specific musical works and styles.

Strategy

Prior to class, three or four methods students, working as a team, have selected two instrumental pieces from a set of masterworks for young children and have prepared a videotape on which they or their peers have performed each instrumental work. The performances should be musically excellent and include the same instruments, but they should differ in style.

One student, acting as the teacher, plays one of the videotaped performances and solicits a description of the performance from the students. The class views the second videotaped example and describes the performance. Finally, the class watches both examples again, one after the other, and describes similarities and differences between the two performances.

The teaching student lists the similarities and differences on the chalkboard as they are mentioned and asks the class to categorize the differences. Then the teaching student makes a chart of the class responses and notes the number of students who preferred each of the two performances.

The teaching student leads the class in a discussion of why they preferred the particular instrumental performance, encouraging students to express their perceptions in their own most descriptive language and offering musical terms.

Methods students discuss the appropriateness of the process for K–4 students, based on their perceptual, linguistic, and musical development.

Suggested Resources

Chuska, Kenneth R. *Teaching the Process of Thinking, K–12.* Bloomington, IN: Phi Delta Kappa Educational Foundation, 1986.

Johnson, Tony. *Philosophy for Children: An Approach to Critical Thinking.* Bloomington, IN: Phi Delta Kappa Educational Foundation, 1984.

◆ ◆ ◆ ◆ ◆ ◆ ◆

Understanding relationships between music, the other arts, and disciplines outside the arts: Students identify similarities and differences in the meanings of common terms used in the various arts.

Strategy

The instructor divides the methods class into small groups with three to six students per group. Two art prints from different stylistic eras are displayed (e.g., a Monet and a Pollock).

Each group first creates a list of ten words that describe each print and then shares its list with the other groups. The class then listens to musical excerpts from the same stylistic eras as those represented in the paintings (e.g., Ravel or Debussy and Webern or Penderecki). Each group then creates a list of ten words that describe each musical excerpt.

Based on both sets of word lists, students in their groups pair each art print with a musical excerpt and find words within their word lists that are the same or similar for the music and the art (e.g., motion, bright, clear, jagged, calming, dark). They also find works that are different (e.g., for music: fast notes, dancelike; for art: pictures of men dressed in Greek robes, foggy-looking, far-out).

Finally, from an array of several art prints, students select another art print of the same style as those just studied. And from an array of musical excerpts, they select another musical excerpt of the same era as those just studied.

Methods students discuss the appropriateness of the process for K–4 students, based on their language and perceptual development.

Suggested Resources

Lautzenheiser, Tim. *The Art of Successful Teaching.* Chicago: GIA Publications, 1992.

Mueller, Alice K., and Howard K. Brahmstedt. "Music: A Key to Collaborative Projects." *General Music Today* 10, no. 2 (Winter 1997): 7–11.

STANDARD 8B

Understanding relationships between music, the other arts, and disciplines outside the arts:
Students identify ways in which the principles and subject matter of other disciplines
taught in the school are interrelated with those of music.

Strategy

The instructor divides the methods class into small groups with three to six students per group. Each student has a plastic drinking straw and scissors.

Working in their groups, students discover the various ways the straws can produce sound and how sound can be altered by cutting the straws. Each group performs a short, improvised sound composition with its straws.

After the performances, the class constructs a statement about how sound was produced with the straws (i.e., What was vibrating to make the sound?), how cutting the straws altered the sound (i.e., Did the sound get higher or lower?), and how this knowledge might generalize to another sound source (e.g., What happens to the sound produced by a rubber band when it is stretched more tightly? Does a rubber band vibrate faster or slower when it is stretched very tightly? Does the sound of a rubber band change when it is stretched over different size resonator boxes? Why?).

The class applies what they learned from the drinking straw experiment to explain how a piccolo and a flute compare in size and pitch. Students explain how a recorder's air column can be made "shorter" without cutting it and how the pitch changes when the air column is shortened.

(continued)

Methods students discuss the effectiveness of this procedure for K–4 students, based on their musical understandings of pitch and of sound sources that produce pitches (musical or otherwise).

Suggested Resources

Berger, Melvin. *The Science of Music.* New York: HarperCollins Publishers, 1989.

Nash, Grace, Geraldine Jones, Barbara Potter, and Patsy Smith. *Do It My Way.* Van Nuys, CA: Alfred Publishing Company, 1977.

◆ ◆ ◆ ◆ ◆ ◆

STANDARD 9A

Understanding music in relation to history and culture: Students identify by genre or style aural examples of music from various historical periods and cultures.

Strategy

Methods students tap the rhythm to the Irish song "Mitty Matty" (Meek, 1985) and learn to sing the chant. Then they sing the English folk song "This Old Man" with gestures.

Students view a map of Ireland in relationship to the United States and listen to virtuosic tin whistle (perhaps from Bergin recording). While listening, students look at pictures of Celtic designs, especially colorful ones of interlocking animals from *The Book of Kells.*

After students have listened to the tin whistle recording, they discuss the following questions: Do you notice a relationship between the intricate interlocking shapes and Irish music? What do you see in the shapes? Do you hear patterns in the music?

Working in groups, students then formulate a listening lesson for K–4 students using music from historical periods (such as medieval European, romantic Western classical, or twentieth-century atonal) and music from specific cultures (such as Japanese, Ghanaian, Peruvian, or Tex-Mex, Polish polka, Chicago blues). Each group gives an overview of its lesson to the class, and a student from each group teaches the lesson to the class. The groups provide everyone with copies of their lessons.

Suggested Resources

Bergin, Mary. *Feadóga Stáin 2.* Shanachie 79083.

Broughton, Simon, Mark Ellingham, David Muddyman, and Richard Trillo, eds. *Rough World Music.* Bergenfield, NJ: Penguin USA, 1994.

Campbell, Patricia Shehan, Ellen McCullough-Brabson, and Judith Cook Tucker. *Roots and Branches: A Legacy of Multicultural Music for Children.* Danbury, CT: World Music Press, 1994. Book and recording.

Meek, Bill. *Moon Penny: A Collection of Rhymes, Songs and Play-verse for and by Children.* Cork, Ireland: Ossian Publications, 1985.

STANDARD 9B

Understanding music in relation to history and culture: Students describe in simple terms how elements of music are used in music examples from various cultures of the world.

Strategy

The instructor writes on the chalkboard the names of three pieces that will be played (see Suggested Resources) and divides the methods class into three groups. Students listen carefully to: (a) "Marilli," in which a young singer from Ghana produces two and sometimes three pitches simultaneously by a controlled buzzing at the back of the roof of her mouth; (b) "I Walk in Beauty" (Burton, 1993), sung by an Apache woman in Flagstaff, Arizona; and (c) "Sylfest Mork," in which a violin and a woman's soprano voice blend in a single melody.

Groups disperse to separate stations in the room that are furnished with paper, crayons and colored pens, a chalkboard, and a tape player with a tape of one of the three selections. Each group plays its recording and then represents the timbre of its piece with descriptive words, drawings, or movements.

Students display their drawings and lists of descriptive words, and they perform their movements at their stations. The groups then take a few minutes to discuss their performances, make changes as they desire, and perform again.

Finally, the groups come together as a class to discuss how timbre is used in each of the pieces. Students reflect upon the fit between the activities and the listenings and how they would work with K–4 students. They discuss related projects that might focus on other elements of music.

Suggested Resources

Burton, J. Bryan. *Moving within the Circle: Contemporary Native American Music and Dance.* Danbury, CT: World Music Press, 1993. Book and audiocassette.

Campbell, Patricia Shehan, and Carol Scott-Kassner. "Music, Multiculturalism and Children." Chapter 13 in *Music in Childhood: From Preschool through the Elementary Grades.* Old Tappan, NJ: Schirmer Books/Simon & Schuster, 1995. See especially Table 13.1 "Guide to Authenticity in the Selection of Music," p. 321.

"Marilli." On *Africa: Ancient Ceremonies.* Produced by Stephen Jay. Elektra Nonesuch 972082-2.

"Sylfest Mork." On *Nordisk Sang.* Produced by Han Wendl. New Albion Records NA 031.

STANDARD 9C

Understanding music in relation to history and culture: *Students identify various uses of music in their daily experiences and describe characteristics that make certain music suitable for each use.*

Strategy

In preparation for class, methods students have read excerpts of *My Music,* which explores the place music holds in people's lives. They also have interviewed a child, perhaps from another culture (aged five to ten years), about his or her music, focusing on singing activities, for example.

In class, students share their findings with each other. They consider whether musical experiences are similar for children of the same age and perhaps from different cultures, and whether there are patterns of preference. Using Merriam's ten uses and functions of music as a point of departure (see Suggested Resources), students brainstorm about specific music that might be heard on particular occasions or at different times and in different places. They describe the characteristics that make it suitable for that purpose.

Students then discuss how they might adapt this activity to develop a lesson for teaching students at the K–4 level.

Suggested Resources

Crafts, Susan D., Daniel Cavicchi, Charles Keil, and the Music in Daily Life Project. *My Music.* Hanover, NH: Wesleyan University Press, 1993.

Merriam, Alan P. Chapter 11 in *The Anthropology of Music.* Evanston, IL: Northwestern University Press, 1964.

Slobin, Mark. *Subcultural Sounds: Micromusics of the West.* Hanover, NH: Wesleyan University Press, 1993.

Titon, Jeff Todd, ed. "The Music-culture as a World of Music" and "Discovering and Documenting a World of Music." In *Worlds of Music: An Introduction to the Music of the World's Peoples,* 3d ed. Old Tappan, NJ: Schirmer Books/Simon & Schuster, 1996. Book and recordings.

CHORAL MUSIC
GRADES 5–8

STANDARD 1A

Singing, alone and with others, a varied repertoire of music: Students sing accurately and with good breath control throughout their singing ranges, alone and in small and large ensembles.

Strategy

Methods students have completed assigned readings about effective warm-ups. Students also have been observing physical and vocal warm-ups used by their university choral directors and voice teachers. In class, they discuss the importance of using physical and vocal warm-ups in the choral rehearsal. Also, based on their reading and observations, students list criteria for proper warm-ups and dangers to look for in warm-ups, particularly with middle-level students.

After modeling how to lead a class through various vocal warm-ups, the instructor, using good breath control and pure vocal sounds, demonstrates a five-note descending warm-up on the piano. Students line up at the piano and, in turn, play and sing the five-note descending warm-up (*sol, fa, mi, re, do*) in successively higher keys (moving up by half steps). Students then repeat the activity, this time with the first student improvising a new five-note pattern using the notes *do* to *sol*. Other students, in turn, play and sing the same pattern in successively higher keys.

The instructor then asks students to (a) create a vocal warm-up based on a brief motive from one of the pieces in the *Choral Music Packet* that is appropriate for middle-level students, (b) teach the warm-up to the class, and (c) play and lead the class in singing the warm-up in several keys. Viewing a video-tape that the instructor makes of their presentations, students then discuss the effectiveness of the warm-ups they have created and their effectiveness in teaching them to the class.

Suggested Resources

Choral Music Packet: Supplement to Teaching Choral Music. Reston, VA: Music Educators National Conference, 1991.

Herman, Sally. *Building a Pyramid of Musicianship.* San Diego, CA: Neil A. Kjos Music Company, 1988.

MENC Task Force on Choral Music Course of Study. *Teaching Choral Music: A Course of Study.* Reston, VA: Music Educators National Conference, 1991.

Phillips, Kenneth H. *Teaching Kids to Sing.* Old Tappan, NJ: Schirmer Books/Simon & Schuster, 1992.

Phillips, Kenneth H. "Twelve Crucial Minutes for Voice Building." *Teaching Music* 2, no. 3 (December 1994): 40–41, 62.

STANDARD 1B

Singing, alone and with others, a varied repertoire of music: *Students sing with expression and technical accuracy a repertoire of vocal literature with a level of difficulty of 2, on a scale of 1 to 6, including some songs performed from memory.*

Strategy

Students have completed assigned reading on Reimer's four criteria for determining artistic merit and suitability: (1) craftsmanship, (2) imagination, (3) authenticity, and (4) sensitivity. Each student has selected two new pieces with a level of difficulty of 2, one piece that meets Reimer's criteria and one that does not. They also consider vocal range, tessitura, and text in their selections.

Prior to class, each student has written a brief critical analysis of his or her selected pieces. In class, each student provides the class with copies of the written critical analyses to serve as a guide to the ensuing discussion. In turn, students lead discussions based on their analyses. The class then discusses the merits of each analysis, as well as expressive possibilities and technical challenges inherent in the choral selections.

Suggested Resource

Reimer, Bennett. *A Philosophy of Music Education,* 2d ed. Englewood Cliffs, NJ: Prentice-Hall, 1989.

STANDARD 1C

Singing, alone and with others, a varied repertoire of music: *Students sing music representing diverse genres and cultures, with expression appropriate for the work being performed.*

Strategy

The instructor divides the methods class into groups of four students each. Each group is assigned one piece (see Suggested Resources, for example) from an array of pieces that includes several historical eras and represents diverse genres, styles, and cultures.

The instructor then engages students in a discussion of similarities and differences in vocal style, the extent to which middle-level students should be expected to sing in authentic style, strategies for teaching appropriate performance style, the suitability of range for middle-level students, and the possibility of adding instrumental accompaniments and movement to enhance the songs.

Finally, the groups prepare a twenty-minute lesson that includes the following: (1) a warm-up derived from melodic or rhythmic motives within the piece, or a solfège exercise based on the key of the piece; (2) a movement activity that will either enhance the performance or aid in the teaching of the song; (3) techniques appropriate to the particular genre or style that efficiently and sequentially lead class in the discovery of the music (e.g., a song from Ghana could be learned by rote; in call and response; sung against a bell pattern; and, ultimately, sung while walking and clapping the polyrhythmic layers); and (4) a performance of the piece.

One of the groups presents its lesson to the class. Students then write reflections in their journals based on the teaching presentation.

Suggested Choral Literature

Nyberg, Anders. *Freedom Is Coming: Songs of Protest and Praise from South Africa.* Edited by Henry H. Leck. Fort Lauderdale, FL: Walton Music Corporation. WW1149, three-part, Level 2; WW1174, SAB, Level 2.

Rao, Doreen, arr. "Siyahamba." New York: Boosey & Hawkes. OCTB6656. Three-part. Level 2.

Suggested Resources

Nketia, Joseph H. K. *Music of Africa.* New York: W. W. Norton, 1974.

"Shaka Zulu." On *Ladysmith Black Mambazo.* Warner Bros. Recordings 9 25582-2.

STANDARD 1D

Singing, alone and with others, a varied repertoire of music: Students sing music written in two and three parts.

Strategy

After a class discussion and demonstration of several appropriate and accessible choral selections for middle-level choirs, the instructor divides the methods class into three small groups and assigns each a song in a two- or three-part arrangement (e.g., "On My Journey," see Suggested Resources).

The instructor gives each group a list of questions (e.g., Is text appropriate for the age group? Is music challenging enough to hold interest through several rehearsals? Is music in appropriate range and tessitura?) and asks groups to analyze why their selection would or would not be appropriate for middle-level students. A student from each group presents the group findings to the class.

Then the instructor asks each group, as follows, to create a concert program of music in two or three parts: Group 1—SAB repertoire appropriate for an auditioned seventh- and eighth-grade chorus; Group 2—unison/SA repertoire suitable for a fifth- and sixth-grade beginning chorus; and Group 3—two or three-part music appropriate for a male chorus in grades 6–8.

Finally, the class analyzes the repertoire chosen by each group and discusses its appropriate use at the middle level.

Suggested Resources

Collins, Donald L. *Teaching Choral Music.* Englewood Cliffs, NJ: Prentice-Hall, 1993.

Hylton, John B. *Comprehensive Choral Music Education.* Englewood Cliffs, NJ: Prentice-Hall, 1995.

"On My Journey." In *The Music Connection,* Grade 7 (Parsippany, NJ: Silver Burdett Ginn, 1995); or *The World of Music,* Grade 7 (Parsippany, NJ: Silver Burdett Ginn, 1991).

Singing, alone and with others, a varied repertoire of music: Students sing with expression and technical accuracy a varied repertoire of vocal literature with a level of difficulty of 3, on a scale of 1 to 6, including some songs performed from memory.

Strategy

The instructor divides the methods class into small groups and assigns each group one movement of a large work with a level of difficulty of 3, such as *Three Hungarian Folk Songs* by M. Seiber (Milwaukee: G. Schirmer/Hal Leonard Corporation), OC10715, SATB, Level 3—or one of various single octavos at that level. Each group appoints a coordinator who then assigns each group member one of the following tasks that will lead toward an accurate and expressive performance of the piece.

1. Analyze the movement for tonality, form, range, meter(s), rhythms, style, teaching possibilities, vocal and musical challenges.

2. Devise specific vocal warm-ups and ear-training exercises appropriate to the demands of the movement.

3. Devise specific movement exercises that enhance the teaching of the melody or rhythm.

4. Lead the class through reading the notation of each voice part in sol-fa.

5. Prepare the pronunciation and movements.

6. Conduct the group as they perform the movement for the class.

7. Rehearse class in the singing of the movement, first in solfège, then with text.

8. Isolate and correct rhythmic and pitch errors.

Then, in their groups, students organize and prepare presentations of the piece, including as many of these specific tasks as possible.

Suggested Resources

Jordanoff, Christine, and Robert Page. *The Choral Triad Video Workshop.* Produced by QED Communications. Reston, VA: Music Educators National Conference, 1994. Book and six videocassettes.

May, William V., and Craig Tolin. *Pronunciation Guide for Choral Literature.* Reston, VA: Music Educators National Conference, 1987.

Phillips, Kenneth H. *Teaching Kids to Sing.* Old Tappan, NJ: Schirmer Books/Simon & Schuster, 1992.

◆ ◆ ◆ ◆ ◆ ◆

STANDARD 2A

Performing on instruments, alone and with others, a varied repertoire of music: Students perform on at least one instrument accurately and independently, alone and in small and large ensembles, with good posture, good playing position, and good breath, bow, or stick control.

Strategy

After reviewing a 5/8 conducting pattern with the methods class, the instructor distributes "Gloria Tibi," from *Mass* by Leonard Bernstein (New York: Boosey & Hawkes), OCTB6344, SA with tenor solo and bongos, Level 4. As the instructor plays a recording of the piece, methods students conduct using the 5/8 conducting pattern.

The instructor then divides the class into three groups (soprano, alto, and bongo accompaniment). Each group rehearses its rhythm pattern using body percussion before the class combines and performs all three parts. After all parts are performed accurately, the students transfer the rhythms to various classroom percussion instruments.

Students review proper playing techniques for the various instruments. Then instructor selects a student conductor. Students trade parts to experience playing the various rhythm patterns and instruments as the student conductor leads. Then, led by the student conductor, the class sings "Gloria Tibi" while several students play the bongo accompaniment.

The class concludes with a discussion of how a similar approach to using instruments in a choral rehearsal would work with a sixth-grade choir.

Suggested Resources

Bernstein, Leonard. "Gloria Tibi." On *Mass.* Norman Scribner, Leonard Bernstein, Berkshire Boys' Choirs. CBS M2K 44593.

Frazee, Jane. *Discovering Orff: A Curriculum for Music Teachers.* Paoli, PA: Schott/European American, 1987.

Walker, David S. "Using Instruments in Today's General Music Classroom." *General Music Today* 3, no. 1 (Fall 1989): 14–17.

STANDARD 2C

Performing on instruments, alone and with others, a varied repertoire of music: Students perform music representing diverse genres and cultures, with expression appropriate for the work being performed.

Strategy

The instructor distributes the octavo "J'entends le Moulin" by Donald Patriquin (Long Beach, CA: Earthsongs), S-06, SATB or SA—or a similar choral selection that has a simple instrumental accompaniment appropriate for middle-level singers. Class members identify and play the wood block and triangle parts, working toward expressive playing of the instrumental accompaniment. Then the class sings the piece with various members of the class playing the instrumental parts.

(continued)

Students discuss effective ways to distribute instruments to classroom students and proper playing techniques for classroom percussion instruments. They consider various strategies for teaching middle-level students simple instrumental rhythm accompaniments. Also, they discuss ways to adapt or rewrite instrumental accompaniments to fit the needs of students with differing abilities and ways to rehearse singers and instrumentalists together. They then compile a list of middle-level choral pieces that use instrumental accompaniments.

Considering the techniques they have discussed, students take turns conducting, singing, and playing expressively the instrumental accompaniment to "J'entends le Moulin."

Suggested Resource

Walker, David S. "Using Instruments in Today's General Music Classroom." *General Music Today* 3, no. 1 (Fall 1989): 14–17.

STANDARD 2D

Performing on instruments, alone and with others, a varied repertoire of music: Students play by ear simple melodies on a melodic instrument and simple accompaniments on a harmonic instrument.

Strategy

Methods students make a list of five simple folk songs that are familiar to all class members. The instructor then gives each student a simple melodic or harmonic instrument (for example, a tin whistle, soprano recorder, guitar, chorded zither—such as Autoharps or ChromAharps—and various Orff mallet instruments) and, on a small piece of paper, the title of one of the five folk songs.

Playing by ear, students rehearse their songs on their assigned instruments. Students playing the accompaniments should be asked to devise accompaniments that are particularly unique to the style of their songs. After students have been given ample time to rehearse alone, the instructor asks students to walk around the room while playing their individual instruments and locate a classmate who is playing the accompaniment or melody to the same selection that they are playing.

After students find the partners who have been assigned the same piece, each group rehearses its folk song together. Each group then performs for the class. Following the performances, students discuss the skills that middle-level students must have to play simple melodies by ear.

Suggested Resource

Hackett, Patricia. *The Melody Book: 300 Selections from the World of Music for Autoharp, Guitar, Piano, Recorder and Voice,* 2d ed. Englewood Cliffs, NJ: Prentice-Hall, 1992.

◆ ◆ ◆ ◆ ◆ ◆

STANDARD 3A

Improvising melodies, variations, and accompaniments: Students improvise simple harmonic accompaniments.

Strategy

The instructor assigns methods students a simple melody, such as "This Land Is Your Land." Working in small groups, students devise chordal accompaniments for the melody using keyboard, guitar, choirchimes, resonator bells, Orff mallet instruments, or chorded zither (such as Autoharp or ChromAharp). Each group then lists the aspects of the melody it had to consider in selecting the appropriate chords. The groups then present their findings, and the class makes a composite list on the chalkboard.

Each student then chooses a simple melody that can be harmonized with only the I, IV, and V chords, adds an improvised harmony for either guitar or keyboard, and plays his or her harmony for the class. The instructor asks each student to list the skills he or she used in completing this task. Then the class compares their individual skill lists with the earlier list of tasks the class developed.

The class discusses the following questions: (1) What prior musical knowledge would a middle-level student need to devise an accompaniment to a melody? (2) How does this knowledge base interact with the skills students need to play the accompaniment? (3) If the chording is limited to tonic, subdominant, and dominant, how can further tasks be increased in complexity? (4) What is the difference between planning chordal accompaniments and improvising such accompaniments?

Suggested Resources

Anderson, William M., and Joy E. Lawrence. *Integrating Music into the Elementary Classroom,* 3d ed. Belmont, CA: Wadsworth Publishing Company, 1995.

Atterbury, Betty W., and Carol P. Richardson. *The Experience of Teaching General Music.* New York: McGraw-Hill, 1995.

Hackett, Patricia, and Carolynn A. Lindeman. *The Musical Classroom: Backgrounds, Models, and Skills for Elementary Teaching,* 4th ed. Englewood Cliffs, NJ: Prentice-Hall, 1997.

❖ ❖ ❖ ❖ ❖ ❖ ❖

STANDARD 4A

Composing and arranging music within specific guidelines: Students compose short pieces within specified guidelines, demonstrating how elements of music are used to achieve unity and variety, tension and release, and balance.

Strategy

The instructor divides the methods class into groups of four students and assigns all groups the same brief poem that will serve as the text for an original vocal composition (the poem may be original). The instructor gives groups ten minutes to rhythmically set the text. After the rhythm is set, the instructor gives groups ten more minutes to set the text to an original melody. (The instructor might recommend that groups use a three-note cell, a five-tone row, or a pentatonic scale in major or minor mode.)

Groups then transcribe and arrange their tunes using a computer program (see Suggested Computer Programs). The software provides a harmonic progression that can then be performed for evaluation. Students can alter and evaluate chords as they perform their compositions.

Students reflect in their journals about the learning process they used, evaluate the effectiveness of their compositions (e.g., Did the rhythms capture natural speech inflections? Did the melody heighten the meaning of the text? In what way did the harmonic accompaniment add to the artistic experience of the text?), and evaluate the effectiveness of the performances of their peers' compositions.

Finally, students discuss as a class how a middle-school chorus could use this process to learn how elements of music are used to achieve unity and variety, tension and release, and balance.

Suggested Literature

Angelou, Maya. *Maya Angelou Poems*. New York: Bantam Books, 1986.

Hughes, Langston. *Selected Poems of Langston Hughes*. New York: Knopf, 1977.

Jones, Bessie, and Bess Lomax Hawes. *Step It Down: Games, Plays, Songs, and Stories from the Afro-American Heritage*. Athens, GA: University of Georgia Press, 1987.

Myers, Walter Dean. *The Mouse Rap*. New York: HarperCollins Publishers, 1990.

Silverstein, Shel. *Where the Sidewalk Ends*. New York: HarperCollins Publishers, 1974.

Suggested Computer Programs

Deluxe Music Construction Set. Petaluma, CA: Electronic Arts Productions, 1990. Amiga.

Encore. Half Moon Bay, CA: Passport Designs, 1989. IBM or Macintosh.

Finale. Eden Prairie, MN: Coda Music Technology, 1990. IBM or Macintosh.

Songworks. Kirkland, WA: Ars Nova, 1993. Macintosh.

STANDARD 4C

Composing and arranging music within specified guidelines: Students use a variety of traditional and nontraditional sound sources and electronic media when composing and arranging.

Strategy

Using a middle-level choral octavo that the methods class has previously studied, the instructor assigns groups of four students each to create movements or actions for selected words of the piece, create body and vocal sounds to accompany the song (for example, sirens, wind sounds), and identify environmental or electronic sounds that might enhance the song.

The instructor asks the groups to notate their compositions using invented notation on a large sheet of paper and to perform them for the class. Each group's notated composition is displayed in the classroom.

After listening to suggestions as to the effectiveness of the composition from their peers, groups prepare a final version that includes body sounds, voice sounds, environmental sounds, and electronic sounds. Students refine their notated compositions and share the finished compositions with the class.

After hearing all of the compositions, the class discusses the feasibility of a similar composition/arranging assignment for middle-level students, considering how to give clear and simple directions for this assignment. Finally, the instructor assigns students to write a self-reflection of the process they followed in completing the composition, assessing each member of the group and the student's specific contribution to the finished product.

Suggested Resources

Paynter, John J. *Sound and Structure.* New York: Cambridge University Press, 1992.

Wiggins, Jackie. *Composition in the Classroom: A Tool for Teaching.* Reston, VA: Music Educators National Conference, 1990.

◆ ◆ ◆ ◆ ◆ ◆ ◆

STANDARD 5A

Reading and notating music: Students read whole, half, quarter, eighth, sixteenth, and dotted notes and rests in 2/4, 3/4, 4/4, 6/8, and 3/8 and alla breve meter signatures.

Strategy

In a previous session, the methods class has been divided into groups, and each group of students has located an octavo, in 4/4 meter, that is appropriate for middle-level singers and that has various rhythmic patterns using quarter notes, half notes, and comparable rests. The methods class becomes a chorus, and students take turns leading the class in echo clapping using various aural and written rhythmic patterns. In an octavo—e.g., Palestrina's "O Bone Jesu," arr. Hans Harthan (Bryn Mawr, PA: Theodore

(continued)

Presser Company), 332-03070, SATB, Level 3—students identify selected rhythmic patterns that can be isolated to use as examples for reading rhythmic patterns. Using rhythmic syllables, students clap and speak the selected patterns.

The instructor then divides the methods class into groups and asks each group to develop a strategy for teaching rhythmic patterns in its selected piece. The strategy should enable middle-level students to read a short rhythmic pattern using half notes, quarter notes, and comparable rests in 4/4 meter through movement activities, playing percussion or other instruments, chanting word rhythms, or using syllables or related mnemonic devices. Also, the instructor asks the groups to describe the effect on the complexity of patterns when two additional note or rest values are included; and the effect on the complexity of the patterns when the meter is changed.

As time allows, members from each group demonstrate their strategies for the class, and the class discusses the effectiveness of each strategy. They consider how the strategies might need to be modified for use with middle-level students.

Suggested Resources

Atterbury, Betty W., and Carol P. Richardson. *The Experience of Teaching General Music.* New York: McGraw-Hill, 1995.

Gelineau, R. Phyllis. *Experiences in Music,* 3d ed. Englewood Cliffs, NJ: Prentice-Hall, 1995.

STANDARD 5B

Reading and notating music: Students read at sight simple melodies in both the treble and bass clefs.

Strategy

The instructor presents methods students with some basic principles of developing sightsinging skills, including consistent practice; small, sequenced steps; positive motivation; sound before symbol (development of aural vocabulary before reading); and writing before reading. Based on assigned readings, the class then discusses the relative advantages and disadvantages of rhythmic and pitch-reading systems (e.g., solmization, numbers). Then the instructor encourages discussion of specific sightsinging strategies, such as Kodály and Gordon approaches, as well as current sightsinging resources.

Using an instructor-generated evaluation form, the class works together to evaluate one of the current sightsinging texts. They consider questions such as the following: Does the approach have clear and complete instructions? Does it have a logical and sequential presentation of material? Does it have quality exercises? Also, they comment on any concerns, positive aspects, or special features of the text, and whether they would use it. If they agree that they would use the text, they describe how they would incorporate the approach into their ensemble curriculum. Students then individually evaluate one other sightsinging text using the evaluation form.

Suggested Resources

Cappers, Paul K. "Sightsinging Makes Middle School Singers into High School Musicians." *Music Educators Journal* 72, no. 2 (October 1985): 45–48.

Choksy, Lois. *The Kodály Context.* Englewood Cliffs, NJ: Prentice-Hall, 1981.

Fowler, Charles, ed. *Sing!* Houston: Hinshaw Music Textbook, 1988.

Smith, Timothy. "A Comparison of Pedagogical Resources in Solmization Systems." *Journal of Music Theory Pedagogy* 5, no. 1 (Spring 1991): 1–23.

Telfer, Nancy. "Sight-singing in the Choral Rehearsal." *Choral Journal* 34, no. 1 (August 1993): 39–40.

STANDARD 5C

Reading and notating music: *Students identify and define standard notation symbols for pitch, rhythm, dynamics, tempo, articulation, and expression.*

Strategy

The instructor leads the class in reading an octavo in three parts, such as "Turtle Dove," arr. Linda Spevacek (Milwaukee: Jensen/Hal Leonard Corporation), 43720070, three-part mixed, Level 2. Working together, the students identify salient musical terms, symbols, concepts, and skills relating to the piece. Students give suggestions for rehearsal activities related to each concept or skill. The instructor then distributes and reviews an instructor-generated model study guide that includes musical terminology used in the piece and musical concepts and related activities.

From an array of works provided by the instructor, students work in groups to select a choral work appropriate for a middle-level choral ensemble. They analyze the work as the instructor modeled using "Turtle Dove" and develop a study guide that includes a minimum of ten salient terms and their notation symbols.

Suggested Resources

Brunner, David L. "Choral Repertoire: A Director's Checklist." *Music Educators Journal* 79, no. 1 (September 1992): 29–32.

Grashel, John. "An Integrated Approach: Comprehensive Musicianship." *Music Educators Journal* 79, no. 8 (April 1993): 38–41.

Rohwer, Debbie. "Making Rehearsals Comprehensive." *Teaching Music* 1, no. 3 (December 1993): 29–30, 51.

Wolverton, Vance D. "Comprehensive Musicianship Revisited: Research-based Applications for Choral Music Classroom." *Update: Applications of Research in Music Education* 10, no. 2 (Spring/Summer 1992): 10–15.

STANDARD 5E

Reading and notating music: Students sightread, accurately and expressively, music with a level of difficulty of 2, on a scale of 1 to 6.

Strategy

Prior to class, students have interviewed choral directors and middle-school students who have used various sightreading sources. In class, the instructor discusses with methods students the value of sightreading exercises and practice with middle-level choruses. Then the instructor invites methods students to discuss sightreading methods that they may have experienced in middle school or high school.

Students examine major sightsinging methods and sources and briefly outline each, comparing them as to interest, difficulty, cost, effectiveness, and appropriateness for the ranges of middle-level choral students. They then construct a set of sightsinging exercises, equivalent to a level of difficulty of 2, appropriate for a cambiata voice.

Suggested Resources

Adams, Charlotte. *Daily Workout for a Beautiful Voice.* Santa Barbara, CA: Santa Barbara Music Publishing, 1991. Videocassette.

Anderson, Tom. *Sing Choral Music at Sight.* Reston, VA: Music Educators National Conference, 1992.

Phillips, Kenneth H. *Teaching Kids to Sing.* Old Tappan, NJ: Schirmer Books/Simon & Schuster, 1992.

Snyder, Audrey. *The Sight-Singer.* Miami: Warner Bros. Publications, 1993.

Telfer, Nancy. *Successful Sight-Singing: A Creative, Step-by-Step Approach.* San Diego: Neil A. Kjos Music Company, 1992.

◆ ◆ ◆ ◆ ◆ ◆

STANDARD 6A

Listening to, analyzing, and describing music: Students describe specific music events in a given aural example, using appropriate terminology.

Strategy

Working in groups of four, methods students have selected a choral excerpt (approximately one minute) for which they can provide a commercial recording. In class, groups present their excerpts to the rest of the class using the following lesson plan:

1. Direct class to listen "in terms of the notes themselves and of their manipulation" in order to increase their "awareness of what is going on insofar as the notes are concerned" (Copland, p. 21–22).

2. Have class members listen again and create a graphic-line notation that reflects the rhythmic motive, place icons of instruments in a series that reflects an awareness of the instrumental timbres, or build a wooden block sculpture that reflects the form of the piece. Display visual descriptions in a central spot.

3. Have students give their perceptions of specific music events in the music example. Offer musical terminology in response to class members' attempts to share their perceptions.

4. On a third listening, have students follow the music using the visual descriptions of the class members.

After the presentations, methods students discuss changes that they would make in presenting the lesson to a middle-level chorus.

Suggested Resource

Copland, Aaron. *What to Listen for in Music.* New York: McGraw-Hill, 1939.

STANDARD 6B

Listening to, analyzing, and describing music: Students analyze the uses of elements of music in aural examples representing diverse genres and cultures.

Strategy

The instructor divides the methods class into groups of four students and assigns each group one choral excerpt, appropriate for middle-school voices, from an African, Mexican, Indonesian, or European-American ethnic tradition. Groups then prepare teaching presentations that include performances of their pieces. As groups prepare teaching presentations, the instructor encourages them to reflect on their learning strategies and describe the learning process in their journals.

For their presentations, students (1) explain the importance and character of each element in the overall piece (e.g., the Indonesian melody—based on a five-tone scale—overlays three polyrhythms that are chanted; the Mexican melody is tonal and supported by homophonic chords); and (2) perform the piece for the class, asking them to listen to a particular element, such as melody. After listening to the performance, class members share their perceptions of the function of the particular element within the excerpt.

After each group has performed and class members have shared their perceptions, groups perform their musical excerpts one after another in an uninterrupted sequence. The instructor then leads a discussion, assisting methods students in comparing the use of a particular element in each excerpt.

Suggested Resources

Anderson, William M., and Patricia Shehan Campbell. *Multicultural Perspectives in Music Education,* 2d ed. Reston, VA: Music Educators National Conference, 1996.

Campbell, Patricia Shehan. *Lessons from the World.* Old Tappan, NJ: Schirmer Books/Simon & Schuster, 1991.

Titon, Jeff Todd, ed. *Worlds of Music: An Introduction to the Music of the World's Peoples,* 3d ed. Old Tappan, NJ: Schirmer Books/Simon & Schuster, 1996. Book and recordings.

◆ ◆ ◆ ◆ ◆ ◆ ◆

Evaluating music and music performances: Students develop criteria for evaluating the quality and effectiveness of music performances and compositions and apply the criteria in their personal listening and performing.

Strategy

Methods students have completed assigned reading in preparation for a discussion focusing on criteria for evaluating middle-school choral ensemble performances. The instructor divides the class into small groups to develop lists of specific criteria. After the groups have completed their lists, each group shares its ideas with the class, and the instructor compiles a master list on the chalkboard.

The instructor then presents and explains standard evaluation forms that are traditionally used at state contests and festivals. Using one of these standard forms, students critique a recorded performance of a middle-level choral ensemble. Then they discuss various techniques for having middle-level students develop criteria and for involving them in a similar evaluation process (e.g., listening to other choral ensembles at festivals or to recordings of their own ensemble and completing critique forms).

Suggested Resources

Radocy, Rudolf E. "Evaluating Student Achievement." *Music Educators Journal* 76, no. 4 (December 1989): 30–33.

Robinson, Charles R. "Choral Performance: Do You Hear What I Hear?" *Music Educators Journal* 77, no. 4 (December 1990): 47–51.

Wurgler, Pamela S. "An Adjudicator Lists Ten Common Vocal Sins." *Choral Journal* 34, no. 10 (May 1994): 31–34.

Evaluating music and music performances: Students evaluate the quality and effectiveness of their own and others' performances, compositions, arrangements, and improvisations by applying specific criteria appropriate for the style of the music and offer constructive suggestions for improvement.

Strategy

The instructor divides the methods class into groups of three or four mixed voices in each group. Groups choose, then prepare, perform, and videotape a performance of a choral piece from a set of masterworks appropriate for middle-school voices. The instructor should make sure that each team's piece is stylistically different (e.g., "El Grillo," by Des Prez; "Hosanna in Excelsis," by Di Lasso; "Hist Whist," by Cummings and Jones; "Ride the Chariot," arr. Melton, all from *World of Choral Music*).

After the class has viewed each group's performance, the instructor leads the methods students in reviewing the stylistic characteristics of music from this genre on the basis of their own performances, observed performances, or recordings. Using these criteria as the basis for their evaluation of the performance, students then give descriptions that are nonjudgmental and richly descriptive, listing descriptions on the chalkboard. They develop categories for these descriptions (e.g. "upbeat," "precise," and "halting" may fit under "rhythm"). The instructor notes that in teaching middle-level students, they would lead the students to use musical terminology to describe their impressions.

Methods students then suggest strategies for improvement of the performance using terminology that would be appropriate and understandable to middle-level students. They consider how middle-level students could use a similar procedure to evaluate and improve their performances.

Suggested Resources

Chuska, Kenneth R. *Teaching the Process of Thinking, K–12*. Bloomington, IN: Phi Delta Kappa Educational Foundation, 1986.

Hausmann, Charles S., Hunter C. March, Samuel D. Miller, and Betty G. Roe, eds. *World of Choral Music*. Parsippany, NJ: Silver Burdett Ginn, 1988.

◆ ◆ ◆ ◆ ◆ ◆ ◆

STANDARD 8A

Understanding relationships between music, the other arts, and disciplines outside the arts:
Students compare in two or more arts how the characteristic materials of each art can be used to transform similar events, scenes, emotions, or ideas into works of art.

Strategy

Methods students listen to recordings of two different storm choruses: "He Gave Them Hailstones for Rain," from Handel's *Israel and Egypt,* and the opening chorus of Verdi's *Otello.*

Students use a listening grid to discover the following: What means did the composer use to create the mood of the storm (large orchestra, small choir, etc.)? How were the elements of music used? How did the form and structure of the music create a mood? What was the origin and original function of the music? Which setting of the storm chorus was the most subtle or the most literal, and why?

The instructor then shows students John Turner's painting, "Steamer in the Snowstorm." Students discuss how Turner used the elements of art to create the mood of a storm. They compare the characteristics that are common to the storm choruses and the Turner painting.

Finally, students discuss how they would lead middle-level students in using a similar procedure.

Suggested Resource

Fogarty, Robin. "Ten Ways to Integrate the Curriculum." *Educational Leadership* 49, no. 2 (October 1991): 61–65.

STANDARD 8B

Understanding relationships between music, the other arts, and disciplines outside the arts:
Students describe ways in which the principles and subject matter of other disciplines
taught in the school are interrelated with those of music.

Strategy

Methods students have read a novel appropriate for middle-level students (see Suggested Children's Literature). In class, they discuss ways in which the various elements of the novel (character, setting, repetition and contrast, style, and motive) lead toward the artistic climax of the story.

Students then watch a videotape of the opera *Amahl and the Night Visitors,* by Menotti, in which, as with many musical works, the musical climax and the emotional climax of the work are different. Working in small groups, students identify ways in which the composer uses the elements of music as the piece builds to a musical and to an emotional climax. They also discuss and prepare to present to the rest of the class ways in which both music and literature use their respective elements to build to an artistic climax.

Students discuss advantages and challenges of using a similar activity in a middle-school choral setting. They also discuss the possibility of teaching such an activity in coordination with a middle-school language arts teacher.

Suggested Children's Literature

Lowry, Lois. *The Giver.* Boston: Houghton-Mifflin, 1993.

Lowry, Lois. *Number the Stars.* Boston: Houghton-Mifflin, 1993.

Suggested Resources

McCoy, Clair. "Music and Children's Literature: Natural Partners." *General Music Today* 7, no. 3 (Spring 1994), 15–19.

Thomas, Troy. "Interart Analogy: Practice and Theory in Comparing the Arts." *Journal of Aesthetic Education* 25, no. 2 (Summer 1991): 17–36.

◆ ◆ ◆ ◆ ◆ ◆ ◆

STANDARD 9A

Understanding music in relation to history and culture: Students describe distinguishing characteristics
of representative music genres and styles from a variety of cultures.

Strategy

Students have completed research into various musical traditions performed in wedding ceremonies within the American culture (e.g., Jewish weddings, slave weddings, and Asian weddings). In class, the instructor leads methods students in a discussion of various rites and rituals of American culture (baptism, weddings, funerals, etc.) and the role that music plays in those rituals. Special focus is drawn to the ritual of the wedding ceremony.

Students relate examples of various styles of music that are heard or performed in weddings; examples will range from "Ave Maria" to current country and popular tunes. Because many college students have performed as musicians for numerous weddings, they are encouraged to describe the various moods that certain music sets before, during, and after the ceremony.

The instructor then plays recordings of the "Bridal Chorus" from Wagner's *Lohengrin* and portions of Stravinsky's *Les Noces* ("The Wedding"), which was based on a Russian pagan wedding. The class discusses distinguishing stylistic characteristics of these works and compares their own experiences with music of the German and Russian depictions of the wedding ceremony. The instructor then asks the class to write a reflection on ways such an activity might enable middle-level students to describe and recognize distinguishing characteristics of representative music genres and styles from a variety of cultures.

Suggested Resources

Borroff, Edith. "A New Look at Teaching Music History." *Music Educators Journal* 79, no. 4 (December 1992): 41–43.

Fulghum, Robert. *From Beginning to End: The Rituals of Our Lives.* New York: Villard Books, 1995.

STANDARD 9B

Understanding music in relation to history and culture: *Students classify by genre and style (and, if applicable, by historical period, composer, and title) a varied body of exemplary (that is, high-quality and characteristic) musical works and explain the characteristics that cause each work to be considered exemplary.*

Strategy

Methods students examine, listen to, and discuss a wide variety of choral music, from Western and non-Western sources, that is appropriate for middle-level students' voices. They classify the pieces according to genre, style, and historical period.

Based on Reimer's four criteria for determining artistic merit and suitability (craftsmanship, imagination, authenticity, and sensitivity), students explain the characteristics that make each of the pieces exemplary or characteristics that keep the work from being exemplary. The instructor and students then discuss how these procedures could be modified for students in a middle-level classroom.

Suggested Resources

Prescribed Music List. Austin, TX: University Interscholastic League, 1995.

Reimer, Bennett. *A Philosophy of Music Education,* 2d ed., Englewood Cliffs, NJ: Prentice-Hall, 1989.

CHORAL MUSIC
GRADES 9-12

STANDARD 1A

Proficient

Singing, alone and with others, a varied repertoire of music: *Students sing with expression and technical accuracy a large and varied repertoire of vocal literature with a level of difficulty of 4, on a scale of 1 to 6, including some songs performed from memory.*

Strategy

The instructor has assigned methods students to act as student conductors of short SATB works with a level of difficulty of 4. After studying and preparing the scores outside class, student conductors lead the methods class in sightreading the works.

Using error detection skills to facilitate technically accurate choral singing, student conductors isolate rhythmic errors after the initial reading of each piece and isolate pitch errors after a second reading. After the student conductor has noted errors and suggested specific corrections to musical mistakes, the class reads through the piece a third time.

The student conductor then turns attention to the vocal and expressive challenges presented by level 4 literature, including well-developed technical skills, attention to phrasing and interpretation, and the ability to perform various meters and rhythms in a variety of keys. Methods students add the literature from this session to their list of moderately difficult repertoire for use with high school students to develop expression and technical accuracy in singing.

Suggested Resources

Grunow, Richard, and Lois Fargo. *The Choral Score Reading Program.* Chicago: GIA Publications, 1983. Book and audiocassette.

Paine, Gordon. "Score Selection, Study, and Interpretation." In *Up Front! Becoming the Complete Choral Conductor,* edited by Guy Webb. Boston: E. C. Schirmer Music Company, 1993.

STANDARD 1B

Proficient

Singing, alone and with others, a varied repertoire of music: *Students sing music written in four parts, with and without accompaniment.*

Strategy

The instructor divides the methods class into small groups. Each group is assigned to create a genre- or style-based "concert" of four-part music, with and without accompaniment, based on specific music selection criteria (e.g., appropriate ranges, tessitura, difficulty, suitability of text, suitability to teach musical concepts). Styles may include Western European sacred music, secular art music, multicultural selections, chamber music, jazz/show, and so on. Students may choose from class texts, repertoire lists, and music they already know.

(continued)

The class then analyzes the repertoire chosen by each group, noting suitability and discussing its appropriate use at the high school level. Each "concert program" is duplicated and provided to all class members.

Suggested Resources

Collins, Donald L. *Teaching Choral Music.* Englewood Cliffs, NJ: Prentice-Hall, 1993.

Garretson, Robert L. *Choral Music: History, Style, and Performance Practice.* Englewood Cliffs, NJ: Prentice-Hall, 1993.

Hylton, John B. *Comprehensive Choral Music Education.* Englewood Cliffs, NJ: Prentice-Hall, 1995.

May, William V., ed. *Something New to Sing About,* Level II. Mission Hills, CA: Glencoe/McGraw-Hill, 1989.

STANDARD 1C
Proficient
Singing, alone and with others, a varied repertoire of music: Students demonstrate well-developed ensemble skills.

Strategy

The instructor plays recorded examples of high school choirs for methods students. After listening, the students discuss the extent to which well-developed ensemble skills were demonstrated, including: listening within the choir, accurate intonation, balance, blend, and uniform pronunciation.

Students discuss the importance of a unison sound within each section of the choir, and they demonstrate how to develop that sound. They discuss how to use seating placement and vowel modification to facilitate well-blended and in-tune singing with a group of singers of like range.

Using the methods class as the high school chorus, students demonstrate vertical tuning of the sections of the ensemble on a simple homophonic vocalise for the purpose of unified balance and blend. The instructor emphasizes the importance of listening by both the singers and the conductor for the development of ensemble skills.

Suggested Resources

Finn, W. J. *The Art of the Choral Conductor.* Boston: C. C. Birchard, 1939.

Nesheim, Paul, and Weston Noble. *Building Beautiful Voices.* Dayton, OH: Roger Dean/The Lorenz Corporation, 1995.

STANDARD 1D

Advanced

Singing, alone and with others, a varied repertoire of music: *Students sing with expression and technical accuracy a large and varied repertoire of vocal literature with a level of difficulty of 5, on a scale of 1 to 6.*

Strategy

Using repertoire from a variety of historical periods and styles, the instructor has assigned each methods student a piece with a level of difficulty of 5 to be analyzed and presented in class. Each student provides the class with copies of a written analysis to serve as a guide to the ensuing discussion.

Students lead discussions of their pieces, paying particular attention to the challenges presented by level 5 literature, including advanced technical and interpretive skills, key signatures with numerous sharps or flats, unusual meters, complex rhythms, and subtle dynamic requirements. When possible, students play recordings of contrasting performances of the pieces, followed by critical analysis and discussion of the interpretive decisions involved.

The instructor demonstrates rehearsal techniques that would help high school students deal with the technical and expressive requirements of level 5 music. Discussion should include the time requirements for learning music of this level and how to balance these selections with high quality music that is less challenging.

Finally, students conduct their pieces, working to realize the performance practices and expressive details discussed in class.

Suggested Resources

Robinson, Ray, and Allen Winold. *The Choral Experience: Literature, Materials, and Methods.* Prospect Heights, IL: Waveland Press, 1992.

Swan, Howard. "The Development of a Choral Instrument." In *Choral Conducting Symposium,* 2d ed., edited by Harold A. Decker and Julius Herford. Englewood Cliffs, NJ: Prentice-Hall, 1987.

STANDARD 1E

Advanced

Singing, alone and with others, a varied repertoire of music: *Students sing music written in more than four parts.*

Strategy

The instructor divides the methods class into two groups and assigns each group to create a concert program of music in more than four parts for advanced mixed choir based on previously discussed music selection criteria (e.g., appropriate ranges, tessitura, difficulty, suitability of text, suitability to teach musical concepts).

(continued)

Group 1 creates a program of multipart music, noting which, if any, of the standard four voice parts have been divided. Group 2 constructs a program of works for double-choir. Students can choose class texts, repertoire lists, or previously learned music for the programs. The class then analyzes and discusses repertoire chosen by each group in regard to its appropriate use at the high school level. Each "concert program" is duplicated and provided to all class members.

Suggested Resources

Collins, Donald L. *Teaching Choral Music.* Englewood Cliffs, NJ: Prentice-Hall, 1993.

Garretson, Robert L. *Choral Music: History, Style and Performance Practice.* Englewood Cliffs, NJ: Prentice-Hall, 1993.

Hylton, John B. *Comprehensive Choral Music Education.* Englewood Cliffs, NJ: Prentice-Hall, 1995.

May, William V., ed. *Something New to Sing About,* Level II, Mission Hills, CA: Glencoe/McGraw-Hill, 1989.

STANDARD 1F

Advanced

Singing, alone and with others, a varied repertoire of music: Students sing in small ensembles with one student on a part.

Strategy

The instructor assigns methods students to various types of small ensembles with one student on a part. Each ensemble analyzes literature, appropriate for the 9–12 level, from a variety of "suggested lists" to indicate the type of small ensemble and level(s) for which the selected literature would be most appropriate. Working all together as a chorus and also in their small ensembles, students demonstrate how music of various voicings is applicable to both full choral and chamber ensemble settings.

Each small ensemble then selects a piece to perform for the class and rehearses its selection. As each small ensemble performs, the rest of the class, acting as teachers, evaluates individual ensemble members' mastery of the selected literature.

The class discusses the use of small ensembles in grades 9–12 for assessment and for encouraging student leadership, musical independence, and actively taking part in making informed musical judgments about the expressive potential of the piece being performed.

Suggested Resources

New York State School Music Association. *NYSSMA Manual of Graded Solo and Ensemble Music.* Westbury, NY: NYSSMA, 1991.

Prescribed Music List. Austin, TX: University Interscholastic League, 1995.

Schmid, Will, ed. *Something to Sing About,* Level I. Mission Hills, CA: Glencoe/McGraw-Hill, 1989.

◆ ◆ ◆ ◆ ◆ ◆ ◆

STANDARD 2B

Proficient

Performing on instruments, alone and with others, a varied repertoire of music: Students perform an appropriate part in an ensemble, demonstrating well-developed ensemble skills.

Strategy

The instructor introduces methods students to the basic techniques of recorder playing and the ranges of soprano, alto, tenor, and bass recorders.

After introductory playing experiences with simple unison pieces, methods students select from standard madrigal repertoire three to five works that have ranges appropriate for a quartet of recorders and that are easy enough for high school students who are relatively inexperienced in recorder playing.

The instructor allows rehearsal time and then leads the group either in singing the pieces, having some doubling of voice parts on recorder, or in playing the parts on recorders without voices. Methods students then determine ensemble skills (e.g., listening, intonation, rhythmic precision and balance) that can be developed by high school students when playing in instrumental ensembles.

Suggested Resource

Burakoff, Gerald and Sonya. *Introducing the Recorder: Information and Guidelines for Teachers.* Jackson, NJ: American Recorder Society, 1993.

◆ ◆ ◆ ◆ ◆ ◆ ◆

STANDARD 3A

Proficient

Improvising melodies, variations, and accompaniments: Students improvise stylistically appropriate harmonizing parts.

Strategy

The instructor plays selected recordings for methods students to introduce the African-derived approach to performance of African-American spirituals and gospel songs. Selections include Sweet Honey in the Rock's "Study War No More" (see Suggested Resources). Students listen for characteristics, including call-and-response structures; syncopated rhythms; polyrhythms; blue notes; and the blend of prepared and improvised melodic, rhythmic, and harmonic components.

The instructor guides students in repeated listenings of "Study War No More," asking them to give particular attention to the text, melody, rhythm, harmony, and vocal nuances of the performance style. Using the traditional African-American approach to song acquisition, the class learns aurally at least one verse and the chorus. Students sing with the recording, including singing the choral response ("Down by the riverside") and adding a rhythmic clapping accompaniment.

(continued)

Without the recording, students attempt to emulate the model but experiment freely with harmonic accompaniments in the style. Then, various students improvise melodically on the solo melody as the full group sings a harmonic response worked out by the group.

Finally, students discuss the challenges of learning by listening and its advantages for building high school students' musicianship skills in melodic and harmonic improvisation and their respect for this traditional system of transmission.

Suggested Resources

Campbell, Patricia Shehan. "Mellonee Burnim on African American Music." *Music Educators Journal* 82, no. 1 (July 1995): 41–48. Also in *Music in Cultural Context: Eight Views on World Music Education.* Reston, VA: Music Educators National Conference, 1996.

"Oh, Happy Day," performed by Edwin Hawkins' Singers. On *Jubilation!: Great Gospel Performances.* Vol. 1, *Black Gospel.* Rhino Entertainment R2 70288.

Southern, Eileen. *The Music of Black Americans,* 3d ed. New York: W. W. Norton, 1997.

Sweet Honey in the Rock. "By the Waters of Babylon." On *Feel Something Drawing Me On.* Flying Fish FF 70375.

Sweet Honey in the Rock. "Study War No More." On *Breaths.* Flying Fish 70105.

STANDARD 3B

Proficient

Improvising melodies, variations, and accompaniments: Students improvise rhythmic and melodic variations on given pentatonic melodies and melodies in major and minor keys.

Strategy

Methods students have each completed an assignment to list five easy, unison songs (including pentatonic, major, and minor melodies) that can be used with high school singers for melodic and rhythmic improvisation. Songs might include "All Night, All Day," "Candy," "Five Hundred Miles," "Mary Had a Baby," "Rock-a-My Soul," "Swing Low Sweet Chariot," and "This Land Is Your Land." In class, each student provides copies of his or her list for the other students and brings music for one of the songs.

Students take turns leading the class in the songs for which they brought music, encouraging the singers to improvise rhythmic and melodic variations on the melodies. Discussion follows regarding effective techniques that were used to help singers improvise, whether these techniques would work with high school singers, and other possible means for including such an activity in a high school choral setting. Methods students also discuss how to help high school students overcome inhibitions about singing alone and improvising and what the musical benefits of this activity are.

Suggested Resources

Campbell, Patricia Shehan, ed. "Special Focus: Improvisation." *Music Educators Journal* 78, no. 4 (December 1991): 21–44.

Fredrickson, Scott. "Teaching Beginning Vocal Improvisation." *Music Educators Journal* 80, no. 4 (January 1994): 21–23.

Henry, Robert E. "Improvisation Through Guided Self-Study." *Music Educators Journal* 79, no. 8 (April 1993): 33–37.

STANDARD 3C

Proficient

Improvising melodies, variations, and accompaniments: *Students improvise original melodies over given chord progressions, each in a consistent style, meter, and tonality.*

Strategy

In class, methods students listen to blues examples that use the traditional 12-bar blues harmonic pattern:

I7	I7	I7	I7
IV7	IV7	I7	I7
V7	IV7	I7	I7

The instructor then demonstrates the blues pattern on piano or plays a recorded example. Students follow the chord pattern written on the chalkboard; sing chord roots on neutral syllables, chord numbers, or note names; and then sing all members of each chord in arpeggiated style. The instructor divides the class and has some sing the root pattern while others improvise by moving from chord member to chord member on changes and then by intoning simple "scat" rhythms.

While students continue the blues pattern, they take turns as soloists, experimenting with improvising at a comfortable level. Some may sing the chord roots only, improvising rhythmically; others may continue to work through the arpeggiated chord style and begin to fill in scale passages; and those with more experience may begin to actively move within the tonal framework but push the melodic and rhythmic content.

The class discusses how they would use this procedure with high school students. They also discuss the value of having the high school students listen frequently to professional examples, having them analyze and discuss the style and the rhythmic and melodic content. They consider possible next steps—e.g., having high school students expand their improvisation experiences to include other styles of jazz, gospel, and other genres.

Suggested Resources

Caffey, David. "Beginning Improvisation for the Vocal Jazz Ensemble." *Jazz Educators Journal* 14, no. 1 (October–November 1981): 10–13.

Campbell, Patricia Shehan, ed. "Special Focus: Improvisation." *Music Educators Journal* 78, no. 4 (December 1991): 21–44.

Fredrickson, Scott. "Teaching Beginning Vocal Improvisation." *Music Educators Journal* 80, no. 4 (January 1994): 21–23.

(continued)

Henry, Robert E. "Improvisation Through Guided Self-Study." *Music Educators Journal* 79, no. 8 (April 1993): 33–37.

Wilcox, Ella, ed. "Start with the Melody." *Teaching Music* 2, no. 5 (April 1995): 32–33.

STANDARD 3D
Advanced

Improvising melodies, variations, and accompaniments: *Students improvise stylistically appropriate harmonizing parts in a variety of styles.*

Strategy

The instructor begins the methods class by having students perform simple harmonizing exercises (see Fowler, 1988). The class then discusses the intervals that result in consonant harmony, and the instructor leads them to discover that simple I, IV, V chord structures can be harmonized with as few as two different notes.

Students suggest techniques for helping high school singers improvise harmony parts in various styles. They identify criteria for model songs to use as resources for early harmonizing experience; for example, familiarity of the song, simple harmonic vocabulary, slow harmonic rhythm, and repetitiveness of melody. Students then suggest songs that meet these criteria.

Finally, students develop a list of songs that fit their criteria and that are in a variety of styles, including folk songs, art songs, hymns and carols, patriotic songs, and songs from diverse cultures. For selected songs, students sing the melody together with piano accompaniment to become familiar with the melody and harmonic structure. Some students then improvise harmonizing parts, limiting the number of different notes they use at first, while all others sing the melody.

The class discusses the relative success of the improvisers and suggests ideas for improving the improvisations, and then repeats the improvisation procedure with other songs. They review the techniques they suggested earlier for helping high school students to improvise, and they discuss possible modifications of their ideas.

Suggested Resource

Fowler, Charles, ed. *Sing!* Houston: Hinshaw Music Textbook, 1988.

◆ ◆ ◆ ◆ ◆ ◆

Proficient

Composing and arranging music within specified guidelines: *Students compose music in several distinct styles, demonstrating creativity in using the elements of music for expressive effect.*

Strategy

The instructor leads methods students in a discussion about various compositional styles in the music they have been studying for high school choirs. The discussion focuses on elements that create stylistic differences, including harmonic structure, specific rhythmic patterns, text setting, and textural characteristics.

Working in groups, methods students create pieces that demonstrate their understanding of style characteristics in choral works they have been studying (for example, setting a short poem with block chords if a work studied has predominantly block chords, or creating a call-and-response piece in connection with a gospel piece). Some groups might use keyboard or guitar to generate a chord progression; others might generate a melodic or bass line and then use their voices and ears to create harmonies.

Students notate their works and then lead the class in sightreading them. The class evaluates the pieces in terms of success in demonstrating the particular style characteristic.

Students discuss modifications for using this activity with high school choirs. For example, some high school groups might indicate the melodic lines for each voice part with scale numbers or syllables; or, groups could perform their compositions for the choir, instead of having the choir sightread them.

Suggested Resources

Paynter, John J. *Sound and Structure*. New York: Cambridge University Press, 1992.

Upitis, Rena. *This Too Is Music*. Portsmouth, NH: Heinemann Educational Books, 1990.

Webster, Peter, and Maud Hickey. "Challenging Children to Think Creatively." *General Music Today* 8, no. 3 (Spring 1995): 4–10.

Wiggins, Jackie. *Composition in the Classroom: A Tool for Teaching*. Reston, VA: Music Educators National Conference, 1990.

Proficient

Composing and arranging music within specified guidelines: *Students arrange pieces for voices or instruments other than those for which the pieces were written in ways that preserve or enhance the expressive effect of the music.*

Strategy

The instructor and methods students discuss and detail the ages and vocal ranges of high school choirs. Students then sing through a variety of age- and range-appropriate folk-song arrangements, noting how each arranger has used musical and expressive techniques to preserve or enhance the expressive effect of the original music.

Each student selects a folk melody from any national, regional, or ethnic source and creates a simple arrangement for it. Creative limitations can be imposed; for example: two-part beginning male chorus with several unchanged voices; three-part beginning female chorus with limited alto range; three-part intermediate male chorus with all changed voices; three-part beginning mixed chorus with no tenors.

If notation software is available, students can use it for arranging and printing. The instructor discusses with students the ease or difficulty of using this software as a creative resource for high school students.

Finally, the class discusses the appropriate setting for using a similar lesson with high school students, considering particular techniques that would be used and how the assignment would change with and without notation software.

Suggested Resources

Ades, Hawley. *Choral Arranging.* Delaware Water Gap, PA: Shawnee Press, 1966.

Ostrander, Arthur. *Contemporary Choral Arranging.* Englewood Cliffs, NJ: Prentice-Hall, 1986.

◆ ◆ ◆ ◆ ◆ ◆

STANDARD 5A

Proficient

Reading and notating music: *Students demonstrate the ability to read an instrumental or vocal score of up to four staves by describing how the elements of music are used.*

Strategy

The instructor distributes the choral octavo "Tambur," arr. Lajos Bardos (New York: Boosey & Hawkes), OCTB6055, SATB, Level 4—or another four-part work appropriate for the high school level—and asks methods students to demonstrate their score-reading skills by writing a brief description of the way the elements of music are used in the work. Emphasis should be on the manner in which voices relate to one another (who has the melody) and on how the elements relate to one another (what changes in timbre or texture occur when the melody moves to the tenor voice).

Then the methods students work in pairs, one student in each pair acting as teacher. The teaching student uses direct questioning, leading the student to discover and verbalize how the elements of music are used in the score. The instructor encourages discussion between partners, especially when only one of the partners has discovered a certain event or relationship in the music.

Afterward, the class discusses the importance of discussion and directed questioning as a regular teaching technique with high school choral students. They consider how it helps develop score-reading skills and increases understanding of the music being studied.

Suggested Resources

Hoffer, Charles. *Teaching Music in the Secondary Schools,* 4th ed. Belmont, CA: Wadsworth Publishing Company, 1991.

Lamb, Gordon. *Choral Techniques,* 3d ed. Columbus, OH: Wm. C. Brown Communications/McGraw-Hill, 1988.

Roach, Donald. *Complete Secondary Choral Music Guide.* Englewood Cliffs, NJ: Center for Applied Research and Education/Simon & Schuster, 1990.

STANDARD 5B
Proficient
Reading and notating music: *Students sightread, accurately and expressively, music with a level of difficulty of 3, on a scale of 1 to 6.*

Strategy

The instructor discusses with methods students when and how they learned to sightread. They discuss the relative success of the methods they experienced, and they consider the importance of teaching reading skills.

Through demonstration and discussion, the instructor introduces a sequence for teaching reading skills, including: reinforcing tonal and pitch memory; hearing, singing, and identifying the tonic triad and other harmonic "markers" when beginning each piece; learning and associating pitches with solfège or numbers while singing a variety of melodic exercises; practicing from prenotational symbols, such as Curwen hand signs or icons from the board or charts, with the teacher directing eye movement and guiding rhythm reading; and integrating reading skills consistently with the chosen method (solfège or numbers) in all rehearsal and class activities.

After demonstration of these procedures, methods students read examples of music with a level of difficulty of 3 and discuss the extent to which the suggested approach would prepare high school singers to read music of this level.

Suggested Resources

Bauguess, David Jenson, arr. *Sight Singing Course.* Milwaukee: Jenson Publishing/Hal Leonard Corporation, 1984.

(continued)

Crocker, Emily, and Joyce Eilers. *The Choral Approach to Sight-Singing*. Milwaukee: Jenson Publishing/Hal Leonard Corporation, 1990.

Snyder, Audrey. *The Sight-Singer*. Miami, FL: Warner Bros. Publications, 1993.

Telfer, Nancy. *Successful Sight-Singing: A Creative, Step by Step Approach*. San Diego: Neil A. Kjos Music Company, 1992.

STANDARD 5C
Advanced

Reading and notating music: *Students demonstrate the ability to read a full instrumental or vocal score by describing how the elements of music are used and explaining all transpositions and clefs.*

Strategy

The instructor distributes the octavo "The Water Is Wide" by Rene Clausen (Champaign, IL: Mark Foster Music Company), MF3038, SATB, Level 4—or another choral work (appropriate for high school choir) that has instrumental parts for transposing instruments. For this lesson, methods students work in pairs, with one student acting as teacher in each pair. Using directed questioning, the teaching students lead the other students to discover and verbalize how the elements of music are used in "The Water Is Wide." The instructor encourages discussion between partners, especially when only one of the partners has discovered a certain event or relationship in the music.

The instructor asks the class to demonstrate their understanding of clefs and transpositions in the work by transposing four- to eight-measure excerpts of the instrumental parts to concert pitch. Methods students break into groups of three or four and practice mini-lessons and demonstrations of how to teach transposition to high school students. Group members and the instructor critique the lessons for clarity of presentation and accuracy.

Suggested Resource

Kohut, Daniel L., and Joe Grant. *Learning to Conduct and Rehearse*. Englewood Cliffs, NJ: Prentice-Hall, 1990.

STANDARD 5D
Advanced

Reading and notating music: *Students interpret nonstandard notation symbols used by some 20th-century composers.*

Strategy

The instructor divides the class into choral sections and distributes an octavo that uses nonstandard notation—e.g., "Down a Different Road: The Sea" by Brent Pierce (Fort Lauderdale, FL: Walton Music Corporation), W2915, SATB, Level 5; or "Epitaph for Moonlight" by R. Murray Schafer

(Toronto: Berandol Music), BER1094, SSSSAAAATTTTBBBB, Level 5. The sections are given time to read the composer's explanation of the notation system, and each section works out its part. The class then discusses the nonstandard notation used for each voice part and performs them in turn. Finally, the class performs the entire work.

Methods students discuss ways to introduce high school students to works with nonstandard and standard notation. These may include having students listen to recordings while following the score of such a composition or having students develop their own notation for vocal and "found sound" sources.

Suggested Resources

Cacavas, John. *The Art of Writing Music.* Van Nuys, CA: Alfred Publishing Company. 1993.

Cope, David. *New Music Notation.* Dubuque, IA: Kendall/Hunt Publishing, 1976.

Stone, Kurt. *Music Notation in the 20th Century.* New York: W. W. Norton, 1980.

◆ ◆ ◆ ◆ ◆ ◆

STANDARD 6A

Proficient

Listening to, analyzing, and describing music: Students analyze aural examples of a varied repertoire of music representing diverse genres and cultures, by describing the uses of elements of music and expressive devices.

Strategy

The instructor introduces methods students to several choral works appropriate for high school choirs and several listening selections, all of which have either shifting meters or a simple, expressive melodic line (see suggested choral works and listening selections). The examples should be representative of diverse genres and cultures. Working in two groups, methods students identify and discuss how the musical elements and expressive devices are used in the selections and try to determine whether certain elements are highlighted in the music of each culture.

After exploring the commonalities of the octavos and listening examples, the groups come together to discuss how they would lead high school choral students in a similar activity.

Suggested Choral Literature

Shifting meter: "Now Welcome Summer" by Robert Washburn. New York: Oxford University Press. 95.202. SATB. Level 5.

Simple, expressive melodic line: "The Huron Carol," arr. Steve Schuch. Night Heron Music (267 Center Rd., Hillsboro, NH 03244; phone 603-464-4321). SATB. Level 4.

(continued)

Suggested Listening

Shifting meter: "San Juan Pueblo Dance Song." On *Native American Traditions—Music of New Mexico.* Smithsonian/Folkways SF-40408.

Simple, expressive melodic line: Mozart, Wolfgang Amadeus. "Batti, batti, o bel Masetto," from *Don Giovanni.*

Suggested Resources

Anderson, William M., ed. *Teaching Music with a Multicultural Approach,* 2d ed. Reston, VA: Music Educators National Conference, 1991. Book and videocassettes.

Titon, Jeff Todd, ed. *Worlds of Music: An Introduction to the Music of the World's Peoples,* 3d ed. Old Tappan, NJ: Schirmer Books/Simon & Schuster, 1996. Book and recordings.

STANDARD 6B
Proficient

Listening to, analyzing, and describing music: *Students demonstrate extensive knowledge of the technical vocabulary of music.*

Strategy

From an array of high school choral literature of varying levels of difficulty, methods students compile a list of technical and expressive terms, citing the choral pieces in which they find them. The instructor tells methods students to use simple, concise definitions for younger, inexperienced students, noting that high school students should be encouraged to keep such a list of terms and definitions encountered in their own music; this may be a simple list in the students' choral folders or in their portfolios.

If some students have had opportunities for classroom observation, they may note current slang or informal terminology used by students to describe musical events and elements. The class discusses techniques for bridging the gap between language and terms used by high school students and correct technical vocabulary.

Suggested Resource

Randel, Don Michael, ed. *The New Harvard Dictionary of Music.* Cambridge: Belknap Press of Harvard University Press, 1986.

STANDARD 6C

Proficient

Listening to, analyzing, and describing music: Students identify and explain compositional devices and techniques used to provide unity and variety and tension and release in a musical work and give examples of other works that make similar uses of these devices and techniques.

Strategy

Methods students listen to a recording of and then sing the "Hallelujah" chorus from Handel's *Messiah*. After examining the score, students discuss how Handel used repetition, contrast, and developmental ideas in the themes and motives of the work. Students sing the chorus again, observing how the melodic, harmonic, and rhythmic devices have been used to create tension and release.

For contrast, students next listen to "Hallelujah" from *Handel's Messiah: A Soulful Celebration*. The class then considers the following questions: Is this the same composition as the original "Hallelujah"? Why or why not? In what ways is it the same or different? Why do you think someone might want to arrange and perform this work in this way? Has the new arrangement used compositional devices and techniques to create unity and variety and tension and release in the same way as Handel's original composition?

Methods students list other choral works in which musical elements are used in a similar way to create unity and variety and tension and release. They then discuss how they would lead high school choral students through a similar process of discovery. They consider the prior knowledge that would be required and how they would direct their students' listening.

Suggested Resources

Roach, Donald. *Complete Secondary Choral Music Guide.* Englewood Cliffs, NJ: Center for Applied Research and Education/Simon & Schuster, 1990.

Warren, Mervyn, Michael O. Jackson, and Mark Kibble, arr. "Hallelujah." On *Handel's Messiah: A Soulful Celebration.* Warner Alliance 26980.

STANDARD 6D

Advanced

Listening to, analyzing, and describing music: Students demonstrate the ability to perceive and remember music events by describing in detail significant events occurring in a given aural example.

Strategy

The instructor leads methods students in a brief discussion focusing on the importance of developing listening skills in the high school choral classroom. Students listen to (or sing) three to five excerpts from choral works and then identify and describe the significant musical events (e.g., modulations, fugal entrances, developmental devices, meter changes, and textural changes). After each musical event has been identified, the instructor plays the excerpt again to help class members who have not yet identified the event.

(continued)

Finally, the instructor plays a recording of a relatively brief but complete choral work (for example, Schubert's "Benedictus," from Mass in G) and asks students to list each significant music event in the order in which the events occur. After listening, students share their observations. They then compile a list of pieces, in a variety of voicings, that could be used in a similar lesson with advanced high school choral students.

Suggested Choral Literature

Fugal entrances: "Cum Sancto Spiritu," from *Gloria* by Antonio Vivaldi. Fort Lauderdale, FL: Walton Music Corporation. W2047. SATB. Level 4.

Meter changes: "O Magnum Mysterium" by Tomas Victoria. Milwaukee: Schirmer/Hal Leonard Corporation. 10193. SATB. Level 4.

Modulation: "Do You Hear What I Hear?" arr. Harry Simeone. Delaware Water Gap, PA: Shawnee Press. B218. SATB. Level 3.

Modulation: "Play for Me a Simple Melody" by Irving Berlin, arr. Kirby Shaw. Milwaukee: Hal Leonard Corporation. 0870794. SATB. Level 3.

Relative major/minor: "My Lord" by Joyce Eilers. Milwaukee: Hal Leonard Corporation. 08545500. Three-part. Level 2.

Texture changes: "Sing We and Chant It" by Thomas Morley. Milwaukee: Schirmer/Hal Leonard Corporation. 50310800. SATB. Level 3.

STANDARD 6E
Advanced

Listening to, analyzing, and describing music: Students compare ways in which musical materials are used in a given example relative to ways in which they are used in other works of the same genre or style.

Strategy

Methods students have brought to class recorded examples of Renaissance and Baroque choral pieces that use melisma. The instructor discusses with methods students the use of these melismatic passages, emphasizing the difference between Renaissance secular works, in which melismas highlighted the poetry or a specific word (text painting), and Baroque compositions, where melismatic passages were derived from an instrumental, nontextual viewpoint.

For contrast, methods students compare the use of musical materials in a Kyrie from the Renaissance, Classical, and Romantic periods by three different composers.

Working in groups, students prepare a mini-lesson that includes listening examples and work sheets appropriate for high school choral students. The objective of each lesson should be to have students compare the use of melismas in two of the works (one from each era) for which students have brought recordings to class. A student from each group presents a sample lesson to the class. The class then discusses the teaching presentations and considers any changes that would need to be made in presenting the lessons to high school choral students.

Suggested Resources

Garretson, Robert L. *Choral Music: History, Style and Performance Practice*. Englewood Cliffs, NJ: Prentice-Hall, 1993.

Robinson, Ray, and Allen Winold. *The Choral Experience: Literature, Materials, and Methods*. Prospect Heights, IL: Waveland Press, 1992.

STANDARD 6F

Advanced

Listening to, analyzing, and describing music: *Students analyze and describe uses of the elements of music in a given work that make it unique, interesting, and expressive.*

Strategy

The instructor asks methods students to list the elements of music (rhythm, melody, harmony, form, timbre, tempo, dynamics, and texture) on the chalkboard. Students then discuss how composers manipulate these elements to make a work unique, interesting, and expressive.

Through recordings or by singing in class, the instructor presents choral works that emphasize the manipulation of one or two specific elements (see Suggested Resources). Students identify and describe the way(s) in which the elements make the work interesting and expressive.

Finally, the instructor plays a recording of a work that exhibits the manipulation of a variety of elements—for example, Randall Thompson's "Last Words of David" (Boston: E. C. Schirmer Music Company), 2294, SATB, Level 5. Students then analyze and describe in writing the unique and expressive use of elements in this piece. They discuss any modifications needed to adapt the lesson demonstrated in class for use with high school students.

Suggested Choral Literature

"Saul" by Egil Hovland. Fort Lauderdale, FL: Walton Music Corporation. WM 126. Mixed chorus with narrator. Level 4.

"Shepherd Me Lord" by G. Kingsley. New York: Bourne Company. 932. SAB. Level 3.

"When Jesus Wept" by William Billings. Milwaukee: Schirmer/Hal Leonard Corporation. 11145. SATB. Level 2.

Suggested Listening

Billings, William. "When Jesus Wept." On *William Billings: The Continental Harmonist*. Gregg Smith Singers. Premier PRCD 1008.

◆ ◆ ◆ ◆ ◆ ◆ ◆

STANDARD 7A

Proficient

Evaluating music and music performances: Students evolve specific criteria for making informed, critical evaluations of the quality and effectiveness of performances, compositions, arrangements, and improvisations and apply the criteria in their personal participation in music.

Strategy

Methods students listen to recorded examples of high school singers performing appropriate choral works. The instructor then asks them to write comments and suggestions about the quality of the performances.

After each example, the instructor asks students to report and discuss their written comments. Through the discussion, the class develops criteria for making judgments and establishes a means of organizing their reactions to the performance, composition, arrangement, or improvisation. The general categories established should adequately encompass the many specific reactions to the performance or composition. Categories might include tone quality, intonation, accuracy of pitch and rhythm, expressive quality, and diction.

Methods students discuss how they would lead high school choral students in developing evaluative criteria and have them develop an evaluation form using their criteria. They also consider how they would guide students in applying the criteria in their personal participation in music.

Suggested Resource

Garretson, Robert L. *Conducting Choral Music,* 7th ed. Englewood Cliffs, NJ: Prentice-Hall, 1993.

STANDARD 7B

Proficient

Evaluating music and music performances: Students evaluate a performance, composition, arrangement, or improvisation by comparing it to similar or exemplary models.

Strategy

Methods students listen to recorded performances, compositions, arrangements, or improvisations of high school choirs. Either individually or in groups, students use copies of a standard evaluation form based on criteria that they have developed, to evaluate each listening selection. After making their evaluations, students compare their opinions.

The instructor also challenges students to make specific recommendations for improvement, asking questions such as the following: If there is poor intonation, diction, or phrasing, what are some suggestions to improve that specific aspect of performance? Which of the problems will take long-range solutions, and which can be solved quickly? If there are multiple problems, which should be corrected first? Are there suggestions that might improve more than one problem simultaneously?

The class discusses how they would use this lesson with high school students. In a high school lesson, the students would first listen to exemplary models of performances, compositions, arrangements, or improvisations, similar to those used in their classrooms. They would then compare their own efforts to those of the models.

Suggested Resources

Decker, Harold A., and Colleen J. Kirk. *Choral Conducting: Focus on Communication.* Prospect Heights, IL: Waveland Press, 1988.

Kohut, Daniel L., and Joe Grant. *Learning to Conduct and Rehearse.* Englewood Cliffs, NJ: Prentice-Hall, 1990.

STANDARD 7C
Advanced

Evaluating music and music performances: Students evaluate a given musical work in terms of its aesthetic qualities and explain the musical means it uses to evoke feelings and emotions.

Strategy

The instructor plays recordings of two or three contrasting choral works and engages methods students in an evaluation of each piece based on aesthetic qualities. Students are asked to list in musical terms what, in each composition, may have generated their responses; for example, interaction of musical elements; specific expressive techniques (dynamic variety, articulation); manipulation of formal elements (repetition, contrast, unifying themes); meaning of text; combining musical setting with text; quality of the technical aspects of the performance (i.e., beauty of tone, intonation, blend, balance).

Following the discussion, the instructor divides the class into small groups to develop questions that could be asked of high school students to guide them in evaluating musical works in terms of their aesthetic qualities. As a class, students share the questions they developed. The class discusses questioning and response techniques appropriate for high school students and how those differ from techniques used at other levels.

Suggested Resources

Tanner, Michael L. "Let the Concert Begin." *Music Educators Journal* 70, no. 4 (December 1983): 40–45.

Tuley, Robert J. "Framework for Performance Evaluation." *Music Educators Journal* 71, no. 7 (March 1985): 32–33.

Veech, Michael W. "The Connection Between Feeling and Thinking in High School General Music." *Update: Applications of Research in Music Education* 11, no. 2 (Spring/Summer 1993): 23–26.

◆ ◆ ◆ ◆ ◆ ◆ ◆

STANDARD 8A

Proficient

Understanding relationships between music, the other arts, and disciplines outside the arts:
Students explain how elements, artistic processes, and organizational principles are used
in similar and distinctive ways in the various arts and cite examples.

Strategy

The instructor prepares and distributes a table with the following headings across the top: Music, Poetry, Dance, Painting, and Sculpture. The left side of the table lists the following categories and sub-categories: General Principles and Processes (representational/abstract, repetition and contrast, tension/release, unity/variety, structure, balance); Analogous Relationships (sensual properties of sound, sensual properties of sight, sensual properties of movement, accent/rhythm/meter); Common Terms/Different Phenomena (rhythm, texture, line, gesture, color, consonance/dissonance).

Methods students individually consider whether and how each of these relationships or terms applies across the art forms and indicate the valid relationships with a check in the cells under each of the appropriate art forms. They then present their ideas to the class, citing specific examples to support their contentions. For example, all of the art forms use the General Principles and Processes, while music, poetry, and dance emphasize the sensual properties of sound and movement. By contrast, dance, painting, and sculpture are more directly involved with sight.

The class considers how they could use a similar procedure with high school choral students. They also discuss how they might implement such a procedure working with teachers of other arts disciplines and disciplines outside the arts.

Suggested Resources

McCoy, Clair. "Music and Children's Literature: Natural Partners." *General Music Today* 7, no. 3 (Spring 1994): 15–19.

Thomas, Troy. "Interart Analogy: Practice and Theory in Comparing the Arts." *Journal of Aesthetic Education* 25, no. 2 (Summer 1991): 17–36.

STANDARD 8C

Proficient

Understanding relationships between music, the other arts, and disciplines outside the arts:
Students explain ways in which the principles and subject matter of various disciplines
outside the arts are interrelated with those of music.

Strategy

Students have completed assigned readings on curriculum integration. In class, they discuss the interrelationships between music and other disciplines. Then, the instructor distributes the octavo "Simple Gifts" by Aaron Copland, arr. Irving Fine (New York: Boosey & Hawkes), 17115, SATB, Level 3.

The instructor plays three recorded versions of the work: the choral arrangement; a solo version by African-American opera singer William Warfield (see Suggested Resources); and the Copland orchestral composition, *Appalachian Spring*, which incorporates the melody. Students then discuss how to incorporate listening to these works into the high school choral class, specifically to teach concepts of style and arrangement in the music as well as information about the composer, the solo singer, and the historical and cultural context of African Americans in the world of opera.

Students then brainstorm in small groups to devise other ways to teach "Simple Gifts" comprehensively to a high school choir, incorporating not only various aspects of music but also dance/movement (studying history of dance among Shakers, watching ballet *Appalachian Spring*), visual arts (studying Shaker furniture, photo essays), global studies/world geography (locating Shaker settlements and other small, isolated cultures), creative writing (writing an essay), and history (of the Shakers, other religious groups, and Copland).

Suggested Resources

Copland, Aaron. "Simple Gifts," performed by William Warfield. On *Old American Songs*. CBS Masterworks CD MK 42430.

Fogarty, Robin. "Ten Ways to Integrate the Curriculum." *Educational Leadership* 49, no. 2 (October 1991): 61–65.

Gratto, Sharon Davis. "Performance-Based Arts Education: A Study of Music in Inter-Arts Programs for Secondary Students." D.M.A. diss., The Catholic University of America, 1994.

Jacobs, Heidi H., ed. *Interdisciplinary Curriculum: Design and Implementation.* Alexandria, VA: Association for Supervision and Curriculum Development, 1989.

Reimer, Bennett. "A Comprehensive Arts Curriculum Model." *Design for Arts Education* 90, no. 6 (July/August 1989): 2–16.

STANDARD 8D

Advanced

Understanding relationships between music, the other arts, and disciplines outside the arts: Students compare the uses of characteristic elements, artistic processes, and organizational principles among the arts in different historical periods and different cultures.

Strategy

The instructor and methods students have located examples of lullabies from a variety of cultures and times. In class, students examine the lyrics of each lullaby, asking the following questions: Who is singing the lullaby? How does the singer show care and concern for the child? Are there images that seem to recur in several lullabies? What do the lyrics tell you about the time and/or culture from which they emerged?

(continued)

Next, students examine the music of the lullabies, asking: What musical characteristics are common to all of them? Which characteristics are unique to the time and place of origin? The class then examines poems, paintings, or sculpture from a variety of times and cultures that depict the relationship between parents and children. Several examples of these can be found in *Talking to the Sun* (see Suggested Resources). Students discuss the following questions: How is the family bond depicted? Are fathers included? How do time and place influence the representations of the family?

Finally, the class discusses how to transfer this activity to a high school choral class. They consider how they might work with teachers of other arts or of literature to implement the lesson.

Suggested Choral Literature

"A La Nanita Nan," arr. Roger Folstrom. Champaign, IL: Mark Foster Music Company. MF547 SATB. Spanish carol. Level 2.

"Allunde' Alluya" by Salli Terri. New York: Lawson-Gould Music Publishers. 52245. Two-part. African prayer lullaby. Level 2.

"Cape Breton Lullaby" by Kenneth Leslie. Miami: Gordon V. Thompson Music/Warner Bros. Publications. VG327. SSA. Level 4.

"Lullaby, Oh Lullaby!" by Gerald Finzi. New York: Boosey & Hawkes. OCTB6147. Two-part. Level 1.

"Winter's Lullaby" by Malcolm Dalglish. New York: Boosey & Hawkes. OCTB6690. Two-part. Level 2.

Suggested Resource

Koch, Kenneth, and Kate Ferrell. *Talking to the Sun: An Illustrated Anthology of Poems for Young People.* New York: The Metropolitan Museum of Art/Henry Holt, 1985.

STANDARD 8E

Advanced

Understanding relationships between music, the other arts, and disciplines outside the arts: Students explain how the roles of creators, performers, and others involved in the production and presentation of the arts are similar to and different from one another in the various arts.

Strategy

Using American musical theatre or opera as a starting point, methods students develop a list of the various types of artists, designers, composers, arrangers, performers, and technicians needed to create a full production.

The instructor leads a discussion on the role of the composer, designers (set, lighting, and costume), choreographer, and others during the initial phases of a production. They consider how those roles affect the performers of the work. Then, the class examines the way that the performers' interpretive work alters and enhances the creators' original intentions. They also compare this model of creation and performance to that of a visual artist and those who exhibit works of art in a museum, such as curators and technical crews.

To amplify the discussions, the instructor may bring in from the campus or community creators, performers, and those involved behind the scenes to describe their roles and how they interact to bring a full production to life.

The class discusses how they can adapt this lesson for teaching a high school choral class about these relationships.

Suggested Resources

Gratto, Sharon Davis. "Performance-Based Arts Education: A Study of Music in Inter-Arts Programs for Secondary Students." D.M.A. diss., The Catholic University of America, 1994.

Munro, Thomas. *The Arts and Their Interrelations.* Cleveland: The Press of Case Western Reserve, 1967.

◆ ◆ ◆ ◆ ◆ ◆

STANDARD 9A

Proficient

Understanding music in relation to history and culture: *Students classify by genre or style and by historical period or culture unfamiliar but representative aural examples of music and explain the reasoning behind their classifications.*

Strategy

Methods students have each done research on a representative example of choral music. In class, the instructor plays examples of a wide variety of choral music from diverse genres, styles, and cultures and then leads methods students in a discussion focusing on the genre, style, culture, and historical period of the works. Students are encouraged to integrate information from courses in music history, music literature, and world music.

Students then present reports on works they have researched, discussing the style, genre, historical background, and use in the culture in which the works originated. They highlight the vocal and musical requirements of each piece in relation to the capabilities of high school singers.

The instructor divides the methods students into groups and gives each group a packet of sample octavos. Each group classifies the works by genre, style, culture of origin, and historical period. Then, the class discusses the group responses, with representatives from each group explaining the reasoning behind their classifications.

Finally, students discuss how they could adapt this procedure for use in a high school choral class. They consider how such an activity would contribute to comprehensive teaching of choral music.

Suggested Resources

Borroff, Edith. "A New Look at Teaching Music History." *Music Educators Journal* 79, no. 4 (December 1992): 41–43.

Collins, Donald L. *Teaching Choral Music.* Englewood Cliffs, NJ: Prentice-Hall, 1993.

Proficient

Understanding music in relation to history and culture: *Students identify sources of American music genres, trace the evolution of those genres, and cite well-known musicians associated with them.*

Strategy

The instructor presents to methods students two choral jazz arrangements: Duke Ellington's "Satin Doll," arr. Kirby Shaw (Milwaukee: Hal Leonard Corporation), 08745839, SATB, Level 4; and George Gershwin's "S'Wonderful," arr. Phil Mattson (Miami: Warner Bros. Publications), 463-19014, SATB, Level 4. Students discuss Ellington and Gershwin as examples of composer/performers who worked during the same time period but in different genres.

Prior to class, the instructor has compiled a tape that includes early recordings of the pieces, as well as instrumental and solo arrangements and other representative recordings of music by Ellington and Gershwin. The instructor uses the tape in class to demonstrate the type of resource needed for effective listening lessons.

The methods class then designs a "portfolio assignment" on jazz, appropriate for high school choral students. The assignment should include research on the lives of the composers, their influences, and their subsequent impact on popular American music.

Students discuss how similar procedures could be used for a high school choral lesson comparing and contrasting composers and works from musical theatre, gospel, blues, and rock.

Suggested Resources

Dorough, Prince. *Popular-Music Culture in America.* New York: Ardsley House Publishers, 1992.

Gridley, Mark C. *Jazz Styles: History & Analysis,* 3d ed. Englewood Cliffs, NJ: Prentice-Hall, 1988.

Tirro, Frank. *Jazz: A History,* 2d ed. New York: W. W. Norton, 1993.

Williams, Martin, ed. *The Smithsonian Collection of Classic Jazz,* rev. ed. Smithsonian Collection of Classic Jazz RJ 0010.

Proficient

Understanding music in relation to history and culture: *Students identify various roles that musicians perform, cite representative individuals who have functioned in each role, and describe their activities and achievements.*

Strategy

The instructor has invited representatives of the collegiate music faculty that could include a performer, educator, musicologist, composer, or audio technician to take part in a panel discussion during methods class. Local church musicians, private instructors, commercial musicians, and music business representatives might also be invited.

The participants talk to methods students about the history of their discrete profession, their own early musical training, people who influenced their career paths, and specific areas of expertise needed to do their present jobs.

After the panel discussion, students discuss how the same activity could be adapted for use with high school students.

Suggested Resources

Bjorneberg, Paul, ed. *Exploring Careers in Music.* Reston, VA: Music Educators National Conference, 1990.

Cowden, Robert, ed. "Careers in Music." Reston, VA: Music Educators National Conference, 1989. Brochure.

STANDARD 9D

Advanced

Understanding music in relation to history and culture: *Students identify and explain the stylistic features of a given musical work that serve to define its aesthetic tradition and its historical or cultural context.*

Strategy

In class, the instructor leads methods students in singing the octavo "Mata del Anima Sola" by Antonio Estevez (Long Beach, CA: Earthsongs), SATB with tenor solo, Level 5. After singing, they discuss how the composer's use of the soloist, the instrumentally based choral accompaniment, and the text setting provide a musical portrait of the Venezuelan llanos (plains).

The instructor explains that Estevez and the poet Alberto Arvelo Torrealbar are considered to be the leading nationalistic artists of twentieth-century Venezuela. Students note specific examples in the music where this nationalism is apparent (use of dance rhythms from *joropo* [a Venezuelan folk-dance rhythm based on combined 3/4 and 6/8 meters], specific choral syllables imitating native instruments, etc.).

The instructor distributes an octavo that exemplifies the United States—its composers, poets, and indigenous musical forms. Using this octavo, the class discusses how they can develop a lesson for high school choirs that is similar to the one presented by the instructor.

Suggested Resources

Machlis, Joseph. *Introduction to Contemporary Music,* 2d ed. New York: W. W. Norton, 1979.

McIntyre, John. "Twentieth-Century Latin American Choral Music: An Introductory Survey." *Choral Journal* 33, no. 10 (May 1993): 27–37.

Advanced

Understanding music in relation to history and culture: *Students identify and describe music genres or styles that show the influence of two or more cultural traditions, identify the cultural source of each influence, and trace the historical conditions that produced the synthesis of influences.*

Strategy

The instructor leads methods students in a discussion of South African choral music, using the examples "Nkosi, Nkosi" and "Singabahamayo," from *Freedom Is Coming: Songs of Protest and Praise from South Africa* by Anders Nyberg, ed. Henry H. Leck (Fort Lauderdale, FL: Walton Music Corporation), WW1149, three-part, Level 2; WW1174, SAB, Level 2. Although the hymn-like form of these pieces comes from the European Christian missionary songs taught in the nineteenth century, the harmonic and rhythmic treatment of the chorales are distinctly South African.

The class then examines the contrasting uses of the music in each original cultural context (for worship in the Euro-Christian setting and as political protest in the contemporary South African setting). Finally, they discuss how this lesson could be taught effectively to a high school choral class.

Suggested Resources

Campbell, Patricia Shehan. "Christopher Waterman on Yoruba Music of Africa." *Music Educators Journal* 81, no. 6 (May 1995): 35–43. Also in *Music in Cultural Context: Eight Views on World Music Education.* Reston, VA: Music Educators National Conference, 1996.

Kazarow, Patricia. "Contemporary African Choral Art Music: An Intercultural Perspective." *Choral Journal* 33, no. 10 (May 1993): 19–27.

Choral Music

"A La Nanita Nan," arr. Roger Folstrom. Champaign, IL: Mark Foster Music Company. MF547. SATB. Spanish carol. Level 2.

"Allunde' Alluya" by Salli Terri. New York: Lawson-Gould Music Publishers. 52245. Two-part. African prayer lullaby. Level 2.

"Cape Breton Lullaby" by Kenneth Leslie. Miami: Gordon V. Thompson Music/Warner Bros. Publications. VG327. SSA. Level 4.

"Cock-a-doodle-doo!" arr. Betty Bertaux. New York: Boosey & Hawkes. OCTB6480. Two-part treble. Level 2.

"Cum Sancto Spiritu," from *Gloria* by Antonio Vivaldi. Fort Lauderdale, FL: Walton Music Corporation. W2047. SATB. Level 4.

"Do You Hear What I Hear?" arr. Harry Simeone. Delaware Water Gap, PA: Shawnee Press. B218. SATB. Level 3.

"Down a Different Road: The Sea" by Brent Pierce. Fort Lauderdale, FL: Walton Music Corporation. W2915. SATB. Level 5.

"Epitaph for Moonlight" by R. Murray Schafer. Toronto: Berandol Music. BER1094. SSSSAAAA-TTTTBBBB. Level 5.

Freedom Is Coming: Songs of Protest and Praise from South Africa by Anders Nyberg. Edited by Henry H. Leck. Fort Lauderdale, FL: Walton Music Corporation. WW1149, three-part, Level 2; WW1174, SAB, Level 2.

"Gloria Tibi," from *Mass* by Leonard Bernstein. New York: Boosey & Hawkes. OCTB6344. SA with tenor solo and bongos. Level 4.

"The Huron Carol," arr. Steve Schuch. Night Heron Music (267 Center Rd., Hillsboro, NH 03244; phone 603-464-4321). SATB. Level 4.

"J'entends le Moulin" by Donald Patriquin. Long Beach, CA: Earthsongs. S-06. SATB or SA.

"Jubilate Deo" by Michael Praetorius, arr. Doreen Rao. New York: Boosey & Hawkes. OCTB6350. Unison and round. Level 1.

"Last Words of David" by Randall Thompson. Boston: E.C. Schirmer Music Company. 2294. SATB. Level 5.

"Lullaby, Oh Lullaby!" by Gerald Finzi. New York: Boosey & Hawkes. OCTB6147. Two-part. Level 1.

"Mata del Anima Sola" by Antonio Estevez. Long Beach, CA: Earthsongs. SATB with tenor solo. Level 5.

"My Lord" by Joyce Eilers. Milwaukee: Hal Leonard Corporation. 08545500. Three-part. Level 2.

"Now Welcome Summer" by Robert Washburn. New York: Oxford University Press. 95.202. SATB. Level 5.

"O Bone Jesu" by Giovanni Pierluigi Palestrina, arr. Hans Harthan. Bryn Mawr, PA: Theodore Presser Company. 332-03070. SATB. Level 3.

"O Magnum Mysterium" by Tomas Victoria. Milwaukee: Schirmer/Hal Leonard Corporation. 10193. SATB. Level 4.

"Play for Me a Simple Melody" by Irving Berlin, arr. Kirby Shaw. Milwaukee: Hal Leonard Corporation. 0870794. SATB. Level 3.

"Satin Doll" by Duke Ellington, arr. Kirby Shaw. Milwaukee: Hal Leonard Corporation. 08745839. SATB. Level 4.

"Saul" by Egil Hovland. Fort Lauderdale, FL: Walton Music Corporation. WM 126. Mixed chorus with narrator. Level 4.

"Shepherd Me Lord" by G. Kingsley. New York: Bourne Company. 932. SAB. Level 3.

"Simple Gifts" by Aaron Copland, arr. Irving Fine. New York: Boosey & Hawkes. 17115. SATB. Level 3.

"Sing We and Chant It" by Thomas Morley. Milwaukee: Schirmer/Hal Leonard Corporation. 50310800. SATB. Level 3.

"Siyahamba," arr. Doreen Rao. New York: Boosey & Hawkes. OCTB6656. Three-part. Level 2.

"S'Wonderful" by George Gershwin, arr. Phil Mattson. Miami: Warner Bros. Publications. 463-19014. SATB. Level 4.

"Tambur," arr. Lajos Bardos. New York: Boosey & Hawkes. OCTB6055. SATB. Level 4.

Three Hungarian Folk Songs by M. Seiber. Milwaukee: G. Schirmer/Hal Leonard Corporation. OC10715. SATB. Level 3.

"Turtle Dove," arr. Linda Spevacek. Milwaukee: Jenson Publishing/Hal Leonard Corporation. 43720070. Three-part mixed. Level 2.

"The Water Is Wide" by Rene Clausen. Champaign, IL: Mark Foster Music Company. MF3038. SATB. Level 4.

"When Jesus Wept" by William Billings. Milwaukee: Schirmer/Hal Leonard Corporation. 11145. SATB. Level 2.

"Winter's Lullaby" by Malcolm Dalglish. New York: Boosey & Hawkes. OCTB6690. Two-part. Level 2.

Books

Ades, Hawley. *Choral Arranging.* Delaware Water Gap, PA: Shawnee Press, 1966.

*Anderson, Tom. *Sing Choral Music at Sight.* Reston, VA: Music Educators National Conference, 1992.

*Anderson, William M., ed. *Teaching Music with a Multicultural Approach,* 2d ed. Reston, VA: Music Educators National Conference, 1991. Book and videocassettes.

*Anderson, William M., and Patricia Shehan Campbell. *Multicultural Perspectives in Music Education,* 2d ed. Reston, VA: Music Educators National Conference, 1996.

Anderson, William M., and Joy E. Lawrence. *Integrating Music into the Elementary Classroom,* 3d ed. Belmont, CA: Wadsworth Publishing Company, 1995.

Angelou, Maya. *Maya Angelou Poems.* New York: Bantam Books, 1986.

*Atterbury, Betty W., ed. *Elementary General Music: The Best of MEJ.* Reston, VA: Music Educators National Conference, 1992.

Atterbury, Betty W., and Carol P. Richardson. *The Experience of Teaching General Music.* New York: McGraw-Hill, 1995.

Bartle, Jean Ashworth. *Lifeline for Children's Choir Directors,* rev. ed. Miami: Gordon V. Thompson Music/Warner Bros. Publications, 1993.

Bauguess, David Jenson, arr. *Sight Singing Course.* Milwaukee: Jenson Publishing/Hal Leonard Corporation, 1984.

Berger, Melvin. *The Science of Music.* New York: HarperCollins Publishers, 1989.

Biasini, Americole, and Lenore Pogonowski. *MMCP Interaction.* Bellingham, WA: Americole, 1979.

*Bjorneberg, Paul, ed. *Exploring Careers in Music.* Reston, VA: Music Educators National Conference, 1990.

Broughton, Simon, Mark Ellingham, David Muddyman, and Richard Trillo, eds. *Rough World Music.* Bergenfield, NJ: Penguin USA, 1994.

Burakoff, Gerald and Sonya. *Introducing the Recorder: Information and Guidelines for Teachers.* Jackson, NJ: American Recorder Society, 1993.

Burton, J. Bryan. *Moving within the Circle: Contemporary Native American Music and Dance.* Danbury, CT: World Music Press, 1993. Book and audiocassette.

Cacavas, John. *The Art of Writing Music.* Van Nuys, CA: Alfred Publishing Company. 1993.

Campbell, Patricia Shehan. *Lessons from the World.* Old Tappan, NJ: Schirmer Books/Simon & Schuster, 1991.

*———. *Music in Cultural Context: Eight Views on World Music Education.* Reston, VA: Music Educators National Conference, 1996.

Campbell, Patricia Shehan, and Carol Scott-Kassner. *Music in Childhood: From Preschool through the Elementary Grades.* Old Tappan, NJ: Schirmer Books/Simon & Schuster, 1995.

Campbell, Patricia Shehan, Ellen McCullough-Brabson, and Judith Cook Tucker. *Roots and Branches: A Legacy of Multicultural Music for Children.* Danbury, CT: World Music Press, 1994. Book and recording.

Choksy, Lois. *The Kodály Context.* Englewood Cliffs, NJ: Prentice-Hall, 1981.

———. *Teaching Music Effectively in the Elementary School.* Englewood Cliffs, NJ: Prentice-Hall, 1991.

Choksy, Lois, Robert M. Abramson, Avon E. Gillespie, and David Woods. *Teaching Music in the Twentieth Century.* Englewood Cliffs, NJ: Prentice-Hall, 1986.

**Choral Music Packet: Supplement to Teaching Choral Music.* Reston, VA: Music Educators National Conference, 1991.

Chuska, Kenneth R. *Teaching the Process of Thinking, K–12.* Bloomington, IN: Phi Delta Kappa Educational Foundation, 1986.

Collins, Donald L. *Teaching Choral Music.* Englewood Cliffs, NJ: Prentice-Hall, 1993.

*Colwell, Richard, ed. *Handbook of Research on Music Teaching and Learning.* Old Tappan, NJ: Schirmer Books/Simon & Schuster, 1992.

Cope, David. *New Music Notation.* Dubuque, IA: Kendall/Hunt Publishing, 1976.

Copland, Aaron. *What to Listen for in Music.* New York: McGraw-Hill, 1939.

Crafts, Susan D., Daniel Cavicchi, Charles Keil, and the Music in Daily Life Project. *My Music.* Hanover, NH: Wesleyan University Press, 1993.

Crocker, Emily, and Joyce Eilers. *The Choral Approach to Sight-Singing.* Milwaukee: Jenson Publishing/ Hal Leonard Corporation, 1990.

Decker, Harold A., and Julius Herford. *Choral Conducting Symposium,* 2d ed. Englewood Cliffs, NJ: Prentice-Hall, 1987.

Decker, Harold A., and Colleen J. Kirk. *Choral Conducting: Focus on Communication.* Prospect Heights, IL: Waveland Press, 1988.

Dorough, Prince. *Popular-Music Culture in America.* New York: Ardsley House Publishers, 1992.

Durland, Frances Caldwell. *Creative Dramatics for Children.* Kent, OH: Kent State University Press, 1975.

Elliott, David J. *Music Matters: A New Philosophy of Music Education.* New York: Oxford University Press, 1995.

Erdei, Peter. *150 American Folk Songs to Sing, Read and Play.* New York: Boosey & Hawkes, 1974.

Finn, W. J. *The Art of the Choral Conductor.* Boston: C.C. Birchard, 1939.

Fowler, Charles, ed. *Sing!* Houston: Hinshaw Music Textbook, 1988.

Frazee, Jane. *Discovering Orff: A Curriculum for Music Teachers.* Paoli, PA: Schott/European American, 1987.

Fulghum, Robert. *From Beginning to End: The Rituals of Our Lives.* New York: Villard Books, 1995.

Garretson, Robert L. *Choral Music: History, Style, and Performance Practice.* Englewood Cliffs, NJ: Prentice-Hall, 1993.

———. *Conducting Choral Music,* 7th ed. Englewood Cliffs, NJ: Prentice-Hall, 1993.

Gelineau, R. Phyllis. *Experiences in Music,* 3d ed. Englewood Cliffs, NJ: Prentice-Hall, 1995.

Goodman, Nelson. *Languages of Art: An Approach to a Theory of Symbols.* Indianapolis: Hackett Publishing Company, 1976.

Gordon, Edwin. *Learning Sequences in Music: Skill, Content, and Patterns.* Chicago, IL: GIA Publications, 1993.

Gridley, Mark C. *Jazz Styles: History & Analysis,* 3d ed. Englewood Cliffs, NJ: Prentice-Hall, 1988.

Grunow, Richard, and Lois Fargo. *The Choral Score Reading Program.* Chicago: GIA Publications, 1983. Book and audiocassette.

Hackett, Patricia. *The Melody Book: 300 Selections from the World of Music for Autoharp, Guitar, Piano, Recorder and Voice,* 2d ed. Englewood Cliffs, NJ: Prentice-Hall, 1992.

Hackett, Patricia, and Carolynn A. Lindeman. *The Musical Classroom: Backgrounds, Models, and Skills for Elementary Teaching,* 4th ed. Englewood Cliffs, NJ: Prentice-Hall, 1997.

*Hamann, Donald L., ed. *Creativity in the Music Classroom: The Best of* MEJ. Reston, VA: Music Educators National Conference, 1991.

Hausmann, Charles S., Hunter C. March, Samuel D. Miller, and Betty G. Roe, eds. *World of Choral Music.* Parsippany, NJ: Silver Burdett Ginn, 1988.

Heffernan, Charles W. *Choral Music.* Englewood Cliffs, NJ: Prentice-Hall, 1982.

Herman, Sally. *Building a Pyramid of Musicianship.* San Diego, CA: Neil A. Kjos Music Company, 1988.

Hoffer, Charles. *Teaching Music in the Secondary Schools*, 4th ed. Belmont, CA: Wadsworth Publishing Company, 1991.

Hughes, Langston. *Selected Poems of Langston Hughes*. New York: Knopf, 1977.

Hylton, John B. *Comprehensive Choral Music Education*. Englewood Cliffs, NJ: Prentice-Hall, 1995.

Jacobs, Heidi H., ed. *Interdisciplinary Curriculum: Design and Implementation*. Alexandria, VA: Association for Supervision and Curriculum Development, 1989.

Johnson, Tony. *Philosophy for Children: An Approach to Critical Thinking*. Bloomington, IN: Phi Delta Kappa Educational Foundation, 1984.

Jones, Bessie, and Bess Lomax Hawes. *Step It Down: Games, Plays, Songs, and Stories from the Afro-American Heritage*. Athens, GA: University of Georgia Press, 1987.

Kemp, Helen. *Of Primary Importance*. Dayton, OH: The Lorenz Corporation, 1989.

Koch, Kenneth, and Kate Ferrell. *Talking to the Sun: An Illustrated Anthology of Poems for Young People*. New York: The Metropolitan Museum of Art/Henry Holt, 1985.

Kohut, Daniel L., and Joe Grant. *Learning to Conduct and Rehearse*. Englewood Cliffs, NJ: Prentice-Hall, 1990.

Lamb, Gordon. *Choral Techniques*, 3d ed. Columbus, OH: Wm. C. Brown Communications/McGraw-Hill, 1988.

Lautzenheiser, Tim. *The Art of Successful Teaching*. Chicago: GIA Publications, 1992.

Locke, Eleanor. *Sail Away: 155 American Folk Songs*. New York: Boosey & Hawkes, 1989.

Machlis, Joseph. *Introduction to Contemporary Music*, 2d ed. New York: W. W. Norton, 1979.

May, William V., ed. *Something New to Sing About*, Level II. Mission Hills, CA: Glencoe/McGraw-Hill, 1989.

*May, William V., and Craig Tolin. *Pronunciation Guide for Choral Literature*. Reston, VA: Music Educators National Conference, 1987.

McRae, Shirley, W. *Directing the Children's Choir*. Old Tappan, NJ: Schirmer Books/Simon & Schuster, 1991.

Meek, Bill. *Moon Penny: A Collection of Rhymes, Songs and Play-verse for and by Children*. Cork, Ireland: Ossian Publications, 1985.

*MENC Task Force on Choral Music Course of Study. *Teaching Choral Music: A Course of Study*. Reston, VA: Music Educators National Conference, 1991.

Merriam, Alan P. *The Anthropology of Music*. Evanston, IL: Northwestern University Press, 1964.

Munro, Thomas. *The Arts and Their Interrelations*. Cleveland: The Press of Case Western Reserve, 1967.

The Music Connection, Grades K–8. Parsippany, NJ: Silver Burdett Ginn, 1995.

Music and You, Grades K–8. New York: Macmillan/McGraw-Hill, 1991.

Nash, Grace, Geraldine Jones, Barbara Potter, and Patsy Smith. *Do It My Way*. Van Nuys, CA: Alfred Publishing Company, 1977.

Nesheim, Paul, and Weston Noble. *Building Beautiful Voices*. Dayton, OH: Roger Dean/The Lorenz Corporation, 1995.

New York State School Music Association. *NYSSMA Manual of Graded Solo and Ensemble Music.* Westbury, NY: NYSSMA, 1991.

Nketia, Joseph H. K. *Music of Africa.* New York: W. W. Norton, 1974.

O'Brien, James P. *Teaching Music.* Fort Worth, TX: Holt, Rinehart & Winston, 1983.

Ostrander, Arthur. *Contemporary Choral Arranging.* Englewood Cliffs, NJ: Prentice-Hall, 1986.

Paynter, John J. *Sound and Structure.* New York: Cambridge University Press, 1992.

Phillips, Kenneth H. *Teaching Kids to Sing.* Old Tappan, NJ: Schirmer Books/Simon & Schuster, 1992.

Prescribed Music List. Austin, TX: University Interscholastic League, 1995.

Randel, Don Michael, ed. *The New Harvard Dictionary of Music.* Cambridge: Belknap Press of Harvard University Press, 1986.

Rao, Doreen. *The Artist in Every Child.* New York: Boosey & Hawkes, 1987.

———. *The Young Singing Voice.* New York: Boosey & Hawkes, 1987.

Regner, Hermann, ed. *Music for Children: Orff-Schulwerk, American Edition.* Vol. 1, *Preschool;* vol. 2, *Primary,* 2d ed. Paoli, PA: Schott/European American. 1982; 1991.

Reimer, Bennett. *A Philosophy of Music Education,* 2d ed. Englewood Cliffs, NJ: Prentice-Hall, 1989.

Roach, Donald. *Complete Secondary Choral Music Guide.* Englewood Cliffs, NJ: Center for Applied Research and Education/Simon & Schuster, 1990.

Robinson, Ray, and Allen Winold. *The Choral Experience: Literature, Materials, and Methods.* Prospect Heights, IL: Waveland Press, 1992.

Rozmajzl, Michon, and Rene Boyer-White. *Music Fundamentals, Methods and Materials for the Elementary Classroom Teacher,* 2d ed. White Plains, NY: Longman Publishing Group, 1995.

Saliba, Konnie K. *Accent on Orff: An Introductory Approach.* Englewood Cliffs, NJ: Prentice-Hall, 1991.

Sawyer, Ruth. *The Way of the Storyteller.* New York: Viking Press, 1962.

Schafer, R. Murray. *Creative Music Education.* New York: Schirmer Books, 1976.

Schmid, Will, ed. *Something to Sing About,* Level I. Mission Hills, CA: Glencoe/McGraw-Hill, 1989.

Share the Music, Grades K–8. New York: Macmillan/McGraw-Hill, 1995, 1997.

Slobin, Mark. *Subcultural Sounds: Micromusics of the West.* Hanover, NH: Wesleyan University Press, 1993.

Snyder, Audrey. *The Sight-Singer.* Miami: Warner Bros. Publications, 1993.

Southern, Eileen. *The Music of Black Americans,* 3d ed. New York: W. W. Norton, 1997.

Stone, Kurt. *Music Notation in the 20th Century.* New York: W. W. Norton, 1980.

Swears, Linda. *Teaching the Elementary School Chorus.* Old Tappan, NJ: Prentice-Hall, 1985.

Tacka, Philip, and Michael Houlahan. *Sound Thinking.* Vol. 1. New York: Boosey & Hawkes, 1995.

Telfer, Nancy. *Successful Sight-Singing: A Creative, Step-by-Step Approach.* San Diego: Neil A. Kjos Music Company, 1992.

Tirro, Frank. *Jazz: A History,* 2d ed. New York: W. W. Norton, 1993.

Titon, Jeff Todd, ed. *Worlds of Music: An Introduction to the Music of the World's Peoples,* 3d ed. Old Tappan, NJ: Schirmer Books/Simon & Schuster, 1996. Book and recordings.

Upitis, Rena. *This Too Is Music.* Portsmouth, NH: Heinemann Educational Books, 1990.

Warner, Brigitte. *Orff-Schulwerk: Applications for the Classroom.* Englewood Cliffs, NJ: Prentice-Hall, 1991.

Webb, Guy, ed. *Up Front! Becoming the Complete Choral Conductor.* Boston: E. C. Schirmer Music Company, 1993.

*Wiggins, Jackie. *Composition in the Classroom: A Tool for Teaching.* Reston, VA: Music Educators National Conference, 1990.

Winner, Ellen. *Invented Worlds: The Psychology of the Arts.* 1982. Reprint, Cambridge: Harvard University Press, 1985.

Winslow, Robert W., and Leon Dallin. *Music Skills for the Classroom Teacher,* 8th ed. Columbus, OH: Wm. C. Brown Communications/McGraw-Hill, 1991.

The World of Music, Grades K–8. Parsippany, NJ: Silver Burdett Ginn, 1991.

Children's Literature

Bulla, Clyde Robert. *What Makes a Shadow?* New York: Crowell, 1962.

Cowcher, Helen. *Rain Forest.* New York: Farrar, Strauss, and Giroux, 1988.

Freeman, Don. *A Rainbow of My Own.* New York: Viking Press, 1966.

Keats, Ezra Jack. *Regards to the Man in the Moon.* New York: Four Winds Press, 1981.

Lowry, Lois. *The Giver.* Boston: Houghton-Mifflin, 1993.

————. *Number the Stars.* Boston: Houghton-Mifflin, 1993.

Martin, Bill, and John Archambault. *Chicka Chicka Boom Boom.* New York: Simon & Schuster Books for Young Readers, 1989.

McNulty, Faith. *How to Dig a Hole to the Other Side of the World.* New York: HarperCollins Publishers, 1990.

Myers, Walter Dean. *The Mouse Rap.* New York: HarperCollins Publishers, 1990.

Servozo, Mary. *Rain Talk.* New York: Margaret K. McElderry Books, 1990.

Showers, Paul. *The Listening Walk.* New York: Crowell, 1961.

Silverstein, Shel. *Where the Sidewalk Ends.* New York: HarperCollins Publishers, 1974.

Vozar, David. *Yo, Hungry Wolf!* New York: Doubleday Books for Young Readers, 1993.

Periodicals

Arts Education Policy Review (formerly *Design for Arts Education*), Heldref Publications, 1319 18th Street NW, Washington, DC 20036-1802.

Choral Journal, American Choral Directors Association, PO Box 6310, Lawton, OK 73506.

Educational Leadership, Association for Supervision and Curriculum Development, 1250 N. Pitt Street, Alexandria, VA 22314-1453.

General Music Today, Music Educators National Conference, 1806 Robert Fulton Drive, Reston, VA 20191.

Jazz Educators Journal, International Association of Jazz Educators, 2803 Claflin Road, Manhattan, KS 66502.

Journal of Aesthetic Education, University of Illinois Press, 1325 S. Oak Street, Champaign, IL 61820.

Journal of Music Theory Pedagogy, School of Music, University of Oklahoma, Norman, OK 73019.

**Journal of Research in Music Education,* Music Educators National Conference, 1806 Robert Fulton Drive, Reston, VA 20191.

**Music Educators Journal,* Music Educators National Conference, 1806 Robert Fulton Drive, Reston, VA 20191.

**Teaching Music,* Music Educators National Conference, 1806 Robert Fulton Drive, Reston, VA 20191.

**Update: Applications of Research in Music Education,* Music Educators National Conference, 1806 Robert Fulton Drive, Reston, VA 20191.

Recordings

Africa: Ancient Ceremonies. Produced by Stephen Jay. Elektra Nonesuch 972082-2.

Bergin, Mary. *Feadóga Stáin 2.* Shanachie 79083.

Bernstein, Leonard. *Mass.* Norman Scribner, L. Bernstein, Berkshire Boys' Choirs. CBS M2K 44593.

Billings, William. *William Billings: The Continental Harmonist.* Gregg Smith Singers. Premier PRCD 1008.

Copland, Aaron. *Old American Songs.* CBS Masterworks CD MK 42430.

Jubilation! Great Gospel Performances. Vol. 1, *Black Gospel.* Edwin Hawkins' Singers. Rhino Entertainment R2 70288.

Ladysmith Black Mambazo. Warner Bros. Recordings 9 25582-2.

Native American Traditions—Music of New Mexico. Smithsonian/Folkways SF-40408.

Nordisk Sang. Produced by Han Wendl. New Albion Records NA 031.

Sweet Honey in the Rock. *Feel Something Drawing Me On.* Flying Fish FF 70375.

———. *Breaths.* Flying Fish 70105.

Warren, Mervyn, Michael O. Jackson, and Mark Kibble, arr. *Handel's Messiah: A Soulful Celebration.* Warner Alliance 26980.

Williams, Martin, ed. *The Smithsonian Collection of Classic Jazz,* rev. ed. Smithsonian Collection of Classic Jazz RJ 0010.

Videotapes

Abramson, Robert M. *Dalcroze Eurhythmics.* Chicago: GIA Publications, 1992.

Adams, Charlotte. *Daily Workout for a Beautiful Voice.* Santa Barbara, CA: Santa Barbara Music Publishing, 1991.

American Odyssey. Cleveland, OH: American Orff-Schulwerk Association, 1979.

*Jordanoff, Christine, and Robert Page. *The Choral Triad Video Workshop.* Produced by QED Communications. Reston, VA: Music Educators National Conference, 1994. Book and six videocassettes.

Sing! Move! Listen! Music and Young Children. Reston, VA: Music Educators National Conference, 1993.

Computer Programs

Deluxe Music Construction Set. Petaluma, CA: Electronic Arts Productions, 1990. Amiga.

Encore. Half Moon Bay, CA: Passport Designs, 1989. IBM or Macintosh.

Finale. Eden Prairie, MN: Coda Music Technology, 1990. IBM or Macintosh.

Songworks. Kirkland, WA: Ars Nova, 1993. Macintosh.

Other Resources

*Cowden, Robert, ed. "Careers in Music." Reston, VA: Music Educators National Conference, 1989. Brochure.

Gratto, Sharon Davis. "Performance-Based Arts Education: A Study of Music in Inter-Arts Programs for Secondary Students." D.M.A. diss., The Catholic University of America, 1994.

---

*Available from MENC.

INSTRUMENTAL MUSIC

Section compiled and edited by:

John Grashel

INTRODUCTION

The content and achievement standards for music in *National Standards for Arts Education* provide instrumental music educators with a sound framework on which to build innovative and effective instructional programs in their classrooms and rehearsal halls. Because the public often perceives school performing groups as more functional or entertaining than educational, band and orchestra directors have too often structured pedagogical efforts around the performance aspects of their ensembles. Such a position might be a viable one for conductors of professional organizations, for which the mission is to develop a product for musical consumers. Those conductors might be relatively confident that knowledge and skills specified in the National Standards have been assimilated by the participating musicians. Music educators, however, given the task of educating young musicians in elementary, middle, and high schools, must attend to the responsibility of providing instruction that ensures that basic musical competencies are achieved.

This obligation will shift the focus of many current instrumental programs, but such an approach will compel band and orchestra directors to implement, teach, evaluate, and assess musical learnings identified as critical by colleagues in the music education enterprise. It will also provide the opportunity for music to be viewed as a truly essential and basic curricular entity in American schools.

Together with the *Strategies for Teaching* books designed for use in the instrumental classroom, this section of the *Guide for Music Methods Classes* provides an excellent library of resources and strategies. The strategies presented here offer a unique opportunity for instrumental methods instructors to prepare preservice teachers for implementing the standards. It is important to realize, though, that these strategies serve only as illustrations; they are not intended to be prescriptive or formulaic. College methods instructors should adapt them as necessary to accommodate the various ways in which material is presented throughout higher education. Most important, instrumental methods instructors should realize that they have an obligation to the profession in making prospective instrumental music educators aware of the comprehensive nature of the standards and the opportunities they offer for securing music education's prominent position in the educational hierarchy.

Appreciation is extended to the many college and university instrumental music educators who answered the call to submit instructional strategies for this project. Without their efforts, this project would not have been possible.

—John Grashel

INSTRUMENTAL MUSIC
GRADES 5–8

STANDARD 1A

Singing, alone and with others, a varied repertoire of music: Students sing accurately and with
good breath control throughout their singing ranges, alone and in small and large ensembles.

Strategy

As part of their exploration of the content and approaches of beginning and intermediate instrumental
method books, methods students, as an ensemble, sing selected excerpts from the books. Students may
use a neutral syllable, such as "la," or solfège syllables. When investigating string methods, it may be
useful for students to sing "down," "up," and so forth, according to the desired bowing. The instructor
encourages attention to tone quality, proper breathing techniques, and intonation.

After reading the exercises, students discuss how they would use this technique to help instrumental
students in grades 5–8 improve tone quality and intonation and use proper breathing techniques for
singing. They also discuss how it would improve intonation on instruments and promote proper
breathing in playing wind instruments.

Suggested Resource

Colwell, Richard J., and Thomas Goolsby. *The Teaching of Instrumental Music,* 2d ed. Englewood
Cliffs, NJ: Prentice Hall, 1992.

STANDARD 1B

Singing, alone and with others, a varied repertoire of music: Students sing with expression
and technical accuracy a repertoire of vocal literature with a level of difficulty of 2,
on a scale of 1 to 6, including some songs performed from memory.

Strategy

The instructor has selected several scores with a level of difficulty of 2 from the New York and Virginia
instrumental lists (see Suggested Resources) and scores for the same tunes (not necessarily identical
arrangements) with a level of difficulty of 2 from the New York choral lists. As a choral ensemble,
methods students sightsing the choral works accurately and expressively. Students then form an instrumental ensemble, playing their secondary instruments, and perform the corresponding instrumental
works with expression and technical accuracy.

The instructor leads a discussion of similarities and differences between the instrumental and choral
arrangements. Then the class discusses how programming both the instrumental and choral versions of
a selected piece can enhance middle school concerts.

Suggested Resources

Berg, C. Sidney, ed. (for Virginia Band and Orchestra Directors Association/Virginia Music Educators
Association). *The Director's Guide to Contest and Festival Music.* Bandworld Magazine/WIBC (407
Terrace St., Ashland, OR 97520; phone 800-247-2263), 1995.

(continued)

Mayer, Frederick R., ed. *The String Orchestra Super List.* Reston, VA: Music Educators National Conference, 1993.

New York State School Music Association. *NYSSMA Manual of Graded Solo and Ensemble Music.* Westbury, NY: NYSSMA, 1991.

STANDARD 1C

Singing, alone and with others, a varied repertoire of music: Students sing music representing diverse genres and cultures, with expression appropriate for the work being performed.

Strategy

The instructor has assigned methods students to select music, appropriate for grades 5–8 instrumental ensembles, that contains folk songs from various cultures. Suitable band works include "Korean Folk Song," arr. Ralph Gingery (Newington, VA: William Allen Music), FCB182, Level 2½, which is based on the folk song "Arirang"; or "Arabian Suite," arr. Paul Jennings (Milwaukee: Hal Leonard Corporation), 26625026, Level 3, which includes the folk songs "Baladi," "Tafta hindi," and "Walking Song." As part of the assignment, students have found the lyrics for the folk songs contained in their selected pieces.

The instructor asks students to create lessons for middle-level instrumental ensembles in which ensemble members would sing with appropriate expression melodies of folk songs contained in selected works as a means of adding this dimension to a performance. Methods students discuss the extent to which expressive singing may substitute for or add to instrumental performance. Working together, they develop rehearsal procedures for teaching the selected pieces.

The class discusses the extent to which they may use performance techniques characteristic of the culture when using folk songs from non-Western cultures. Students present their findings to the class and place written materials from this project in their portfolios.

Suggested Resources

Anderson, William M., ed. *Teaching Music with a Multicultural Approach.* Reston, VA: Music Educators National Conference, 1990. Book and videocassettes.

"Arirang." In *The Music Connection,* Grade 5 (Parsippany, NJ: Silver Burdett Ginn, 1995); or *Share the Music,* Grade 5 (New York: Macmillan/McGraw-Hill, 1995).

"Baladi." In *Musica Arabia* by Alice Olson. Coralville, IA: Alice Olson Publications/West Music, 1987.

Crocker, Emily, and John Leavitt. *Essential Musicianship,* book 1. Milwaukee: Hal Leonard Corporation, 1995.

"Tafta Hindi." In *Share the Music,* Grade 5; *The World of Music,* Grade 2 (Parsippany, NJ: Silver Burdett Ginn, 1991); or *Musica Arabia* by Alice Olson.

"Walking Music." In *Musica Arabia* by Alice Olson.

◆ ◆ ◆ ◆ ◆ ◆ ◆

STANDARD 2A

Performing on instruments, alone and with others, a varied repertoire of music: Students perform on at least one instrument accurately and independently, alone and in small and large ensembles, with good posture, good playing position, and good breath, bow, or stick control.

Strategy

The instructor assigns methods students the task of designing a sequence of lessons for the beginning instrumental student's first month of instruction. To develop the lessons, methods students work in groups (single reeds, double reeds, flutes, high brass, low brass, pitched percussion, and unpitched percussion), each group being responsible for appropriate strategies for the instruments in its category.

The sequenced lessons should address good posture, good playing position, and good breath, bow, or stick control, including when to introduce each aspect of tone production, methods of introducing information (including appropriate vocabulary level), and the means for monitoring and assessing student progress. One member from each group presents a first lesson for a specific instrument, using another class member as a model beginning student. The instructor asks each group to copy its lessons and distribute them to other groups so that the entire class can use them in field situations or in future teaching of beginning students.

Suggested Resources

Cook, Gary. "Training the Beginning Percussionist." In *Teaching Percussion,* 2d ed. New York: Schirmer Books/Simon & Schuster, 1996.

Hunt, Norman J. *A Guide to Teaching Brass,* 5th ed. Columbus, OH: Wm. C. Brown Communications/McGraw-Hill, 1993.

Lamb, Norman, and Susan Lamb Cook. *Guide to Teaching Strings,* 6th ed. Columbus, OH: Wm. C. Brown Communications/McGraw-Hill, 1993.

McCabe, Donald. "Teaching Procedures and Techniques." In *ASBDA Curriculum Guide: A Reference for School Band Directors.* Miami: Warner Bros. Publications, 1973.

Westphal, Frederick. *A Guide to Teaching Woodwinds,* 5th ed. Columbus, OH: Wm. C. Brown Communications/McGraw-Hill, 1989.

STANDARD 2B

Performing on instruments, alone and with others, a varied repertoire of music: Students perform with expression and technical accuracy on at least one string, wind, percussion, or classroom instrument a repertoire of instrumental literature with a level of difficulty of 2, on a scale of 1 to 6.

Strategy

As part of an ongoing project to develop knowledge of large instrumental ensemble literature appropriate for grades 5–8, the instructor has divided the methods class into groups and has asked each group to choose a level 2 piece for middle school or junior high school band or orchestra. In class, the

(continued)

instructor asks each group to create a sequence of lessons leading middle-level students from first reading of the piece to final performance in a concert or festival. The instructor provides methods students with a checklist based on the proposed sequence, encouraging students to use all steps on the list. Lessons should focus on an accurate and expressive performance and include instructions for sightreading the piece, a sequence of practice to learn the piece, a schedule of lessons and assigned sections of the piece for each lesson, and a means for monitoring and assessing student progress.

With methods students performing as an ensemble on their secondary instruments, students from each group take turns as the teacher to demonstrate lessons, with particular attention to technical accuracy and expressive playing of the selected pieces. Methods students add the selected pieces to their portfolio repertoire lists, and they place the lessons, along with comments from the class discussion, in their portfolios for future reflection.

Suggested Resources

Dvorak, Thomas L., Cynthia Crump Taggart, and Peter Schmalz. *Best Music for Young Band: A Selective Guide to the Young Band/Young Wind Ensemble Repertoire.* Edited by Bob Margolis. Manhattan Beach Music (1595 East 46th St., Brooklyn, NY 11234-3122; phone 718-338-4137), 1986.

Klotman, Robert H. *Teaching Strings: Technique and Pedagogy,* 2d ed. New York: Schirmer Books/ Simon & Schuster, 1996.

Lamb, Norman, and Susan Lamb Cook. *Guide to Teaching Strings,* 6th ed. Columbus, OH: Wm. C. Brown Communications/McGraw-Hill, 1993.

Smith, Norman E., and Albert J. Stoutamire. *Band Music Notes.* Lake Charles, LA: Program Note Press, 1982.

STANDARD 2C

Performing on instruments, alone and with others, a varied repertoire of music: Students perform music representing diverse genres and cultures, with expression appropriate for the work being performed.

Strategy

Previously, working in groups, methods students have selected music for a middle-school band concert, including music representing various cultures (e.g., Quincy C. Hilliard's "Variations on an African Hymn Song" (Oskaloosa, IA: C. L. Barnhouse), 012-2607, Level 3½. In class, students work in the same groups to develop specific plans for an instructional unit based on the selected works. The instructor notes that the groups' units should deal with cultural background and instrumentation, and they should enhance middle-level ensemble members understanding of style and tone color appropriate for the selected works. After developing the units, methods students form an ensemble on their secondary instruments, and a student from each group presents a selected plan from the group's unit as a microteaching experience.

Suggested Resources

Anderson, William M., ed. *Teaching Music with a Multicultural Approach.* Reston, VA: Music Educators National Conference, 1990. Book and videocassettes.

Brown, Thomas A. *Afro-Latin Rhythm Dictionary: A Complete Dictionary for All Musicians.* Van Nuys, CA: Alfred Publishing Company, 1984.

Jessup, Lynne E. *All Hands On.* Danbury, CT: World Music Press, 1996.

Nketia, Joseph H. K. *Music of Africa.* New York: W. W. Norton, 1974.

◆ ◆ ◆ ◆ ◆ ◆ ◆

STANDARD 3A

Improvising melodies, variations, and accompaniments: Students improvise simple harmonic accompaniments.

Strategy

The instructor plays for methods students a recording of a folk song or a currently popular country or rock tune that has a simple and predictable harmonic progression. By ear, students perform along with the music to find chord notes that fit the harmony. Using the chord notes, each student then improvises on his or her major instrument a simple ostinato appropriate for students in grades 5–8. Then each methods student writes out the ostinato he or she has created.

On repeated playing of the recording, students improvise and then write out a second voice for their ostinato accompaniments. Once students have completed their accompaniments, the instructor selects a student to play his or her ostinato accompaniment while another student, on an appropriate instrument, plays the accompaniment for a second voice created by the selected student. The instructor then assigns some students to play each of the accompaniment parts, and students play the complete accompaniment with the recording.

Students discuss how they would modify these procedures for use in the middle-level instrumental classroom.

Suggested Resources

Corpolongo, Richard. "The Foundation of Improvisation." *The Instrumentalist* 49, no. 7 (February 1995): 60–65.

Winslow, Robert W., and Leon Dallin. "Creating Music." In *Music Skills for the Classroom Teacher*, 8th ed. Columbus, OH: Wm. C. Brown Communications/McGraw-Hill, 1991.

STANDARD 3C

Improvising melodies, variations, and accompaniments: Students improvise short melodies, unaccompanied and over given rhythmic accompaniments, each in a consistent style, meter, and tonality.

Strategy

Methods students have completed assigned readings about the Orff approach to music teaching. In class, they suggest ways in which they could teach middle-level students in a beginning instrumental

(continued)

class to improvise short melodies. As part of an exploration of different ways in which an instrumental teacher can use the pentatonic scale for teaching students to improvise, the instructor leads methods students in a demonstration of question-and-answer melodic techniques.

The instructor asks each student to compose a short (four-measure) "question" (antecedent) to use for this activity. A selected student then sings his or her "question" and asks the class first to sing it back and then to play it on their instruments. The class then plays the antecedent and, one at a time, students improvise an "answer" (consequent) based on the pentatonic scale.

After the improvisations, the class discusses how they would use a similar procedure in teaching middle-level students to improvise answers to pentatonic questions. They discuss varying the level of difficulty of the exercise and how they would evaluate students' improvisations.

Suggested Resources

Campbell, Patricia Shehan. "Unveiling the Mysteries of Musical Spontaneity." *Music Educators Journal* 78, no. 4 (December 1991): 21–25.

Choksy, Lois, Robert M. Abramson, Avon E. Gillespie, and David Woods. *Teaching Music in the Twentieth Century.* Englewood Cliffs, NJ: Prentice-Hall, 1986.

Frazee, Jane. *Discovering Orff: A Curriculum for Music Teachers.* Paoli, PA: Schott/European American, 1987.

Orff, Carl, and Gunild Keetman. *Music for Children—Vol. I, Pentatonic.* English version adapted by Margaret Murray. Paoli, PA: Schott/European American, 1982.

◆ ◆ ◆ ◆ ◆ ◆ ◆

STANDARD 4A

Composing and arranging music within specified guidelines: Students compose short pieces within specified guidelines, demonstrating how the elements of music are used to achieve unity and variety, tension and release, and balance.

Strategy

The instructor forms the methods class into a band and introduces Clifton Williams's "Variation Overture" (Cleveland: Ludwig Music Publishing Company), SBS100, Level 3, or another middle-level band piece that uses theme-and-variations compositional techniques.

The class sightreads "Variation Overture" from measure 73 to measure 101. The instructor then calls students' attention to that passage in the score, noting Williams's use of the first five notes of the E♭ scale. Students analyze and discuss the composer's use of this melodic material.

The instructor asks students to compose—as Williams did—an eight-measure melody in 4/4 meter using only the notes E♭, F, G, A♭, and B♭. Students' compositions should include repetition and contrast, tension and release, and symmetry and balance.

Student volunteers then perform their compositions while the ensemble plays the chordal accompaniment from measure 73 to measure 81 of "Variation Overture." The instructor records the performances, and, after listening to each one, students discuss how the elements of music were used in each composition.

The class discusses how they would need to expand these procedures in teaching students in grades 5–8. Finally, they begin a list of other middle-level band literature that uses theme-and-variations compositional techniques.

Suggested Resources

Grashel, John W. "An Integrated Approach to Comprehensive Musicianship." *Music Educators Journal* 79, no. 8 (April 1993): 38–41.

Labuta, Joseph A. *Teaching Musicianship in the High School Band*, rev. ed. Fort Lauderdale, FL: Meredith Music Publications, 1997.

STANDARD 4B

Composing and arranging music within specified guidelines: Students arrange simple pieces for voices or instruments other than those for which the pieces were written.

Strategy

The instructor has selected James Curnow's "African Sketches" (Milwaukee: Hal Leonard Corporation), 861706, Level 2, and John Higgins, "Serengeti, an African Rhapsody" (Milwaukee: Jenson Publishing/ Hal Leonard Corporation), 25519010, Level 3, or other middle-level band music in which parts could be arranged for African instruments. Playing on their secondary instruments, the class reads through the selected pieces. Then the instructor initiates a discussion with the methods class about how to incorporate African instruments into band performances by arranging percussion parts from concert band scores for an ensemble of African instruments.

Either the instructor or some students demonstrate the playing of African instruments. The class discusses the examples, including performance techniques, and determines appropriate substitutions for standard percussion instruments. Then students discuss and list procedures for teaching middle-level students the skills necessary to arrange works for African instruments.

Students place written procedures in their portfolios for their reference in future teaching experiences.

Suggested Resources

Anderson, William M., ed. *Teaching Music with a Multicultural Approach.* Reston, VA: Music Educators National Conference, 1990. Book and videocassettes.

Jessup, Lynne E. *All Hands On.* Danbury, CT: World Music Press, 1996.

Nketia, Joseph H. K. *Music of Africa.* New York: W. W. Norton, 1974.

Sands, Rosita. "What Prospective Music Teachers Need to Know about Black Music." *Black Music Research Journal* 16, no. 2 (Fall 1996): 225–37.

Composing and arranging music within specified guidelines: Students use a variety of traditional and nontraditional sound sources and electronic media when composing and arranging.

Strategy

Methods students have completed an assignment to investigate and develop a list of world music instruments available from manufacturers, importers, and suppliers. This assignment is part of an ongoing project on integrating general knowledge and musical skills pertaining to music from world cultures into concert band. In class, as an example of a composition incorporating traditional instruments from world cultures, students perform John Barnes Chance's "Variations on a Korean Folk Song" (New York: Boosey & Hawkes), QMB348, Level 4. The instructor then assigns students the task of developing compositions appropriate for middle-level band and employing instruments available to them from world cultures.

The class discusses the criteria that they should use for developing their compositions (e.g., length, instrumentation). The instructor specifies minimum and maximum lengths for the composition, instrumentation, and means of assessment for the work that students will compose.

After completing their compositions, students perform them, and the instructor and class evaluate the compositions. Together, they consider appropriate criteria for a similar compositional activity for students in grades 5–8. Students place copies of their compositions and comments from the class discussion in their portfolios.

Suggested Resources

Anderson, William M., ed. *Teaching Music with a Multicultural Approach.* Reston, VA: Music Educators National Conference, 1990. Book and videocassettes.

Jessup, Lynne E. *All Hands On.* Danbury, CT: World Music Press, 1996.

◆ ◆ ◆ ◆ ◆ ◆ ◆

Reading and notating music: Students read whole, half, quarter, eighth, sixteenth, and dotted notes and rests in 2/4, 3/4, 4/4, 6/8, 3/8, and alla breve meter signatures.

Strategy

Methods students have examined three different counting systems (e. g., traditional—1 & 2 &; Eastman—1 te 2 te; and breath impulse—wo-n, two-oo, three, fou-r). Dividing the class into three groups, the instructor gives each group a level 1 or 2 middle-level band composition and asks the groups to count verbally through part of their pieces using one of the counting systems, reading the rhythms as notated.

Each group demonstrates its counting system for the other groups. The class discusses the merits of incorporating and using a particular counting system with students in a middle-level instrumental program.

Suggested Resources

Colwell, Richard J., and Thomas Goolsby. *The Teaching of Instrumental Music*, 2d ed. Englewood Cliffs, NJ: Prentice Hall, 1992.

Crider, Paula A. "Sight-Reading: Is It a Lost Art?" *The Instrumentalist* 43, no. 10 (May 1989): 29–30, 35.

STANDARD 5D

Reading and notating music: Students use standard notation to record their musical ideas and the musical ideas of others.

Strategy

The instructor asks each methods student to name a short folk song or a familiar melody he or she can sing from memory. Once everyone has selected a different tune, the instructor assigns each student to notate the melody for his or her own instrument on manuscript paper, using conventional notation. The instructor collects the examples and redistributes them to other students, who then play the examples to check each writer's notation skills.

The instructor and students discuss how this procedure could be adapted for instrumental students in grades 5–8. They consider, for example, the prior knowledge that would be needed by students in order to play other students' notation if their own instruments are in a different key.

Suggested Resources

Cacavas, John. *The Art of Writing Music*. Van Nuys, CA: Alfred Publishing Company. 1993.

Harder, Paul, and Greg A. Steinke. *Basic Materials in Music Theory*, 8th ed. Englewood Cliffs, NJ: Allyn and Bacon/Prentice-Hall, 1995.

Powell, Steven. "Avoiding Common Manuscript Problems." *The Instrumentalist* 48, no. 9 (April 1994): 50–60.

STANDARD 5E

Reading and notating music: Students sightread, accurately and expressively, music with a level of difficulty of 2, on a scale of 1 to 6.

Strategy

The instructor divides the methods class into two groups and distributes identical materials (level 2 music arrangements or instrumental-ensemble method books that are unfamiliar to the students).

(continued)

Each group studies a selected piece for twenty seconds. Students in one of the two groups, playing their secondary instruments, sightread the piece. The instructor and the listening students give the performing group a score of 10, 20, 30, or 40 points according to the following scale:

10 points = All group members stop playing before reaching the end of the piece.

20 points = At least one player makes it to the end of the piece with reasonable technical and expressive accuracy.

30 points = Most players play the whole piece with reasonable technical and expressive accuracy.

40 points = All players perform the piece with reasonable technical and expressive accuracy.

Play alternates, as groups sightread other pieces, until one group scores 150 points. The instructor then divides the class into new groups and repeats the exercise.

In adapting this strategy for use with grades 5–8 ensembles, the instructor notes, the teacher would attempt to maintain a balance of individual playing skill between the groups. The class considers other adaptations that would need to be made.

Suggested Resources

Dufresne, Gaston. *Develop Sightreading.* New York: Charles Colin Publications, 1972.

Harris, Brian. "Comparisons of Attained Ratings to Instructional Behaviors and Techniques Exhibited by Band Directors in Sight-Reading Performance Situations." Ph.D. diss., The Florida State University, 1991.

Prentice, Barbara. "Rx: Pain Free Sight-Reading." *The Instrumentalist* 40, no. 9 (April 1986): 46–47.

◆ ◆ ◆ ◆ ◆ ◆ ◆

STANDARD 6A

Listening to, analyzing, and describing music: Students describe specific music events in a given aural example, using appropriate terminology.

Strategy

The instructor gives each methods student an assignment to write a lesson focusing on development of aural skills of middle-level band or orchestra students. The lesson should include recognition of melodies, structural features, and instrumental timbres in recordings of band or orchestra repertoire. Methods students should select listening examples, design formats for middle-level students' responses and descriptions of the pieces, and give guidelines for appropriate terminology.

Individual methods students demonstrate portions of the completed assignment for the class, and the class critiques the presentations and discusses any adaptations needed for using the lessons with middle-level students. Students place the materials they have developed in their portfolios.

Suggested Resources

ASBDA Curriculum Guide: A Reference for School Band Directors. Miami: Warner Bros. Publications, 1973.

Smith, Norman E., and Albert J. Stoutamire. *Band Music Notes.* Lake Charles, LA: Program Note Press, 1982.

STANDARD 6B

Listening to, analyzing, and describing music: Students analyze the uses of elements of music in aural examples representing diverse genres and cultures.

Strategy

The methods class is examining means of incorporating the study of world music into beginning and intermediate-level band or orchestra classes. Students have created lists of compositions and arrangements based on music from a variety of cultures and appropriate for performance by beginning and intermediate ensembles (grades 1–2). They have developed a series of lessons teaching both performance skills and comprehensive musicianship.

The instructor divides the methods class into small groups and asks each group to create a written or oral examination to assess the ensemble members' ability to describe how the compositions and arrangements use the elements of music. The completed assignments should include examples of music selected, analyses of the works, sample lesson plans, and the assessment instrument. Students place their work in their portfolios.

Suggested Resource

Fowler, Charles. Chapter 2 in *Music! Its Role and Importance in Our Lives.* Mission Hills, CA: Glencoe/McGraw-Hill, 1994. Book and recordings.

◆ ◆ ◆ ◆ ◆ ◆

STANDARD 7A

Evaluating music and music performances: Students develop criteria for evaluating the quality and effectiveness of music performances and compositions and apply the criteria in their personal listening and performing.

Strategy

The methods class is examining a variety of ways in which to achieve greater involvement of middle-level students in the process of evaluating individual and group performances and recommending possible solutions for performance problems. The instructor gives methods students an assignment to develop a list of criteria by which to assess performance of students in middle-level band and orchestra classes. Each student is asked to create a Likert-type scale or an evaluation grid for monitoring progress

(continued)

and recommending ways in which middle-level students can improve performance. An evaluation grid, for example, could have the following headings: performance skill, observed performance, recommended solutions; students would develop performance skill categories as criteria for evaluating performances.

Students present their lists of criteria to the class, and the class discusses how they would be used. The instructor leads the class in a discussion about how they would guide middle-level instrumental students in developing such criteria and applying them to their own performances.

Suggested Resources

Byo, James. "Teach Your Instrumental Students to *Listen*." *Music Educators Journal* 77, no. 4 (December 1990): 43–46.

Green, Elizabeth A. H. *Teaching Stringed Instruments in Classes,* 2d ed. Reston, VA: American String Teachers Association, 1987.

STANDARD 7B

Evaluating music and music performances: Students evaluate the quality and effectiveness of their own and others' performances, compositions, arrangements, and improvisations by applying specific criteria appropriate for the style of the music and offer constructive suggestions for improvement.

Strategy

The instructor introduces tapes of middle school band and orchestra performances (including poor, mediocre, very good, and outstanding performances) and scores of the pieces performed on the tapes. Working in three groups, methods students compare what they hear on the tapes with what they see in the scores. Using criteria they developed in a previous class session, they listen for pitch or rhythmic errors, inappropriate dynamics, articulation problems, texture imbalances, tone color deficits, and inept phrasing. The instructor rotates tapes and scores until all three groups have evaluated each performance.

The instructor and students compare evaluations and discuss the extent to which the evaluations demonstrate sensitivity, accuracy, and consistency in evaluating musical performance. They then discuss how middle-level instrumental students could use a similar procedure to develop their ability to evaluate performances and suggest improvements.

Suggested Resources

Bassin, Joseph. "The Art of Musicianship in Performance." *Music Educators Journal* 80, no. 5 (March 1994): 30–48.

Boyle, J. David, and Rudolf E. Radocy. *Measurement and Evaluation of Musical Experiences.* New York: Schirmer Books/Simon & Schuster, 1987.

Robinson, Mitchell. "Alternative Assessment Techniques for Teachers." *Music Educators Journal* 81, no. 5 (March 1995): 28–34.

◆ ◆ ◆ ◆ ◆ ◆ ◆

STANDARD 8A

Understanding relationships between music, the other arts, and disciplines outside the arts: Students compare in two or more arts how the characteristic materials of each art can be used to transform similar events, scenes, emotions, or ideas into works of art.

Strategy

The methods class has been studying the means for integrating instrumental music with the other arts and with disciplines outside the arts. In previous methods class sessions, students have heard guest lecturers from the visual arts, literature, dance, or theatre discuss how artworks in their areas of expertise function to provide aesthetic experiences for viewers, readers, observers, or listeners.

In this class session, working in groups, methods students develop a lesson teaching both performance skills and related content, using a level 2 instrumental piece. The lesson plans should include information on how the piece relates to a work in visual art, literature, dance, or theatre; and an analysis of the musical characteristics of the piece. Also, the lesson plans should include how, as teachers, methods students would teach the piece and compare how the composer uses sound with how an artist of the related artwork uses the characteristic materials of his or her art to transform a similar event into a work of art.

Suggested Resources

Garvin, James P. "Merging the Exploratory and Basic Subjects." In *Music at the Middle Level: Building Strong Programs,* edited by June Hinckley. Reston, VA: Music Educators National Conference, 1994.

Haack, Paul A. "Finding Commonalities among the Arts." In *Music at the Middle Level: Building Strong Programs,* edited by June Hinckley. Reston, VA: Music Educators National Conference, 1994.

Nyberg, John L. "Related Arts in the Music Classroom." In *Music at the Middle Level: Building Strong Programs,* edited by June Hinckley. Reston, VA: Music Educators National Conference, 1994.

STANDARD 8B

Understanding relationships between music, the other arts, and disciplines outside the arts: Students describe ways in which the principles and subject matter of other disciplines taught in the school are interrelated with those of music.

Strategy

The instrumental methods class meets with methods classes in language arts and social studies. The instructors for each class present brief summaries of goals and objectives for their respective disciplines on a selected lesson topic. Students form groups with at least one member from each of the three disciplines in each group. Then each group produces a lesson on a topic of mutual importance, such as the use of music and language in advertising, with each member contributing something from his or her area of expertise.

(continued)

A trio of students from each group (one from each discipline) presents its lesson to the other groups. Then, as a class, the groups discuss the presentations and recommend possible adaptations for using the lessons with middle-level students.

Suggested Resource

Reimer, Bennett. "The Philosophy in Action: The Performance Program." In *A Philosophy of Music Education,* 2d ed. Englewood Cliffs, NJ: Prentice Hall, 1989.

◆ ◆ ◆ ◆ ◆ ◆ ◆

STANDARD 9A

Understanding music in relation to history and culture: Students describe distinguishing characteristics of representative music genres and styles from a variety of cultures.

Strategy

In a previous methods class, the instructor has divided the class into groups and each group has selected a specific culture around which they will build a lesson. Students in each group have identified band or orchestra compositions or arrangements, as well as recordings of some of these works and of authentic original examples of music (not for band or orchestra) from the same cultures.

In this class session, the instructor gives the groups an assignment to develop a lesson for intermediate-level instrumental students. The lesson should include a list of compositions or arrangements for the selected culture, a list of identifying characteristics for each musical tradition represented in the pieces, a list of recordings from which excerpts might come, and a listening test.

The listening test should include examples drawn from the band or orchestra pieces that intermediate-level students would have studied and from the authentic original examples of music. The task for intermediate-level students would be to identify the culture on which the recorded excerpt is based and identify characteristics of that culture's music that they hear in the excerpt.

Methods students from each group demonstrate selected test items for the class. All students place the materials in their portfolios for evaluation and for use in their teaching.

Suggested Resource

Fowler, Charles. Chapter 2 in *Music! Its Role and Importance in Our Lives.* Mission Hills, CA: Glencoe/McGraw-Hill, 1994. Book and recordings.

Understanding music in relation to history and culture: *Students classify by genre and style (and, if applicable, by historical period, composer, and title) a varied body of exemplary (that is, high-quality and characteristic) musical works and explain the characteristics that cause each work to be considered exemplary.*

Strategy

Methods students have completed assigned reading. The instructor divides the methods class into small groups, gives each group a copy of either *Schwann Opus* or *Schwann Spectrum*, and asks each group to consider the following:

"You are the director of a middle school band program that currently has no significant listening materials. You have received a grant of $300 to purchase recorded materials for incorporation into the curriculum. What will you buy? Recordings of representative instrumental soloists? If so, which soloists? Examples of band or orchestra music? If so, how will you use them? Recordings of music from each historical period? If so, which ones, and why? Attempt to arrive at a group consensus. List the recordings you will purchase (including company and order number), the cost of each recording, and your justification for selecting it. Be sure to explain what it is about the recording that makes it an exemplary work and an exemplary performance of that work."

After completing their lists, the groups reports to the class. Reports should include which recordings the students selected and why, again focusing on what makes the selected recordings exemplary, whether or not the group obtained a consensus, and insights gained from the exercise. Finally, the instructor leads the class in a discussion about how they would use a similar procedure with students in grades 5–8, including how they would guide such students in making decisions about works as exemplary.

Suggested Resources

Masterson, Michael L. "Moving Beyond 'It's Got a Good Beat'." *Music Educators Journal* 80, no. 6 (May 1994): 24–28.

Rohwer, Debbie, "Making Rehearsals Comprehensive." *Teaching Music* 1, no. 3 (December 1993): 29–30, 51.

Snedeker, Jeffrey L. "Bringing the Past into Music Classrooms." *Music Educators Journal* 80, no. 2 (September 1993): 40, 63.

INSTRUMENTAL MUSIC
GRADES 9–12

STANDARD 1B

Proficient

Singing, alone and with others, a varied repertoire of music: *Students sing music written in four parts, with and without accompaniment.*

Strategy

The methods class has selected literature for a program by a high school concert band, including one work in which band members' singing of four-part music is a performance option—for example, Johann Sebastian Bach, "Who Puts His Trust in God Most Just," arr. James Croft (Delaware Water Gap, PA: Shawnee Press), K 390, Level 3; or Claude T. Smith's "God of Our Fathers" (Kansas City, MO: Wingert Jones Music), 3011421, Level 3/4.

The instructor asks students individually to develop a series of rehearsal procedures that specifically address singing of the parts by instrumentalists. These procedures might include teaching vocal tone production, diction, and balance between singers and instrumentalists. The instructor notes that, as teachers, methods students would execute these lessons in consultation with the choral specialists in their schools. Students also consider appropriateness for performing with or without accompaniment during choral passages.

Methods students form themselves into a band, and students present their procedures by rehearsing the band in the selected piece. Students place their written procedures in their portfolios along with their own comments and instructor evaluations of the effectiveness of the procedures.

Suggested Resources

Collins, Donald L. *Teaching Choral Music.* Englewood Cliffs, NJ: Prentice-Hall, 1993.

Crocker, Emily, and John Leavitt. *Essential Musicianship,* book 1. Milwaukee: Hal Leonard Corporation, 1995.

Telfer, Nancy. *Successful Warm-Ups.* 2 vols. San Diego: Neil A. Kjos Music Company, 1995–96.

STANDARD 1C

Proficient

Singing, alone and with others, a varied repertoire of music: *Students demonstrate well-developed ensemble skills.*

Strategy

The methods class has selected a band composition that uses voices (without text) as part of the instrumental texture—for example, Robert W. Smith's "Africa: Ceremony, Song, and Ritual" (Miami: Warner Bros. Publications), MB9757, Level 5.

(continued)

The instructor divides the methods class into groups and asks each group to create rehearsal procedures that address matching intonation between voices and instruments, establishing correct balance between instruments and voices, and blending vocal and instrumental textures. The instructor notes that, as teachers, methods students would execute these lessons in consultation with the choral specialists in their schools.

Students experiment with various techniques in class demonstrations. They place their written procedures in their portfolios for later evaluation.

Suggested Resources

Collins, Donald L. *Teaching Choral Music.* Englewood Cliffs, NJ: Prentice-Hall, 1993.

Colwell, Richard J., and Thomas Goolsby. "Rehearsal Techniques." In *The Teaching of Instrumental Music,* 2d ed. Englewood Cliffs, NJ: Prentice Hall, 1992.

Crocker, Emily, and John Leavitt. *Essential Musicianship,* book 1. Milwaukee: Hal Leonard Corporation, 1995.

◆ ◆ ◆ ◆ ◆ ◆ ◆

STANDARD 2A

Proficient

Performing on instruments, alone and with others, a varied repertoire of music: *Students perform with expression and technical accuracy a large and varied repertoire of instrumental literature with a level of difficulty of 4, on a scale of 1 to 6.*

Strategy

The instructor divides the methods class into groups and asks each group to select two examples of instrumental music literature with a level of difficulty of 4, appropriate for high school bands or orchestras. The assignment includes giving rationales for their selections, identifying anticipated performance problems and listing possible solutions for each, developing a sequence of instructional plans for teaching and rehearsing the selections with particular focus on expression and technical accuracy, and creating a schedule outlining sections of each work to be studied in each rehearsal.

To give the groups an opportunity to share their work with other members of the class, students in the class act as the band and, in turn, a member from each group acts as teacher. After each performance, the class suggests possible modifications to the plans. Students place the completed work in their portfolios for subsequent evaluation.

Suggested Resources

Del Borgo, Elliot. *The Rehearsal . . . The First Ten Minutes.* Educational Programs Publications (1784 West Schuylkill Road, Douglassville, PA 19518-9100; phone 610-327-3050), 1995. Conductor's score and student books.

Dvorak, Thomas L., Robert Grechesky, and Gary M. Ciepluch. *Best Music for High School Band: A Selective Repertoire Guide for High School Bands and Wind Ensembles.* Edited by Bob Margolis. Manhattan Beach Music (1595 East 46th St., Brooklyn, NY 11234-3122; phone 718-338-4137), 1993.

Garofalo, Robert. *Guides to Band Masterworks.* Fort Lauderdale, FL: Meredith Music Publications, 1992.

New York State School Music Association. *NYSSMA Manual of Graded Solo and Ensemble Music.* Westbury, NY: NYSSMA, 1991.

STANDARD 2B

Proficient

Performing on instruments, alone and with others, a varied repertoire of music: Students perform an appropriate part in an ensemble, demonstrating well-developed ensemble skills.

Strategy

The instructor gives methods students a simple piece and asks them to read the melody, harmony, and accompaniment parts on their secondary instruments. During the course of the exercise, each student should have a chance to play each part.

The instructor leads methods students in a discussion of the ensemble skills required to perform successfully in the ensemble while playing various roles (e.g., playing melody versus playing accompaniment). Using selected pieces as models, they discuss rehearsal techniques to develop all aspects of ensemble skills at the high school level. Following their discussion, they try some of the techniques with selected students acting as conductor of an ensemble formed by class members on their major instruments. They consider how the techniques that are demonstrated will work with high school instrumental students.

Suggested Resources

Hoffer, Charles R. *Teaching Music in the Secondary Schools,* 4th ed. Belmont, CA: Wadsworth Publishing Company, 1991.

Reimer, Bennett. "The Philosophy in Action: The Performance Program." In *A Philosophy of Music Education,* 2d ed. Englewood Cliffs, NJ: Prentice Hall, 1989.

Advanced

Performing on instruments, alone and with others, a varied repertoire of music: Students perform with expression and technical accuracy a large and varied repertoire of instrumental literature with a level of difficulty of 5, on a scale of 1 to 6.

Strategy

To acquaint methods students with a procedure for teaching advanced wind ensemble literature, the instructor presents an overview of the band compositions of Percy Grainger. After listening to recordings of several of Grainger's works, the class discusses his compositional practices and characteristics of his music. The discussion includes how he used native folk songs artistically as the basis for many of his compositions. Also, the class identifies other wind composers who have used this technique.

Citing performance challenges inherent in each composition they have discussed, the class determines the appropriateness of these works for high school wind ensembles. The instructor shows a list of the performance challenges on an overhead transparency, and the class suggests solutions. Playing in ensemble on their major instruments, students perform representative level 5 Grainger compositions—for example, "Irish Tune from County Derry and Shepherd's Hey" (New York: Carl Fischer), J 240; or "Molly on the Shore" (New York: Carl Fischer), J 270. Using procedures evolving from the class discussion, student conductors direct the ensemble.

The instructor asks students to identify other noted composers who have multiple works in the wind-ensemble literature, such as Clifton Williams and Norman Dello Joio. The class discusses stylistic concerns in teaching the works of these composers.

Suggested Resources

Goldman, Richard Franko. *The Wind Band.* Boston: Allyn & Bacon, 1961.

Mellers, Wilfrid H. *Percy Grainger.* New York: Oxford University Press, 1992.

Slattery, Thomas C. *Percy Grainger: The Inveterate Innovator.* Evanston, IL. The Instrumentalist Company, 1974.

◆ ◆ ◆ ◆ ◆ ◆

STANDARD 3B

Proficient

Improvising melodies, variations, and accompaniments: Students improvise rhythmic and melodic variations on given pentatonic melodies and melodies in major and minor keys.

Strategy

The instructor asks methods students to improvise three or more variations on the melody of "America" in the key of F major. Individuals may alter the melody by adding embellishments—such as passing tones, neighboring tones, turns, and trills—in an appropriate and musical manner. They may also alter the melody by changing the rhythm, the mode, or the meter. The class discusses the effectiveness of these improvisations and the reasons for their assessments.

The instructor leads the class in a discussion about how they would adapt this procedure to use it with high school instrumental students. For example, they might have those students first try improvising either all together (playing at the same time) or in small groups before calling on an individual student. They might also have the high school students listen to existing variations on "America," such as Charles Ives' Variations on "America" for Organ; or to variations on another song, such as Jean-Baptiste Arban's Fantasie, Theme and Variations on *The Carnival of Venice*.

Suggested Resources

Baker, David. "Improvisation: A Tool for Music Learning." *Music Educators Journal* 66, no. 5 (January 1980): 42–51.

Lisk, Edward S. *The Creative Director: Alternative Rehearsal Techniques.* Fort Lauderdale, FL: Meredith Music Publications, 1991.

Nolan, Evonne, ed. "Drawing Creativity out of Your Students." *Teaching Music* 2, no. 5 (April 1995): 28–29.

STANDARD 3C

Proficient

Improvising melodies, variations, and accompaniments: *Students improvise original melodies over given chord progressions, each in a consistent style, meter, and tonality.*

Strategy

Methods students review the G minor scale by playing and singing the correct pitches of the scale and of the I, III, V#, and VII chords. The instructor then presents a harmonic progression in G minor and in 3/4 meter, based on a spirited sixteenth- and seventeenth-century Iberian dance, the folia.

							⌐1., 2.		⌐3.		
‖: g	|D	|g	| F	|B♭	|F	|g	|D	:‖D	g ‖
‖: I	|V#	|I	|VII	|III	|VII	|I	|V#	:‖V#	I ‖

Using pitches from the chords, students take turns improvising three melodies over the progression. The instructor or a student plays the chord progression on guitar, the instrument that was often used in early folia. The first melody should contain only quarter notes; the second improvisation should include some moving eighth notes and passing tones; and the third attempt should include eighth notes, sixteenth notes, and possibly dotted-note patterns.

Students discuss the effectiveness of their improvisations and the reasons for their assessments. With the instructor, they outline the steps for using a similar procedure in a high school instrumental class, considering any adaptations they would need to make.

(continued)

Suggested Resources

Bechtel, Ben. "Improvisation in Early Music." *Music Educators Journal* 66, no. 5 (January 1980): 109–112.

Donington, Robert. "Ornaments." In *The New Grove Dictionary of Music and Musicians,* edited by Stanley Sadie. London: Macmillan, 1980.

Lisk, Edward S. *The Creative Director: Alternative Rehearsal Techniques.* Fort Lauderdale, FL: Meredith Music Publications, 1991.

Moe, Lawrence H. "Folia." In *The New Harvard Dictionary of Music,* edited by Don Michael Randel. Cambridge: Belknap Press of Harvard University Press, 1986.

STANDARD 3E

Advanced

Improvising melodies, variations, and accompaniments: Students improvise original melodies in a variety of styles, over given chord progressions, each in a consistent style, meter, and tonality.

Strategy

The instructor plays a recording of a familiar pop song or a 12-bar blues. Methods students determine the chord progression used in the piece. Students then notate the chord progression and score it for an ensemble made up of class members. Playing their major instruments, individual students improvise melodies over the chord changes, in a style, meter, and tonality consistent with the selected piece. Students might also improvise descants for the original melody. They evaluate their own improvisations, considering the criteria (style, meter, and tonality).

The class then discusses any changes they would need to make in using a similar procedure to teach advanced high school instrumental students to improvise original melodies in various styles. They consider additional criteria that might be given, depending on the style of the selected piece.

Suggested Resources

Azzara, Christopher D., Richard F. Grunow, and Edwin E. Gordon. *Creativity in Improvisation.* Books 1 and 2, with recordings. Chicago: GIA Publications, 1997.

Lisk, Edward S. *The Creative Director: Alternative Rehearsal Techniques.* Fort Lauderdale, FL: Meredith Music Publications, 1991.

◆ ◆ ◆ ◆ ◆ ◆ ◆

Standard 4A

Proficient

Composing and arranging music within specified guidelines: *Students compose music in several distinct styles, demonstrating creativity in using the elements of music for expressive effect.*

Strategy

The instructor distributes copies of the Walt Whitman poem "I Hear America Singing," asking methods students to read the poem and think about the literary elements Whitman used to create impact and meaning. Students then list the characteristics of the musical elements (rhythm, pitch, style, and form) that they think parallel the literary elements in the poem. The instructor asks each student to compose a short piece for his or her instrument, using at least three musical elements inspired by the Whitman poem.

After completing their compositions, students perform them for the class. The class identifies how each student has used the elements of music for expressive effect. Also, students discuss how they would modify this procedure in order to use it with instrumental students in grades 9–12. They consider how, as teachers, they could work in coordination with the high school students' literature teacher to present the lesson.

Suggested Resources

Rudaitis, Cheryl, ed. "Your Band Can Compose, Too." *Teaching Music* 2, no. 3 (December 1994): 32–33.

Wiggins, Jackie. *Composition in the Classroom: A Tool for Teaching.* Reston, VA: Music Educators National Conference, 1990.

Standard 4B

Proficient

Composing and arranging music within specified guidelines: *Students arrange pieces for voices or instruments other than those for which the pieces were written in ways that preserve or enhance the expressive effect of the music.*

Strategy

The instructor has asked methods students to bring to class a piece of standard solo literature, which they have performed, for their own major instrument or voice (e.g., Haydn, Concerto in E♭ for Trumpet and Orchestra; or Mozart, Concerto in A for Clarinet and Orchestra). In class, the instructor asks each student to choose a section of sixteen to thirty-two measures that states one of the main themes of the work and to arrange this segment for his or her secondary instrument, keeping in mind ranges and tessitura, and transposing where necessary to produce a version that the student can perform. Each student must also create a suitable piano or instrumental accompaniment that varies from the reference score.

(continued)

After completing the assignment, students perform their pieces for the class with artistic expression, phrasing, and articulation. The class discusses each performance and how effective each student composer was in realizing the expressive intent of the work when transferring the piece to a new instrument. The instructor leads the class in outlining steps for using a similar procedure for a high school instrumental class.

Suggested Resource

Colwell, Richard J., and Thomas Goolsby. *The Teaching of Instrumental Music,* 2d ed. Englewood Cliffs, NJ: Prentice Hall, 1992.

STANDARD 4C
Proficient

Composing and arranging music within specified guidelines: *Students compose and arrange music for voices and various acoustic and electronic instruments, demonstrating knowledge of the ranges and traditional usages of the sound sources.*

Strategy

Methods students form a band and play the chorale-like opening section of "Chester" by William Schuman (Bryn Mawr, PA: Merion Music/Theodore Presser Company), 145400000, Level 6. The instructor asks students which instruments play in which measures.

The instructor distributes a handout with ranges (written and transposed) for each instrument in the string quartet, clarinet quartet, woodwind quintet, brass quintet, and percussion ensemble. Then the instructor demonstrates how to transcribe a selected four-part hymn or chorale for one of the ensembles. Distributing copies of another hymn or chorale, the instructor asks students to outline a procedure for teaching high school instrumental students to transcribe a four- or eight-measure segment of the piece for their own instrument family. The procedure should include having high school students write a score and parts for their transcriptions, rehearse and conduct the transcriptions in their class, and discuss the effectiveness of each transcription.

After students complete their procedures, the instructor divides the class into groups and asks each group to review the plans prepared by the class members and discuss their effectiveness. The class comes together again and discusses how using lessons in transcription with high school students will lead toward lessons in arranging.

Suggested Resources

Colwell, Richard J., and Thomas Goolsby. *The Teaching of Instrumental Music,* 2d ed. Englewood Cliffs, NJ: Prentice-Hall, 1992.

Kennan, Kent W., and Donald Grantham. *The Technique of Orchestration,* 4th ed. Englewood Cliffs, NJ: Prentice-Hall, 1990.

STANDARD 4D

Advanced

Composing and arranging music within specified guidelines: *Students compose music, demonstrating imagination and technical skill in applying the principles of composition.*

Strategy

The instructor asks methods students to create brief (eight-measure) original two-voice compositions. Considering instruments played by members of the class, each student selects an instrument group for which to write a composition. The instructor sets limits on the composition—for example: ABA form, eight measures in length, meter signature, key(s), difficulty level, at least one tempo change. Compositions should include indications of expression, articulation, and dynamics.

Students compose and prepare a score and then extract parts on a computer notation program. They rehearse and perform their works with the class. The class discusses the effectiveness of each composition, including whether it fits the given parameters and how effective the student composer was in demonstrating imagination and technical skill in applying the principles of composition. Also, they consider adaptations that would need to be made to this lesson for teaching students in grades 9–12.

Suggested Resources

Kennan, Kent W., and Donald Grantham. *The Technique of Orchestration,* 4th ed. Englewood Cliffs, NJ: Prentice-Hall, 1990.

Rudaitis, Cheryl, ed. "Your Band Can Compose, Too." *Teaching Music* 2, no. 3 (December 1994): 32–33.

◆ ◆ ◆ ◆ ◆ ◆ ◆

STANDARD 5A

Proficient

Reading and notating music: *Students demonstrate the ability to read an instrumental or vocal score of up to four staves by describing how the elements of music are used.*

Strategy

Methods students review basic score-reading techniques. The instructor divides the methods class into groups and asks each group to design a series of lessons and instructional materials that will provide high school band or orchestra students with the skills necessary to rehearse small ensembles (e.g., string quartet, woodwind quartet, brass quartet, percussion ensemble for four players, or mixed instrument quartet) from a four-part score. One of the instructional materials should be a checklist that would guide high school students in their score reading by directing their attention to the use of elements of music in material that is being rehearsed.

(continued)

After completing the assignment, methods students discuss how preparation of small ensembles in high school differs from their experience with similar groups in higher education. They then compile a list of suitable materials for small ensembles of varying abilities at the high school level.

Suggested Resources

Battisti, Frank, and Robert Garofalo. *Guide to Score Study for the Wind Band Conductor.* Fort Lauderdale, FL: Meredith Music Publications, 1990.

Garofalo, Robert. *Rehearsal Handbook for Band and Orchestra Students.* Fort Lauderdale, FL: Meredith Music Publications, 1983.

"Guides to Score Preparation." In *Conductor's Anthology,* 2d ed. 2 vols. Northfield, IL: The Instrumentalist Company, 1993.

STANDARD 5B
Proficient
Reading and notating music: Students sightread, accurately and expressively, music with a level of difficulty of 3, on a scale of 1 to 6.

Strategy

Playing their secondary instruments, methods students sightread instrumental-ensemble literature with a level of difficulty of 3. They take turns conducting the selections, first having ensemble members identify important rhythms, melodic patterns, structural designs, and potential performance challenges. Student conductors then guide the ensemble through the sightreading process, just as they would do in a festival or contest, or in a school setting, encouraging accurate and expressive playing. (If students are not acquainted with this activity, the instructor demonstrates the procedure first and encourages students to observe it in festivals or contests.)

Suggested Resources

Colwell, Richard J., and Thomas Goolsby. *The Teaching of Instrumental Music,* 2d ed. Englewood Cliffs, NJ: Prentice Hall, 1992.

Crider, Paula A. "Sight-Reading: Is It a Lost Art?" *The Instrumentalist* 43, no. 10 (May 1989): 29–30, 35.

STANDARD 5C

Advanced

Reading and notating music: *Students demonstrate the ability to read a full instrumental or vocal score by describing how the elements of music are used and explaining all transpositions and clefs.*

Strategy

Methods students review basic score-reading techniques. The instructor divides the methods class into groups and gives each group an assignment to create a series of lessons and instructional materials that will provide high school band or orchestra students with skills necessary to serve effectively as student conductors. The assignment also includes developing an assessment instrument.

The class discusses how they would adapt university-level instructional activities for use by high school students. Each group then writes a series of lessons as an introduction to score reading for high school students, describing basic techniques of score analysis, providing a list of listening examples (recordings of band or orchestra pieces playable by high school bands and orchestras), and developing an assessment instrument to evaluate the effects of this instruction.

Students from each group demonstrate selected portions of their group's work, and the groups place all materials in their portfolios for subsequent evaluation.

Suggested Resources

Battisti, Frank, and Robert Garofalo. *Guide to Score Study for the Wind Band Conductor.* Fort Lauderdale, FL: Meredith Music Publications, 1990.

Garofalo, Robert. *Rehearsal Handbook for Band and Orchestra Students.* Fort Lauderdale, FL: Meredith Music Publications, 1983.

"Guides to Score Preparation." In *Conductor's Anthology,* 2d ed. 2 vols. Northfield, IL: The Instrumentalist Company, 1993.

Hunsberger, Donald, and Roy Ernst. *The Art of Conducting,* 2d ed. Columbus, OH: McGraw-Hill, 1992.

STANDARD 5D

Advanced

Reading and notating music: *Students interpret nonstandard notation symbols used by some 20th-century composers.*

Strategy

The instructor leads methods students in a discussion of techniques for teaching high school band or orchestra students to read nonstandard notation. Together, they develop a list of band or orchestra works, appropriate for high school students, using nonstandard notation.

(continued)

Then the instructor divides the methods class into small groups to develop an instructional sequence for introducing nonstandard notation to high school students, including exercises and drills in performing nonstandard notation. The sequence should include teaching aids, such as wall charts or overhead transparencies showing nonstandard notation and instructions for their interpretation.

Upon completion of the assignment, each group teaches an excerpt from its work to the other groups, and the class discusses the effectiveness of the materials and techniques. Students then place all materials, including comments based on the class discussion, in their portfolios for subsequent evaluation.

Suggested Resources

Barry, Malcolm, and Roger Parker. *Score Reading.* Twentieth Century, book 5. New York: Oxford University Press, 1987.

Chew, Geoffrey. "Notation." In *The New Grove Dictionary of Music and Musicians,* edited by Stanley Sadie. London: Macmillan, 1980.

Dallin, Leon. *Techniques of Twentieth-Century Composition,* 3d ed. Columbus, OH: Wm. C. Brown Communications/McGraw-Hill, 1974.

Morgan, Robert P. *Twentieth-Century Music.* Scranton, PA: W. W. Norton, 1991.

◆ ◆ ◆ ◆ ◆ ◆ ◆

STANDARD 6B

Proficient

Listening to, analyzing, and describing music: Students demonstrate extensive knowledge of the technical vocabulary of music.

Strategy

Prior to class, each methods student has selected an excerpt from a work, suitable for use with a high school instrumental ensemble, demonstrating a particular technical challenge in bowing or tone production. Also, each student has found a recording of the selected work.

In class, methods students discuss the music terminology related to bowing and tone production. Methods students form an instrumental ensemble, and each student takes a turn teaching the ensemble. As the teaching student demonstrates the proper technique and teaches it to the ensemble, he or she gives particular emphasis to the technical vocabulary related to the particular technique. Then, the teaching student plays the recorded example.

After listening, students discuss the performance on the recording, demonstrating their aural understanding of the technique by using appropriate technical vocabulary to describe what they hear. Following the teaching demonstrations, students discuss the effectiveness of the demonstrations and consider any adaptations that would need to be made in using the techniques with high school students. They also discuss how they would quiz high school students on their ability to recall and define terms related to these techniques.

Suggested Resources

Green, Elizabeth A. H. *Orchestral Bowings and Routines.* Reston, VA: American String Teachers Association, 1990.

Rabin, Marvin, and Priscilla Smith. *Guide to Orchestral Bowings through Musical Styles,* rev. ed. Madison, WI: Division of University Outreach, Department of Continuing Education in the Arts, University of Wisconsin, 1991.

Randel, Don Michael, ed. *The New Harvard Dictionary of Music.* Cambridge: Belknap Press of Harvard University, 1986.

STANDARD 6E
Advanced

Listening to, analyzing, and describing music: *Students compare ways in which musical materials are used in a given example relative to ways in which they are used in other works of the same genre or style.*

Strategy

Methods students form a band and perform "Lindbergh Variations" by Robert Sheldon (Oskaloosa, IA: C. L. Barnhouse), 012-2369, Level 3. The instructor asks students where in the piece the variations occur and how they differ from, but relate to, the theme. Students replay each variation as needed.

The ensemble then performs "Variations on a Shaker Melody" by Aaron Copland (New York: Boosey & Hawkes), QMB236SB, Level 5. Students identify and describe the variations, using the same procedure as above. The instructor then asks students to compare and contrast variation techniques in the two works.

The instructor plays or sings each of the following, and students play each one back, in turn: a simple folk song, a rhythmic variation of the song, and variations on the song based on other elements (pitch or style). Then the instructor asks for volunteers to create their own variations based on rhythm, pitch, and quality (dynamics, articulation, or tone color).

Methods students discuss how they would use a similar procedure with high school students. They also consider how they would evaluate high school students' understanding.

Suggested Resources

Anderson, William M., and Joy E. Lawrence. "Fundamentals of Music: Understanding How Sounds Are Organized." In *Integrating Music into the Elementary Classroom,* 3d ed. Belmont, CA: Wadsworth Publishing Company, 1995.

Garofalo, Robert. *Blueprint for Band: A Guide to Teaching Comprehensive Musicianship Through School Band Performance,* rev. ed. Portland, ME: J. Weston Walch, 1983.

Green, Douglas. *Form in Tonal Music,* 2d ed. Orlando, FL: Holt, Rinehart & Winston/Harcourt Brace, 1979.

◆ ◆ ◆ ◆ ◆ ◆ ◆

STANDARD 7A
Proficient

Evaluating music and music performances: *Students evolve specific criteria for making informed, critical evaluations of the quality and effectiveness of performances, compositions, arrangements, and improvisations and apply the criteria in their personal participation in music.*

Strategy

Methods students have completed assigned readings. In class, they discuss a recent musical performance experience that all have heard, starting by describing the event in Elliott's terms (1994, pp. 16–18): (i) Who did the performing? (ii) What kind(s) of music performing did they do, in detail? (iii) What music did they perform and what did they intend to accomplish by doing so? (iv) What was the context of the performance and the music?

Students then evaluate the performance they heard in terms of its artistry and creativity, using the following headings: (a) the design of the music and/or the performance, (b) its cultural-ideological authenticity, (c) its expressive or representational success (if appropriate in the context and tradition), and (d) its interpretive quality—artists' and creators' ability (Elliott, 1995, p. 231).

The instructor asks students to generate a list of criteria from factors identified in their evaluations that might serve in critiquing similar performances. Students play recordings of their own musical performances, and the student performing and other members of the class review the performances based on the criteria they have created.

The instructor concludes the lesson with a discussion of how these procedures could be used by students in a high school instrumental class.

Suggested Resources

Abeles, Harold F., Charles R. Hoffer, and Robert Klotman. *Foundations of Music Education,* 2d ed. Old Tappan, NJ: Schirmer Books/Simon & Schuster, 1994.

Elliott, David J. "Rethinking Music: First Steps to a New Philosophy of Music Education." *International Journal of Music Education* 24 (1994): 9–20.

Elliott, David J. *Music Matters: A New Philosophy of Music Education.* New York: Oxford University Press, 1995.

STANDARD 7C
Advanced

Evaluating music and music performances: *Students evaluate a given musical work in terms of its aesthetic qualities and explain the musical means it uses to evoke feelings and emotions.*

Strategy

Methods students have completed assigned reading concerning development of aesthetic sensitivity. In class, students discuss the two parts of music listening: perception and reaction. The instructor explains that, in order to evaluate a musical work, the listener must perceive and understand the work's musical subtleties, regardless of how well the composer and performers project them.

The instructor plays a recording of the first movement of Percy Grainger's "Lincolnshire Posy for Band" (e.g., on *The Spirit of '76 and Ruffles and Flourishes,* Eastman Wind Ensemble, Frederick Fennell, Mercury Living Presence 434386-2), asking students to consider the following questions:

- How would you describe the central mood or character of this movement? How is that achieved musically?

- What portions of the music stimulate strong feelings in you?

- What salient characteristics of the music evoke these feelings?

After listening, students discuss the questions that were presented. The class then breaks into groups to write a lesson plan for teaching high school students to evaluate a piece in terms of its aesthetic qualities. The lesson should include how the teacher would lead students to identifying the aesthetic qualities of the piece and to explaining, in musical terms, how it evokes feelings and emotions. Each group presents a portion of its lesson plan, and the class discusses the effectiveness of the procedures.

Suggested Resources

Reimer, Bennett. "Music Education as Aesthetic Education: Toward the Future." *Music Educators Journal* 75, no. 7 (March 1989): 26–32.

Swanwick, Keith. *Music, Mind, and Education.* London: Routledge, 1989.

Swanwick, Keith. *Musical Knowledge: Intuition, Analysis, and Music Education.* London: Routledge, 1994.

◆ ◆ ◆ ◆ ◆ ◆ ◆

STANDARD 8C

Proficient

Understanding relationships between music, the other arts, and disciplines outside the arts: *Students explain ways in which the principles and subject matter of various disciplines outside the arts are interrelated with those of music.*

Strategy

Methods students have read *The Lord of the Rings* by J. R. R. Tolkien. In class, they discuss the story and consider how the author used the English language to describe personality traits, the setting, and events of the story.

Students then listen to a recording of Symphony no. 1 ("Lord of the Rings") by Johan de Meij (Rondo Grammofon RCD 8346). The instructor guides a discussion focusing on musical elements and techniques the composer used and how those compare and contrast with the literary elements Tolkien used. Students define the term *leitmotif* and explain how the music exemplifies its use.

(continued)

Students discuss how they could adapt these procedures for teaching high school instrumental students to relate the subject matter and compositional techniques of a work they are rehearsing to the subject matter and techniques used by the author of a literary work. They consider the need for consulting the high school literature teacher or teachers in the other arts.

The instructor asks methods students to identify other instrumental works based on literary works—for example, Timothy Broege's "The Headless Horseman" (Manhattan Beach Music, 1595 East 46th St., Brooklyn, NY 11234-3122; phone 718-338-4137), Level 3, which is based on Washington Irving's *The Legend of Sleepy Hollow.*

Suggested Resources

Aaron, Jeffrey. "Integrating Music with Core Subjects." *Music Educators Journal* 80, no. 6 (May 1994): 33–36.

Anderson, William M., and Joy E. Lawrence. "Experiences with Music and Other Arts." In *Integrating Music into the Elementary Classroom,* 3d ed. Belmont, CA: Wadsworth Publishing Company, 1995.

Snyder, Sue. "Language, Movement, and Music—Process Connections." *General Music Today* 7, no. 3 (Spring 1994): 4–9.

STANDARD 8D

Advanced

Understanding relationships between music, the other arts, and disciplines outside the arts: Students compare the uses of characteristic elements, artistic processes, and organizational principles among the arts in different historical periods and different cultures.

Strategy

After the instructor has shown the methods students prints or slides of paintings by Velázquez ("The Ladies in Waiting") and Seurat ("La Grande Jatte"), the instructor and students discuss the differences between the two works. The discussion includes comparison of the materials used, the processes used to create them, and the organization of the materials and processes to create an effect on the viewer.

The instructor makes sure that the students are aware of the Realist characteristics illustrated in the Velázquez painting and the more impressionistic techniques used by Seurat. The students discuss whether one is more "realistic" than the other.

The instructor then plays recordings of Debussy's "Nuages," the opening (approx. five minutes) of Wagner's *Tristan and Isolde,* and Mozart's *Eine kleine Nachtmusik.* Students discuss the similarities and differences between the three examples, drawing analogies in terms of their elements, compositional processes, and organizational principles.

The instructor leads students in a discussion of how they might use similar procedures with high school instrumental students. Together, they outline a high school instrumental strategy based on these procedures, perhaps having the high school art teacher collaborate with the music teacher in teaching such a strategy.

Suggested Resources

Grout, Donald J. and Claude Palisca. *A History of Western Music,* 5th ed. New York: W. W. Norton, 1996.

Haskell, Francis. *History and Its Images: Art and the Interpretation of the Past.* New Haven: Yale University Press, 1993.

Margolis, Joseph. *Interpretation Radical but Not Unruly: The New Puzzle of the Arts and History.* Berkeley: University of California Press, 1995.

◆ ◆ ◆ ◆ ◆ ◆

STANDARD 9A

Proficient

Understanding music in relation to history and culture: *Students classify by genre or style and by historical period or culture unfamiliar but representative aural examples of music and explain the reasoning behind their classifications.*

Strategy

As part of a unit on teaching comprehensive musicianship, the instructor divides students into small groups to design a series of lessons focusing on the classification of music by historical period (Medieval, Renaissance, Baroque, Classic, Romantic, Impressionistic, Modern, and Postmodern). The lessons should include a plan for teaching aids, such as charts of style characteristics for the periods. Each group should also create lists of band or orchestra works suitable for performance by high school students in each of the categories. The instructor notes that arrangements and transcriptions are permissible for some eras.

A member of each group presents the group's work to the class, and the instructor leads the class in making a summary list of techniques for teaching high school instrumental students to classify unfamiliar aural examples and explain the reasoning behind their classifications. Methods students put copies of all materials in their portfolios.

Suggested Resources

Dvorak, Thomas L., Robert Grechesky, and Gary M. Ciepluch. *Best Music for High School Band: A Selective Repertoire Guide for High School Bands and Wind Ensembles.* Edited by Bob Margolis. Manhattan Beach Music (1595 East 46th St., Brooklyn, NY 11234-3122; phone 718-338-4137), 1993.

Grout, Donald J., and Claude Palisca. *A History of Western Music,* 5th ed. New York: W. W. Norton, 1996.

Smith, Norman E., and Albert J. Stoutamire. *Band Music Notes.* Lake Charles, LA: Program Note Press, 1982.

Stolba, K. Marie. *The Development of Western Music: A History,* 2d ed. Dubuque, IA: Brown & Benchmark Publishers/McGraw-Hill, 1993.

Proficient

Understanding music in relation to history and culture: *Students identify sources of American music genres, trace the evolution of those genres, and cite well-known musicians associated with them.*

Strategy

In a previous class, the instructor divided the methods class into small groups and gave each group an assignment related to a different well-known Broadway musical. Each group has investigated the plot and noted any well-known performers who starred in its assigned musical.

In this class session, the instructor presents several band or orchestra arrangements of selections from musicals investigated in the previous assignment—for example, Leonard Bernstein's *West Side Story,* arr. W. J. Duthoit (Milwaukee: G. Schirmer/Hal Leonard Corporation), 50352040, Level 4/5. Students discuss any philosophical, educational, or musical reasons for introducing such pieces in a high school instrumental program. They consider the sources of the genre and its importance in relation to America's history and culture.

The instructor asks the groups formed previously to design an instructional sequence for incorporating the band or orchestra arrangements for their assigned musicals into a high school instrumental program. The sequence should include introducing information on Broadway musicals in general (i.e., the source and evolution of the genre), as well as teaching students about the specific musical and well-known musicians associated with it.

Finally, a member of each group presents an excerpt from its instructional sequence to the class. The class discusses the potential of the techniques for use with high school instrumental students.

Suggested Resource

Hoffer, Charles R. *Teaching Music in the Secondary Schools,* 4th ed. Belmont, CA: Wadsworth Publishing Company, 1991.

Proficient

Understanding music in relation to history and culture: *Students identify various roles that musicians perform, cite representative individuals who have functioned in each role, and describe their activities and achievements.*

Strategy

Methods students have completed assigned reading of articles on music careers. In class, the instructor asks students to give examples of the most unusual music-related career or use of music in a social function of which they are aware. The instructor asks, "What duties or functions do musicians perform in society?" "How many roles does an individual musician fulfill in society?"

The instructor then leads the class in creating a chart of the potential roles a musician fulfills in American society. At the center of the chart is a statement such as "make music," surrounded by concentric rings with progressively higher levels of specificity. At the outer ring are real-life examples of people who make or support music. For each music career listed in one of the rings, students provide a comment about the economic benefits of fulfilling that function in American society.

Students describe how their views on music making have changed during the course of the discussion. The instructor concludes the class with a discussion of how these procedures can be adapted for use with high school instrumental students.

Suggested Resources

Abeles, Harold F., Charles R. Hoffer, and Robert Klotman. *Foundations of Music Education,* 2d ed. Old Tappan, NJ: Schirmer Books/Simon & Schuster, 1994.

Cowden, Robert, ed. "Careers in Music." Reston, VA: Music Educators National Conference, 1989. Brochure.

Merriam, Alan P. *Anthropology of Music.* Evanston, IL: Northwestern University Press, 1964.

National Academy of Recording Arts & Sciences. *The Careers in Music Video.* Santa Monica, CA: NARAS, 1991. Available from Music Educators National Conference, Reston, VA.

STANDARD 9D
Advanced
Understanding music in relation to history and culture: *Students identify and explain the stylistic features of a given musical work that serve to define its aesthetic tradition and its historical or cultural context.*

Strategy

Methods students have completed assigned readings about the migration of Acadians from Nova Scotia to Louisiana after deportation by the British. As a band, they sightread Quincy C. Hilliard's "Acadian Festival" (New York: Carl Fischer), YBS62, Level 2^1/$_2$. From lead sheets (melody and chords) with texts in English and French, students play "Colinda," "J'ai passe devant tu port," and "Dance de Mardi Gras"—tunes from "Acadian Festival."

Methods students then listen to recordings of authentic Cajun performances, such as *Cajun Party,* performed by the Cajun Playboys, Mardi Gras Records (3331 St. Charles Ave., New Orleans, LA 70115; phone 504-895-0441) 1014. The instructor asks students to cite similarities and differences between their own playing and what they heard on the recordings. They note the stylistic features that define the music's tradition and its historical and cultural context.

The class discusses the importance of Cajun music as an artistic expression of the culture, historical events that helped develop the musical style, and the subject matter of Cajun music. Students then view the videotape *Cajun Visits,* with particular attention to the impact of Cajun music on the people's lives.

The instructor leads a discussion of how these activities could be adapted for a high school instrumental ensemble.

(continued)

Suggested Resources

Bernard, Shane, and Julia Girouard. "'Colinda': Mysterious Origins of a Cajun Folksong." *Journal of Folklore Research* 29, 1 (January 1992): 37–52.

Broughton, Simon. "Ultimate Gumbo: Cajun, Zydeco, and Swamp—Sounds of Louisiana." In *Rough World Music,* edited by Simon Broughton, Mark Ellingham, David Muddyman, and Richard Trillo. Bergenfield, NJ: Penguin USA, 1994.

Cajun Visits. Yasha Aginsky Productions. Flower Films, 10341 San Pablo Ave., El Cerrito, CA 94530; phone 800-572-7618.

Kingman, Daniel. "Three Regional Samplings." In *American Music: A Panorama,* 2d ed. New York: Schirmer Books/Simon & Schuster, 1990.

STANDARD 9E
Advanced

Understanding music in relation to history and culture: Students identify and describe music genres or styles that show the influence of two or more cultural traditions, identify the cultural source of each influence, and trace the historical conditions that produced the synthesis of influences.

Strategy

The instructor asks methods students for examples of music from their own lives that reflects culturally diverse musical experiences. Students discuss the stylistic features of the music in each experience. As a class, they make an outline or chart of the musical roots of examples given by class members.

The instructor demonstrates a lesson for high school students using two diverse musical experiences. Then, with the class divided into groups, the instructor asks each group to plan a lesson on a topic that would be both interesting and informative to high school instrumental students and emphasize the influence of two or more cultural traditions on a given music genre or style. The lesson should include having high school students trace the historical conditions that produced the synthesis of influences.

A student from each group summarizes the group's lesson for the class, and the instructor leads a discussion of the potential for each lesson plan.

Suggested Resources

Anderson, William M., ed. *Teaching Music with a Multicultural Approach.* Reston, VA: Music Educators National Conference, 1990. Book and videocassettes.

Gonzo, Carroll. "Multicultural Issues in Music Education." *Music Educators Journal* 79, no. 6 (February 1993): 49–52.

Schmid, Will. "World Music in the Instrumental Program." *Music Educators Journal* 78, no. 9 (May 1992): 41–44.

Instrumental Music

"Acadian Festival" by Quincy C. Hilliard. New York: Carl Fischer. YBS62. Level 2½.

"Africa: Ceremony, Song, and Ritual" by Robert W. Smith. Miami: Warner Bros. Publications. MB9757. Level 5.

"African Sketches" by James Curnow. Milwaukee: Hal Leonard Corporation. 861706. Level 2.

"Arabian Suite," arr. Paul Jennings. Milwaukee: Hal Leonard Corporation. 26625026. Level 3.

"Chester" by William Schuman. Bryn Mawr, PA: Merion Music/Theodore Presser Company. 145400000. Level 6.

"God of Our Fathers" by Claude T. Smith. Kansas City, MO: Wingert Jones Music. 3011421. Level 3/4.

"The Headless Horseman" by Timothy Broege. Manhattan Beach Music (1595 East 46th St., Brooklyn, NY 11234-3122; phone 718-338-4137), Level 3.

"Irish Tune from County Derry and Shepherd's Hey" by Percy Grainger. New York: Carl Fischer. J 240. Level 5.

"Korean Folk Song," arr. Ralph Gingery. Newington, VA: William Allen Music. FCB182. Level 2½.

"Lindbergh Variations" by Robert Sheldon. Oskaloosa, IA: C. L. Barnhouse. 012-2369. Level 3.

"Molly on the Shore" by Percy Grainger. New York: Carl Fischer. J 270. Level 5.

"Serengeti, an African Rhapsody" by John Higgins. Milwaukee: Jenson Publishing/Hal Leonard Corporation. 25519010. Level 3.

"Variation Overture" by Clifton Williams. Cleveland: Ludwig Music Publishing Company. SBS100. Level 3.

"Variations on an African Hymn Song" by Quincy C. Hilliard. Oskaloosa, IA: C. L. Barnhouse. 012-2607. Level 3½.

"Variations on a Korean Folk Song" by John Barnes Chance. New York: Boosey & Hawkes. QMB348. Level 4.

"Variations on a Shaker Melody" by Aaron Copland. New York: Boosey & Hawkes. QMB236SB. Level 5.

West Side Story by Leonard Bernstein, arr. W. J. Duthoit. Milwaukee: G. Schirmer/Hal Leonard Corporation. 50352040. Level 4/5.

"Who Puts His Trust in God Most Just" by Johann Sebastian Bach, arr. James Croft. Delaware Water Gap, PA: Shawnee Press. K 390. Level 3.

Books

Abeles, Harold F., Charles R. Hoffer, and Robert Klotman. *Foundations of Music Education,* 2d ed. Old Tappan, NJ: Schirmer Books/Simon & Schuster, 1994.

*Anderson, William M., ed. *Teaching Music with a Multicultural Approach.* Reston, VA: Music Educators National Conference, 1990. Book and videocassettes.

Anderson, William M., and Joy E. Lawrence. *Integrating Music into the Elementary Classroom*, 3d ed. Belmont, CA: Wadsworth Publishing Company, 1995.

ASBDA Curriculum Guide: A Reference for School Band Directors. Miami: Warner Bros. Publications, 1973.

Azzara, Christopher D., Richard F. Grunow, and Edwin E. Gordon. *Creativity in Improvisation*. Books 1 and 2, with recordings. Chicago: GIA Publications, 1997.

Barry, Malcolm, and Roger Parker. *Score Reading*. Twentieth-Century, book 5. New York: Oxford University Press, 1987.

Battisti, Frank, and Robert Garofalo. *Guide to Score Study for the Wind Band Conductor*. Fort Lauderdale, FL: Meredith Music Publications, 1990.

Berg, C. Sidney, ed. (for Virginia Band and Orchestra Directors Association/Virginia Music Educators Association). *The Director's Guide to Contest and Festival Music*. Bandworld Magazine/WIBC (407 Terrace St., Ashland, OR 97520; phone 800-247-2263), 1995.

Boyle, J. David, and Rudolf E. Radocy. *Measurement and Evaluation of Musical Experiences*. New York: Schirmer Books/Simon & Schuster, 1987.

Broughton, Simon, Mark Ellingham, David Muddyman, and Richard Trillo, eds. *Rough World Music*. Bergenfield, NJ: Penguin USA, 1994.

Brown, Thomas A. *Afro-Latin Rhythm Dictionary: A Complete Dictionary for All Musicians*. Van Nuys, CA: Alfred Publishing Company, 1984.

Cacavas, John. *The Art of Writing Music*. Van Nuys, CA: Alfred Publishing Company. 1993.

Choksy, Lois, Robert M. Abramson, Avon E. Gillespie, and David Woods. *Teaching Music in the Twentieth Century*. Englewood Cliffs, NJ: Prentice-Hall, 1986.

Collins, Donald L. *Teaching Choral Music*. Englewood Cliffs, NJ: Prentice-Hall, 1993.

Colwell, Richard J., and Thomas Goolsby. *The Teaching of Instrumental Music*, 2d ed. Englewood Cliffs, NJ: Prentice Hall, 1992.

Conductor's Anthology, 2d ed. 2 vols. Northfield, IL: The Instrumentalist Company, 1993.

Cook, Gary. *Teaching Percussion*, 2d ed. New York: Schirmer Books/Simon & Schuster, 1996.

Crocker, Emily, and John Leavitt. *Essential Musicianship*, book 1. Milwaukee: Hal Leonard Corporation, 1995.

Dallin, Leon. *Techniques of Twentieth-Century Composition*, 3d ed. Columbus, OH: Wm. C. Brown Communications/McGraw-Hill, 1974.

Del Borgo, Elliot. *The Rehearsal . . . The First Ten Minutes*. Educational Programs Publications (1784 West Schuylkill Road, Douglassville, PA 19518-9100; phone 610-327-3050), 1995. Conductor's score and student books.

Dufresne, Gaston. *Develop Sightreading*. New York: Charles Colin Publications, 1972.

Dvorak, Thomas L., Cynthia Crump Taggart, and Peter Schmalz. *Best Music for Young Band: A Selective Guide to the Young Band/Young Wind Ensemble Repertoire*. Edited by Bob Margolis. Manhattan Beach Music (1595 East 46th St., Brooklyn, NY 11234-3122; phone 718-338-4137), 1986.

Dvorak, Thomas L., Robert Grechesky, and Gary M. Ciepluch. *Best Music for High School Band: A Selective Repertoire Guide for High School Bands and Wind Ensembles*. Edited by Bob Margolis. Manhattan Beach Music (1595 East 46th St., Brooklyn, NY 11234-3122; phone 718-338-4137), 1993.

Elliott, David J. *Music Matters: A New Philosophy of Music Education.* New York: Oxford University Press, 1995.

Fowler, Charles. *Music! Its Role and Importance in Our Lives.* Mission Hills, CA: Glencoe/McGraw-Hill, 1994. Book and recordings.

Frazee, Jane. *Discovering Orff: A Curriculum for Music Teachers.* Paoli, PA: Schott/European American, 1987.

Garofalo, Robert. *Blueprint for Band: A Guide to Teaching Comprehensive Musicianship Through School Band Performance,* rev. ed. Portland, ME: J. Weston Walch, 1983.

————. *Guides to Band Masterworks.* Fort Lauderdale, FL: Meredith Music Publications, 1992.

————. *Rehearsal Handbook for Band and Orchestra Students.* Fort Lauderdale, FL: Meredith Music Publications, 1983.

Goldman, Richard Franko. *The Wind Band.* Boston: Allyn & Bacon, 1961.

Green, Douglas. *Form in Tonal Music,* 2d ed. Orlando, FL: Holt, Rinehart & Winston/Harcourt Brace, 1979.

Green, Elizabeth A. H. *Orchestral Bowings and Routines.* Reston, VA: American String Teachers Association, 1990.

————. *Teaching Stringed Instruments in Classes,* 2d ed. Reston, VA: American String Teachers Association, 1987.

Grout, Donald J., and Claude Palisca. *A History of Western Music,* 5th ed. New York: W. W. Norton, 1996.

Harder, Paul, and Greg A. Steinke. *Basic Materials in Music Theory,* 8th ed. Englewood Cliffs, NJ: Allyn and Bacon/Prentice-Hall, 1995.

Haskell, Francis. *History and Its Images: Art and the Interpretation of the Past.* New Haven: Yale University Press, 1993.

*Hinckley, June, ed. *Music at the Middle Level: Building Strong Programs.* Reston, VA: Music Educators National Conference, 1994.

Hoffer, Charles R. *Teaching Music in the Secondary Schools,* 4th ed. Belmont, CA: Wadsworth Publishing Company, 1991.

Hunsberger, Donald, and Roy Ernst. *The Art of Conducting,* 2d ed. Columbus, OH: McGraw-Hill, 1992.

Hunt, Norman J. *A Guide to Teaching Brass,* 5th ed. Columbus, OH: Wm. C. Brown Communications/McGraw-Hill, 1993.

Jessup, Lynne E. *All Hands On.* Danbury, CT: World Music Press, 1996.

Kennan, Kent W., and Donald Grantham. *The Technique of Orchestration,* 4th ed. Englewood Cliffs, NJ: Prentice-Hall, 1990.

Kingman, Daniel. *American Music: A Panorama,* 2d ed. New York: Schirmer Books/Simon & Schuster, 1990.

Klotman, Robert H. *Teaching Strings: Technique and Pedagogy,* 2d ed. New York: Schirmer Books/Simon & Schuster, 1996.

Labuta, Joseph A. *Teaching Musicianship in the High School Band,* rev. ed. Fort Lauderdale, FL: Meredith Music Publications, 1997.

Lamb, Norman, and Susan Lamb Cook. *Guide to Teaching Strings,* 6th ed. Columbus, OH: Wm. C. Brown Communications/McGraw-Hill, 1993.

Lisk, Edward S. *The Creative Director: Alternative Rehearsal Techniques.* Fort Lauderdale, FL: Meredith Music Publications, 1991.

Margolis, Joseph. *Interpretation Radical but Not Unruly: The New Puzzle of the Arts and History.* Berkeley: University of California Press, 1995.

*Mayer, Frederick R., ed. *The String Orchestra Super List.* Reston, VA: Music Educators National Conference, 1993.

Mellers, Wilfrid H. *Percy Grainger.* New York: Oxford University Press, 1992.

Merriam, Alan P. *Anthropology of Music.* Evanston, IL: Northwestern University Press, 1964.

Morgan, Robert P. *Twentieth-Century Music.* Scranton, PA: W. W. Norton, 1991.

The Music Connection, Grades K–8. Parsippany, NJ: Silver Burdett Ginn, 1995.

New York State School Music Association. *NYSSMA Manual of Graded Solo and Ensemble Music.* Westbury, NY: NYSSMA, 1991.

Nketia, Joseph H. K. *Music of Africa.* New York: W. W. Norton, 1974.

Olson, Alice. *Musica Arabia.* Coralville, IA: Alice Olson Publications/West Music, 1987.

Orff, Carl, and Gunild Keetman. *Music for Children—Vol. I, Pentatonic.* English version adapted by Margaret Murray. Paoli, PA: Schott/European American, 1982.

Rabin, Marvin, and Priscilla Smith. *Guide to Orchestral Bowings through Musical Styles,* rev. ed. Madison, WI: Division of University Outreach, Department of Continuing Education in the Arts, University of Wisconsin, 1991.

Randel, Don Michael, ed. *The New Harvard Dictionary of Music.* Cambridge: Belknap Press of Harvard University Press, 1986.

Reimer, Bennett. *A Philosophy of Music Education,* 2d ed. Englewood Cliffs, NJ: Prentice Hall, 1989.

Sadie, Stanley, ed. *The New Grove Dictionary of Music and Musicians.* London: Macmillan, 1980.

Share the Music, Grades K–8. New York: Macmillan/McGraw-Hill, 1995, 1997.

Slattery, Thomas C. *Percy Grainger: The Inveterate Innovator.* Evanston, IL: The Instrumentalist Company, 1974.

Smith, Norman E., and Albert J. Stoutamire. *Band Music Notes.* Lake Charles, LA: Program Note Press, 1982.

Stolba, K. Marie. *The Development of Western Music: A History,* 2d ed. Dubuque, IA: Brown & Benchmark Publishers/McGraw-Hill, 1993.

Swanwick, Keith. *Music, Mind, and Education.* London: Routledge, 1989.

———. *Musical Knowledge: Intuition, Analysis, and Music Education.* London: Routledge, 1994.

Telfer, Nancy. *Successful Warm-Ups.* 2 vols. San Diego: Neil A. Kjos Music Company, 1995–96.

Westphal, Frederick. *A Guide to Teaching Woodwinds,* 5th ed. Columbus, OH: Wm. C. Brown Communications/McGraw-Hill, 1989.

*Wiggins, Jackie. *Composition in the Classroom: A Tool for Teaching.* Reston, VA: Music Educators National Conference, 1990.

Winslow, Robert W., and Leon Dallin. *Music Skills for the Classroom Teacher,* 8th ed. Columbus, OH:

Wm. C. Brown Communications/McGraw-Hill, 1991.

The World of Music, Grades K–8. Parsippany, NJ: Silver Burdett Ginn, 1991.

Periodicals

Black Music Research Journal, Center for Black Music Research, Columbia College Chicago, 600 South Michigan Avenue, Chicago, IL 60605-1996.

*General Music Today, Music Educators National Conference, 1806 Robert Fulton Drive, Reston, VA 20191.

The Instrumentalist, The Instrumentalist Company, 200 Northfield Road, Northfield, IL 60093.

International Journal of Music Education, ISME International Office, International Centre for Research in Music Education, University of Reading, Bulmershe Court, Reading RG6 1HY, United Kingdom.

Journal of Folklore Research, Indiana University Folklore Institute, 504 N. Fess St., Bloomington, IN 47408; phone 812-855-1027.

*Music Educators Journal, Music Educators National Conference, 1806 Robert Fulton Drive, Reston, VA 20191.

*Teaching Music, Music Educators National Conference, 1806 Robert Fulton Drive, Reston, VA 20191.

Recordings

Cajun Party. Cajun Playboys. Mardi Gras Records (3331 St. Charles Ave., New Orleans, LA 70115; phone 504-895-0441) 1014.

de Meij, Johan. Symphony no. 1 ("Lord of the Rings"). Rondo Grammofon RCD 8346.

The Spirit of '76 and Ruffles and Flourishes. Eastman Wind Ensemble. Frederick Fennell. Mercury Living Presence. 434386-2.

Videotapes

Cajun Visits. Yasha Aginsky Productions. Flower Films, 10341 San Pablo Ave., El Cerrito, CA 94530; phone 800-572-7618.

*National Academy of Recording Arts & Sciences. *The Careers in Music Video.* Santa Monica, CA: NARAS, 1991.

Other Resources

*Cowden, Robert, ed. "Careers in Music." Reston, VA: Music Educators National Conference, 1989. Brochure.

Harris, Brian. "Comparisons of Attained Ratings to Instructional Behaviors and Techniques Exhibited by Band Directors in Sight-Reading Performance Situations." Ph.D. diss., The Florida State University, 1991.

---

* Available from MENC.

Resources on Music and Arts Education Standards

Aiming for Excellence: The Impact of the Standards Movement on Music Education. 1996. #1012.

Implementing the Arts Education Standards. Set of five brochures: "What School Boards Can Do," "What School Administrators Can Do," "What State Education Agencies Can Do," "What Parents Can Do," "What the Arts Community Can Do." 1994. #4022. Each brochure is also available in packs of 20.

Music for a Sound Education: A Tool Kit for Implementing the Standards. 1994. #1600.

National Standards for Arts Education: What Every Young American Should Know and Be Able to Do in the Arts. 1994. #1605.

Opportunity-to-Learn Standards for Music Instruction: Grades PreK–12. 1994. #1619.

Performance Standards for Music: Strategies and Benchmarks for Assessing Progress Toward the National Standards, Grades Pre-K–12. 1996. #1633.

Perspectives on Implementation: Arts Education Standards for America's Students. 1994. #1622.

"Prekindergarten Music Education Standards" (brochure). 1995. #4015 (set of 10).

The School Music Program—A New Vision: The K–12 National Standards, PreK Standards, and What They Mean to Music Educators. 1994. #1618.

"Teacher Education for the Arts Disciplines: Issues Raised by the National Standards for Arts Education." 1996. #1609.

Teaching Examples: Ideas for Music Educators. 1994. #1620.

The Vision for Arts Education in the 21st Century. 1994. #1617.

Strategies for Teaching Series

Strategies for Teaching Prekindergarten Music, compiled and edited by Wendy L. Sims. #1644.

Strategies for Teaching K–4 General Music, compiled and edited by Sandra L. Stauffer and Jennifer Davidson. #1645.

Strategies for Teaching Middle-Level General Music, compiled and edited by June M. Hinckley and Suzanne M. Shull. #1646.

Strategies for Teaching High School General Music, compiled and edited by Keith P. Thompson and Gloria J. Kiester. #1647.

Strategies for Teaching Elementary and Middle-Level Chorus, compiled and edited by Ann Roberts Small and Judy K. Bowers. #1648.

Strategies for Teaching High School Chorus, compiled and edited by Randal Swiggum. #1649.

Strategies for Teaching Strings and Orchestra, compiled and edited by Dorothy A. Straub, Louis S. Bergonzi, and Anne C. Witt. #1652.

Strategies for Teaching Middle-Level and High School Keyboard, compiled and edited by Martha F. Hilley and Tommie Pardue. #1655.

Strategies for Teaching Beginning and Intermediate Band, compiled and edited by Edward J. Kvet and Janet M. Tweed. #1650.

Strategies for Teaching High School Band, compiled and edited by Edward J. Kvet and John E. Williamson. #1651.

Strategies for Teaching Specialized Ensembles, compiled and edited by Robert A. Cutietta. #1653.

Strategies for Teaching Middle-Level and High School Guitar, compiled and edited by William E. Purse, James L. Jordan, and Nancy Marsters. #1654.

Strategies for Teaching: Guide for Music Methods Classes, compiled and edited by Louis O. Hall with Nancy R. Boone, John Grashel, and Rosemary C. Watkins. #1656.

For more information on these and other MENC publications, write to or call MENC Publications Sales, 1806 Robert Fulton Drive, Reston, VA 20191-4348; 703-860-4000 or 800-828-0229.

About the Editors

NANCY R. BOONE is a professor in the Department of Music at Middle Tennessee State University in Murfreesboro.

JOE W. GRANT is an associate professor in the School of Music at the University of Illinois in Urbana.

JOHN GRASHEL is an associate professor in the School of Music at the University of Illinois in Urbana.

JOYCE EASTLUND GROMKO is associate dean for academic affairs in The Graduate College and an associate professor in the College of Musical Arts at Bowling Green State University in Bowling Green, Ohio.

LOUIS O. HALL is an associate professor and coordinator of music education in the School of Performing Arts, Division of Music, at the University of Maine in Orono.

BARBARA LEWIS is an associate professor in the Department of Music at the University of North Dakota in Grand Forks.

CAROLYNN A. LINDEMAN is a professor in the Department of Music at San Francisco State University.

DIANE C. PERSELLIN is a professor in the Department of Music at Trinity University in San Antonio, Texas.

MARY LOU VAN RYSSELBERGHE is a senior instructor in the School of Music at the University of Oregon in Eugene.

ROSEMARY C. WATKINS is an associate professor in the Division of Music at The University of Texas in San Antonio.